GENEALOGY ONLINE FOR DUMMIES®

This Large Print Book carries the
Seal of Approval of N.A.V.H.

GENEALOGY ONLINE FOR DUMMIES®

5th Edition

MATTHEW L. HELM
AND APRIL LEIGH HELM

THORNDIKE PRESS
A part of Gale, Cengage Learning

Detroit • New York • San Francisco • New Haven, Conn • Waterville, Maine • London

Thorndike Press® Large Print Health, Home & Learning.

The text of this Large Print edition is unabridged.

Other aspects of the book may vary from the original edition.

Set in 16 pt. Plantin.

Printed on permanent paper.

LIBRARY OF CONGRESS CATALOGING-IN-PUBLICATION DATA

Helm, Matthew.
  Genealogy online for dummies / by Matthew L. Helm and April Leigh Helm. — 5th ed.
    p. cm.
  Originally published: Indianapolis, IN : Wiley Pub., 2008.
  Includes index.
  ISBN-13: 978-1-4104-1546-2 (hardcover : lg. print : alk. paper)
  ISBN-10: 1-4104-1546-5 (hardcover : lg. print : alk. paper)
  1. Genealogy — Computer network resources — Handbooks, manuals, etc. 2. Genealogy — Databases. 3. Genealogy — Directories. 4. Web sites — Directories. I. Helm, April Leigh. II. Title.
  CS21.H455 2009
  929'.10285—dc22

2009010890

Published in 2009 by arrangement with John Wiley & Sons, Inc.

Printed in the United States of America
1 2 3 4 5 6 7 13 12 11 10 09

Dedication

For Kyleakin and Cambrian.

Authors' Acknowledgments

We wish to acknowledge the following people, without whom this book wouldn't exist: Greg Croy, Linda Morris, Jenny Swisher, Liz Kerstans, and Gary Smith. They logged a lot of hours pulling together this book.

Our respective parents and ancestors, without whom our own genealogies wouldn't be possible.

About the Authors

Matthew L. Helm is the Executive Vice President and Chief Technology Officer for FamilyToolbox.net, Inc. He's the creator and maintainer of the award-winning Helm's Genealogy Toolbox, Helm/Helms Family Research Page, and a variety of other Web sites. Matthew speaks at national genealogical conventions and lectures to genealogical and historical societies. Matthew holds an A.B. in History and an M.S. in Library and Information Science from the University of Illinois at Urbana-Champaign.

April Leigh Helm is the President of FamilyToolbox.net, Inc. April lectures on genealogy and other topics for various conferences and groups. She holds a B.S. in Journalism and an Ed.M. in Higher Education Administration from the University of Illinois at Urbana-Champaign.

Together, the Helms have coauthored several books in addition to the five editions of *Genealogy Online For Dummies*. They include *Family Tree Maker For Dummies, Your Official America Online Guide to Genealogy Online,* and *Get Your Degree Online.*

Although they collected notes on family members and old photographs for many years, it wasn't until 1990, while living and working in the Washington, D.C. area, that the Helms began seriously researching their family lines. Upon returning to central Illinois in 1994, the Helms found themselves with limited historical and genealogical resources for the areas in which their ancestors lived. It was then that they jumped into online genealogy.

Here's a little more information about a few of the genealogical Web sites maintained by the Helms:

Helm's Genealogy Toolbox (www.genealogytoolbox.com): An online clearinghouse of genealogical tools and links.

HistoryKat (www.historykat.com): A subscription online archive of digitized records and documents that enable genealogists to conduct primary research on the Internet.

TreEZy.com (www.treezy.com): A site containing a genealogically focused search engine that index sites of interest to genealogists.

Publisher's Acknowledgments

We're proud of this book; please send us your comments through our online registration form located at www.dummies.com/register/.

Some of the people who helped bring this book to market include the following:

Acquisitions, Editorial, and Media Development
Project Editor: Linda Morris
Acquisitions Editor: Greg Croy
Copy Editor: Linda Morris
Technical Editor: Gary Smith
Editorial Manager: Jodi Jensen
Media Project Supervisor: Laura Moss-Hollister
Media Development Specialist: Jenny Swisher
Media Development Associate Producer: Richard Graves
Editorial Assistant: Amanda Foxworth
Sr. Editorial Assistant: Cherie Case
Cartoons: Rich Tennant, (www.the5thwave.com)

Composition Services for Original Edition
Project Coordinator: Katherine Key
Layout and Graphics: Reuben W. Davis, Christine Williams

11

Proofreaders: Broccoli Information Management, Cynthia Fields, John Greenough

Indexer: Potomac Indexing, LLC

Publishing and Editorial for Technology Dummies

Richard Swadley, Vice President and Executive Group Publisher

Andy Cummings, Vice President and Publisher

Mary Bednarek, Executive Acquisitions Director

Mary C. Corder, Editorial Director

Publishing for Consumer Dummies

Diane Graves Steele, Vice President and Publisher

Joyce Pepple, Acquisitions Director

Composition Services

Gerry Fahey, Vice President of Production Services

Debbie Stailey, Director of Composition Services

Genealogy Online For Dummies®, 5th Edition

Cheat Sheet

Some Genealogical Web Sites to Remember

For news and information about developments in genealogy

Eastman's Online Genealogy Newsletter	http://blog.eogn.com/
Genealogy Insider/Family Tree Magazine	www.familytreemagazine.com/insider/default.aspx

For links to lots of other genealogical sites

Genealogy Home Page	www.genhomepage.com
Helm's Genealogy Toolbox	www.genealogytoolbox.com

For surname resources

Genealogy Resources on the Internet Mailing List	www.rootsweb.com/~jfuller/gen_mail.html
Roots Surname List search page	rsl.rootsweb.com/cgi-bin/rslsql.cgi

To post queries and share genealogical research success

Ancestry Message Boards	boards.ancestry.com
GenCircles	www.gencircles.com
Geni.com	www.geni.com
USGenweb	usgenweb.org
GenForum	genforum.genealogy.com

For United States government resources

Citizenship and Naturalization Service (formerly the Immigration and Naturalization Service)	www.uscis.gov/portal/site/uscis
Library of Congress	www.loc.gov
National Archives and Records Administration	www.nara.gov

How to Use Helm's Genealogy Toolbox

You can use Helm's Genealogy Toolbox to identify genealogical resources on the Internet in two different ways: using the Global Search engine or browsing through categories. To do either, go to Helm's Genealogy Toolbox at www.genealogytoolbox.com.

Using the Global Search engine

1. **In the section called Search for Genealogical and Local History Web Sites, look for the search box labeled Enter Your Keywords.**
2. **Type the keyword that you're looking for in the box, or type the first and/or last names that you're looking for, and click the Search button.**

   The Search Results page contains the results of a full-text search for your terms using the Toolbox.

3. **Choose a link that appears to have information on your topic.**

Browsing by category in the directory

On the home page for Helm's Genealogy Toolbox are three sections of category links. These sections include People, Places, and Topics:

1. **Click the category link that interests you.**

2. If a listing of subcategories appears, browse through it and click the subcategory that interests you.

On subcategory pages, you find lists of hand-picked links relating to that topic, and a list of URLs generated from the Toolbox's full-text search. For each link to another site, you're provided the name and a brief abstract of the link's content.

Here are a couple of hints to remember when you browse through categories:

✔ **Looking for information about a surname?** Click the People category in the main directory.

✔ **Looking for information about a geographic location?** Click the Places category in the main directory.

Contents at a Glance

Table of Contents

Introduction

· ·

Are you interested in knowing more about your family's history? Looking to determine how your ancestors relate to others with the same last name? Wanting to organize your research using your computer? Then this just might be the book for you.

You may be interested in learning about your family history, or genealogy, for various reasons:

✔ Do you want to know what part your ancestors played in history?

✔ Do you need to conduct genealogical research for religious reasons or to join a lineage society?

✔ Do you simply enjoy solving mysteries or puzzles?

No matter what your reason is for research, this is the best time in history to be looking into your genealogy.

In the past, genealogists had to load up the car with all of their notebooks and travel hundreds of miles to find clues about their ancestors. This meant that only a few had the time, energy, and money to do serious research. With the advent of the computer and genealogical resources on the

Internet, and the growing availability of DNA testing and matching, the genealogy landscape completely changed. You can now spend quality time sifting through the many resources available online, at any time of the day, without leaving the comfort of your home. And you can find other researchers who match you on a whole new level to share information with.

Of course, at this point we should give you a couple of warnings. First, genealogy is a very addictive pursuit. You just might find yourself staying up until all hours of the night chasing down that elusive ancestor. Please don't blame us if you start falling asleep at work due to your genealogical research routine. Also, on a more serious note, keep in mind that online research is merely one tool among many for finding information about your family. To thoroughly research your genealogy, you will have to employ a number of tools — many of which we talk about throughout this book.

Now that the disclaimers are out of the way, put the kids to bed, let your pets out, and boot up that computer. Your ancestors are just waiting to be found!

About This Book

Researching your family history online is like being a child in a candy store. There are so many neat things that catch your eye that it's difficult to decide which one to try. That's where this book comes in. We try to help you become a discriminating candy eater — well, a discriminating researcher, anyway — by showing you not only the locations of useful genealogy sites but also how to effectively use them to meet your research goals.

Having said that, you're probably asking yourself how this book differs from the many other genealogy books on the shelf. Some books tell you only the traditional methods of genealogical research — which have you traveling hundreds of miles to visit courthouses and archives in other states. Unfortunately, these books neglect the many opportunities that online research provides. Other books that do cover online genealogy tend to group resources by how users access them (all FTP sites are listed together, all World Wide Web sites are listed together, and so on), rather than telling you how you can integrate the many Internet resources to achieve your genealogical goal. As genealogists, we understand that researchers don't conduct searches by trying all the FTP sites, and then all the World Wide Web sites, and so on. We search by looking for surnames or places anywhere we can find them — through World Wide Web sites, e-mail, or whatever.

Some books become too computer-heavy — overkilling the ins and outs of each kind of Internet resource, and neglecting to help you with basic research techniques online *and offline* that you need to successfully meet your goal. We don't want you to have a bad experience online. So rather than focus on just one thing — genealogy *or* online resources — we try to balance the act. In this book, we show you how to integrate genealogical research with the use of online resources so you can learn to effectively and efficiently use your computer and the Internet in your family research.

Now that we've explained a bit about the book, are you ready to get started and to become an official genealogist? You might be asking yourself, "What are the requirements for becoming an official genealogist?" It's simple — just say out loud, "I declare myself an official genealogist." There you go. Of course, if you prefer, you're welcome to drag your family or pets into the room to witness this historic event. Whether you make your proclamation in a private ceremony for one or you have witnesses, it's official — you're a genealogist, and it's time to start pulling together

31

the puzzle pieces of your family history.

Seriously, being a genealogist has no formal requirements. You simply need an interest in your ancestry and a willingness to devote the rest of your life to pursuing information and documents.

Foolish Assumptions

In writing and revising this book, we made a couple of assumptions. If you fit one of these assumptions, this book is for you:

- ✔ You've done at least a little genealogy groundwork, and now you're ready to use the Internet and DNA testing to pursue (and better prepare yourself for) your genealogy research both online and offline.

- ✔ You have at least a little computer experience, are now interested in pursuing your family tree, and want to know where and how to start.

- ✔ You have a little experience in genealogy and some experience with computers, but you want to learn how to put them together.

Of course, you can have a lot of computer experience and be a novice to genealogy or to online genealogy and still benefit from this book. In this case, you may still want to skim some of the basic sections on computers and the Internet.

How to Use This Book

We don't expect you to read this book from cover to cover, in order. (No, you're not hurting our feelings by skipping through the sections looking only for the information that you're interested in at that particular moment! We want this book to be useful. How you use it is up to you.) In fact, we've tried to write this book to accommodate you. Each section within each chapter can stand alone as a separate entity, so you can pick up the book and flip directly to a section that deals with what you want to know. If we think something relevant in another section can supplement your knowledge on a particular topic, we provide a note or reference telling you the other place(s) we think you should look. However, we've tried very hard to do this referencing in a manner that isn't obnoxious to those of you who choose to read the book from cover to cover. We hope we've succeeded in addressing both types of readers!

We use a couple of conventions in this book to make it easier for you to follow a set of specific instructions. Commands for menus appear with arrows between each selection. (For example, the command Format→Tree Format tells you to choose Tree Format from the Format menu.)

If you need to type something, the **bold type** indicates what you need to type.

How This Book Is Organized

To help you get a better picture of what this book has to offer, we explain a little about how we organized it and what you can expect to find in each part.

Part I: Getting Your Act Together

You need to have a good foundation before starting your online genealogical research. This part explores how to form an online research plan, the fundamental family information that you need to collect first, and how to start or-

33

ganizing your research and placing it into a genealogical database.

Part II: Focusing on Your Ancestor

Searching online for information about your particular ancestors can be a daunting task. Part II examines resources available for locating your ancestor by name and using government resources for the United States and abroad that can assist you in your ancestral hunt.

Part III: Adding Color to Your Research

Your family history is a lot more than just a list of names and birth dates. There are many details to be filled in so that your ancestors' lives are put in context. This part looks at geographical, ethnic, and religious resources that provide an insight into the everyday lives of your ancestors.

Part IV: Share and Share Alike

One of the most important aspects of genealogical research is using a coordinated effort to achieve success. This part takes a look at what goes into this effort, including using all available online resources, cooperating with other researchers, benefiting from groups and societies, and sharing the fruits of your research with the online community.

Part V: The Part of Tens

Ah, the infamous Part of Tens (infamous because every *For Dummies* book has one of these sections with profound advice or lists of things to do). Here you find a series of quick-reference chapters that give you useful genealogical hints and reminders. We include a list of online database sites we think you should know about, some tips for creating a genealogical Web page, hints to keep your online research sailing smoothly, a list of sites that offer help to genealogists, and things to take and useful sites to plan your research-related travels.

Glossary

As you read this book (or skip from chapter to chapter, section to section, looking over only those parts that interest you), you may have additional questions in some areas. That's why we include the glossary. It provides definitions of many terms that you're likely to encounter in your genealogical research.

Icons Used in This Book

To help you get the most out of this book, we created some icons that tell you at a glance if a section or paragraph has important information of a particular kind.

Here we refer you to other books or materials if you'd like additional information.

Here you can find concepts or terms that are unique to genealogy.

When you see this icon, you know we're offering advice or shortcuts to make your researching easier.

We walk readers step by step through an example of something.

Look out! This is something tricky or unusual to watch for.

This icon marks important genealogical stuff, so don't forget it.

Where to Go from Here

Depending on where you're reading this introduction, your next step is one of two possibilities:

- You need to go to the front of the bookstore and pay for this book so that you can take it home and use it. (Many bookstores don't mind if you sit and flip through books to see what they contain — that's why they provide the comfortable chairs, right? But we're not sure they would look highly upon you whipping out your laptop computer, hooking into their wireless Internet service, and proceeding to go through this entire book right there in the store. Then again, we could be mistaken — so use your best judgment, based on your knowledge of the bookstore in which you're standing.)

- If you already bought the book and you're at home (or wherever), you can go ahead and start reading in depth, following the steps for the online activities in the book as they come along.

Part I
Getting Your Act Together

The 5th Wave
By Rich Tennant

"They came here to help me with my genealogical research, but they stayed for the satellite TV."

In this part . . .

So you wanna be an online genealogist? Well, you need to prepare yourself for that first online research trip by finding out about the basics of genealogy and how to form a research plan. Then you need to know how to organize and preserve what you find both online and offline. This part starts you off in the right direction.

Chapter 1

Planning for Genealogical Success

All great projects start with a plan, right? Starting a genealogical project is no exception. A well thought-out plan can help you make efficient use of your time and keep you focused on the goals that you have set for a particular research session. Now, we realize that not everyone enjoys coming up with a plan. Finding your ancestors is the fun part — not the planning. So, to help speed things along, we've come up with a basic process that we hope helps you make the most of your research time.

This chapter covers some of the basic things to keep in mind when you begin your research journey and offers some tips on what you can do when you hit research bumps along the way. Also, we provide some hints on how to select that first ancestor to kick off your genealogical pursuit.

Introducing the Helm Online Family Tree Research Cycle

No book on research would be complete without some sort of model to follow, so we created one just for you. Of course, wanting to take credit for our fabulous model, we like to call it the *Helm Online Family Tree Research Cycle*. Sounds impressive, doesn't it? Well, we have to admit that most of it is common sense. Figure 1-1 shows the five phases of the cycle: planning, collecting, researching, consolidating, and distilling.

Sticking with the *family tree* motif here, we liken the cycle to the steps you take to plant and sustain a tree:

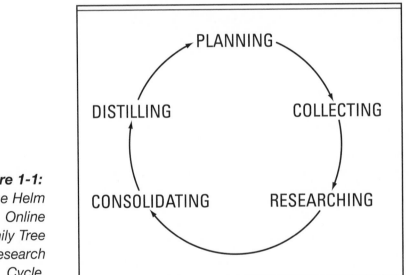

Figure 1-1:
The Helm Online Family Tree Research Cycle.

PLANNING

COLLECTING

RESEARCHING

CONSOLIDATING

DISTILLING

 **Planning:** The first step in planting a tree is figuring out what kind of tree you want and then finding a good place in your yard for the tree to grow. This step in the cycle is the *planning* phase. In genealogy, you want to select a family that you know enough

about to begin a search and then think about the resources that will provide the information that you're looking for.

✔ **Collecting:** After you plan for the tree, you go to a nursery and pick a suitable sapling and other necessary materials to ensure that the tree's roots take hold. The second phase of the cycle, *collecting,* is the same — you collect information on the family that you're researching by conducting interviews in person, on the phone, or through e-mail, and by finding documents in attics, basements, and other home-front repositories.

✔ **Researching:** The next step is to actually plant the tree. You dig a hole, place the tree in it, and then cover the roots. Similarly, you spend the *researching* phase of the cycle digging for clues, finding information that can support your family tree, and obtaining documentation. You can use traditional and technological tools to dig — tools like libraries, courthouses, your computer, and the World Wide Web.

✔ **Consolidating:** You planted the tree and covered its roots. However, to make sure that the tree grows, you put mulch around it and provide the nourishment the tree needs to survive. The *consolidating* phase of the cycle is similar in that you take the information you find and place it into your computer-based genealogical database or your filing system. These systems protect your findings by keeping them in a centralized location and provide an environment in which you can see the fruits of your labor.

✔ **Distilling:** After your tree has taken root and begins to grow, you need to prune the old growth, allowing new growth to appear. Similarly, the *distilling* phase is where you use your computer-based genealogical database to generate reports showing the current state of your research. You can use these reports to prune from your database those individuals you've proven don't fit into your family lines — and perhaps find room for new genealogical growth by finding clues to other lines you want to follow up.

We think that using our research model makes looking for genealogical information a lot easier and more fulfilling. However, this model is merely a guide. Feel free to use whatever methods work best for you — as long as those methods make it possible for someone else to verify your research (through sources you cite and so on).

Planning your research

The Internet puts the world at your fingertips. Discovering all the wonderful online resources that exist makes you feel like a kid in a candy store. You click around from site to site with wide eyes, amazed by what you see, tempted to record everything for your genealogy — whether it relates to one of your family lines or not.

Because of the immense wealth of information available to you, putting together a research plan before going online is very important — it can save you a lot of time and frustration by keeping you focused. Tens of thousands of genealogical sites are on the Internet. If you don't have a good idea of exactly what you're looking for to fill in the blanks in your genealogy, you can get lost online. Getting lost is even easier when you see a name that looks familiar and start following its links, only to discover hours later (when you finally get around to pulling out the genealogical notes you already had) that you've been tracking the wrong person and family line.

Now that we've convinced you that you need a research plan, you're probably wondering exactly what a research plan is. Basically, a *research plan* is a common-sense approach to looking for information about your ancestors online. A research plan entails knowing what you're looking for and what your priorities are for finding information.

If you're the kind of person who likes detailed organization (like lists and steps that you can follow to the tee), you can map out your research plan in a spreadsheet or word processor on your computer or you can write it out on paper. If you're the kind of person who knows exactly what you want and need at all times, and you have an excellent memory of where you leave off when doing projects, your research plan can exist solely in your mind. In other words, your research plan can be as formal or informal as you like — as long as it helps you plot what you're looking for.

For example, say you're interested in finding some information on your great-grandmother. Here are some steps you can take to form a research plan:

1. **Write down what you already know about the person you want to research — in this case, your great-grandmother.**
   Include details like the dates and places of birth, marriage, and death; spouse's name; children's names; and any other details you think may help you distinguish your ancestor from other individuals. Of course, it's possible that all you know at this time is great-grandma's name.

2. **Conduct a search using a genealogically focused search engine to get an overview of what's available.**
   Visit sites like the TreEZy (www.treezy.com) to search for information by name and location. Using

great-grandma's name and the names of some of the locations where she lived provides you with search results that give you an idea of what kind of resources are available. (Chapters 3 and 4 go into more detail about online trips and searching for this type of information.) You may want to make a list of the sites that you find in your word processor, spreadsheet, or on a piece of paper, or download the Web page for offline browsing.

3. **Prioritize the resources that you want to use.**
Your search on a genealogically focused search engine may turn up several different types of resources, such as newsgroups, mailing lists, and Web sites. We recommend that you prioritize which resources you plan to use first. You may want to visit a Web site that specifically names great-grandma prior to signing up for a mailing list for all researchers interested in great-grandma's surname.

4. **Schedule time to use the various resources that you identify.**
Genealogy is truly a lifelong pursuit — you can't download every bit of information and documentation that you need all at once. Because researching your genealogy requires time and effort on your part, we recommend that you schedule time to work on specific parts of your research. If you have a particular evening open every week, you can pencil in a research night on your calendar, setting aside 15-30 minutes at the beginning to review what you have and assess your goals, then spending a couple of hours researching, and ending your evening with another 15-30 minute review in which you organize what you found.

Collecting useful information

After you generate a research plan (see the preceding section, "Planning your research," for more information), you may need to fill in a few details like dates and locations of births, marriages, and deaths. You can collect this information by interviewing family members and by looking through family documents and photographs. (See Chapter 2 for tips on interviewing and using family documents and photographs.) You may also need to look up a few things in an atlas or *gazetteer* (a geographical dictionary) if you aren't sure where certain locations are. (Chapter 7 provides more information on online gazetteers.)

For a list of things that may be useful to collect, see Chapter 2. In the meantime, here are a few online resources that identify items to collect for your genealogy:

- **Suggestions for Beginners**
  www.ngsgenealogy.org/edugetstart.cfm

- **Introduction to Genealogy: First Steps**
  genealogy.about.com/library/lessons/blintro2a.htm

- **Getting Started in Genealogy and Family History**
  www.genuki.org.uk/gs/

- **Get Started in Genealogy: Some tips on how to start your family tree research**
  genealogy.suite101.com/article.cfm/get_started_in_genealogy

Researching: Through the brick wall and beyond

Of course, researching your family history online is the

topic of this entire book, so you can find the necessary resources to do a great deal of your online research in these pages.

A time will undoubtedly come when you run into what genealogists affectionately call the *Brick Wall Syndrome* — when you think you have exhausted every possible way of finding an ancestor. The most important thing you can do is to keep the faith — don't give up! Web sites are known to change frequently (especially as more people come online and share their information); although you may not find exactly what you need today, you may find it next week at a site you've visited several times before or at a new site altogether. The lesson here is to check back at sites that you've visited before.

Another way to get past the brick wall is to ask for help. Don't be afraid to post a message on a mailing list or e-mail other researchers you've corresponded with in the past to see if they have answers or suggestions for finding answers. We provide more information for using mailing lists and e-mail in Chapter 4.

Fortunately, there are also suggestions posted online on how to get through that brick wall when you run up against it. Check out these sites:

- **Breaking Down Walls, Brick by Brick: The Search for Henrietta:** genealogy.about.com/ library/weekly/aa042602a.htm

- **Brick Wall Research:** genealogypro .com/articles/brick-wall-research.html

- **Brick Wall Genealogy Solutions: A Family Heritage Resource:** www.workingdogweb .com/Brick-Wall-Genealogy.htm

Consolidating information in a database

After you get rolling on your research, you often find so much information that it feels like you don't have enough time to put it all into your computer-based genealogical database.

A *genealogical database* is a software program that allows you to enter, organize, store, and use all sorts of genealogical information on your computer.

When possible, try to set aside some time to update your database with information you recently gathered. This process of putting your information together in one central place, which we call *consolidating,* helps you gain a perspective on the work that you've completed and provides a place for you to store all those nuggets you'll need when you begin researching again. By storing your information in a database, you can always refer to it for a quick answer the next time you try to remember something specific, such as where you found a reference to a marriage certificate for your great-great-grandparents, or where your great-grandfather lived during a particular timeframe.

Distilling the information that you gather

The final step in the cycle is distilling the information that you gather into a report, chart, organized database, or detailed research log that you can use to find additional genealogical leads. Frequently, you can complete the distillation process by producing a report from your computer-based genealogical database. Most genealogical software programs allow you to generate reports in a variety of formats. For example, you can pull up a Pedigree chart (a chart showing a primary person with lines representing the relationships to his/her parents, then lines connecting them to their parents, and so on) or an outline of descendants from information that you entered in the database about each ancestor. You can use these reports to see what holes still exist in your research, and you can add these missing pieces to the planning phase for your next research effort — starting the whole cycle over again.

Another advantage to genealogical reports is having the information readily available so that you can *toggle* back to look at the report while researching online, which can help you stay focused. (*Toggling* is flipping back and forth between open programs on your computer. For example, in Windows you press Alt+Tab to toggle, or you can click the appropriate item on the taskbar at the bottom of the screen. On a Macintosh, you can use the Application Switcher in the upper-right corner of the screen.) Of course, if you prefer, printing copies of the reports and keeping them next to the computer while you're researching on the Internet serves the same purpose.

Selecting a Person to Begin Your Search

Selecting a person sounds easy, doesn't it? Just pick your great-great-grandfather's name, and you're off to the races. But what if your great-great-grandfather's name was John Smith? You may encounter millions of sites with information on John Smith — unless you know some facts about the John Smith you're looking for, we can almost guarantee that you will have a frustrating time online.

Trying a unique name

The first time you research online, try to start with a person whose name is, for lack of a better term, semi-unique. By this we mean a person with a name that doesn't take up ten pages in your local phone book, but is still common enough that you can find some information on it the first time you conduct a search. If you're really brave, you can begin with someone with a very common surname such as Smith or Jones, but you have to do a lot more groundwork up-front so you can easily determine whether any of the multiple findings relate to your ancestor. (For more on groundwork, see Chapter 2.)

Also, consider any variations in spelling that your ancestor's name may have. Often, you can find more information on the mainstream spelling of his or her surname than on one of its rarer variants. For example, if you research someone with the surname Helme, you may have better luck finding information under the spellings *Helm* or *Helms.* If your family members immigrated to the United States in the last two centuries, they may have *Americanized* their surname. Americanizing a name was often done so that the name could be easily pronounced in English, or sometimes the surname was simply misspelled and adopted by the family.

To find various spellings of the surname, you may need to dig through some family records or look at a site like Table of Common Surname Variations & Surname Misspellings (www.ingeneas.com/alternate.html).

Narrowing your starting point

If you aren't sure how popular a name is, try visiting a site like Hamrick Software's surname distribution site (www.hamrick.com/names). At Hamrick's site, you can find the distribution of surnames in the United States based on the 1850 Census, 1880 Census, 1920 Census, and phone books from 1990 to the present. Here's what you do:

1. **Open your World Wide Web browser and go to Hamrick Software's surname distribution site**

(www.hamrick.com/names).

The Hamrick site appears with instructions and a form to use for searching.

2. **Type the surname you're researching into the Surname field in the search form.**

   For help choosing a surname, see the preceding section.

3. **Use the drop-down menu to select the year(s) for which you want to see the surname distribution.**

   You can choose 1850, 1880, 1920, 1990, or All Years.

4. **Click Display.**

   A color map displaying the distribution of your surname appears.

Figure 1-2 shows a distribution map for the surname Abell in 1990. According to the map, only one out of every 1,000 individuals uses this surname in two states. In the remaining states, the name is even rarer. This gives you a good indication that the surname Abell is semi-unique. In contrast, during the same year, the surname Smith was held by at least one out of every 300 individuals in each state.

Note: Looking at Figure 1-2, you may find it difficult to determine which two states have one out of 1,000 individuals using the surname Abell because the colors show up as black, white, or shades of gray. If you visit Hamrick's site, the maps come up in color and are easier to read. (And just in case you're curious, the two states were Maryland and Kentucky.)

 A good reason to check out distribution maps is that you can use them to identify potential geographic areas where you can look for your family during the years covered by the site. This is especially true for maps generated from

1850 and 1880 Census data. For example, we generated another map on the Abell surname for the 1880 Census. We discovered that the name appeared more frequently in six states than in the rest of the country. If we hit a wall and can't find additional information online about a particular individual or the surname, we know we can start looking at records in these states to find more clues about families with the name and hopefully, by doing so, we'll find our branch.

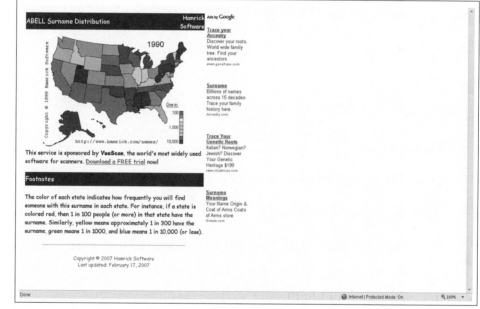

Figure 1-2:
A map of the Abell surname distribution in 1990 from Hamrick Software.

Choosing someone you know about

In addition to picking a person whom you're likely to have success researching, you want to use a person you already know something about. If you have a family line for which you know some basic information on your great-great-grandparents, use one of their names rather than a name for which you only know a few scattered details. The more details that you know about a person, the more successful your initial search is likely to be.

For example, Matthew used his great-grandfather William Abell because he knew more about that side of his family. His grandmother once mentioned that her father was born in Larue County, Kentucky, in 1876. This gives him a point of reference for judging whether a site has any relevant information on his family. A site is relevant if it contains any information on Abells who were located in or near LaRue County, Kentucky, prior to or around the year 1876. Try to use the same technique with your ancestor. For more information on how to extract genealogical information from your family to use in your research, see Chapter 2.

Selecting a grandparent's name

Having trouble selecting a name? Why not try one of your grandparent's names? Using a grandparent's name can have several benefits. If you find some information on an individual but you aren't sure whether it's relevant to your family, you can check with relatives to see whether they know any additional information that can help you. This may also spur interest in genealogy in other family members who can then assist you with some of your research burden or produce some family documents that you never knew existed.

With a name in hand, you're ready to see how much information is currently available on the Internet about that individual. Because this is just one step in a long journey to discover your family history, keep in mind that you want to begin slowly. *Don't try to examine every resource right from the start.* You're more likely to become overloaded with information if you try to find too many resources too quickly. Your best approach is to begin searching a few sites until you get the hang of how to find information about your ancestors online. And keep in mind that you can always book-mark sites in your Web browser or record the URL in a spreadsheet so you can easily return to them later, when you're ready for more in-depth researching.

Too Many Ancestor Irons in the Research Fire

One last piece of advice: When you begin your research, take your time and don't get in a big hurry. Keep things simple and look for one piece of information at a time. If you try to do too much too fast, you risk getting confused, having no online success, and getting frustrated with the Internet. This result isn't very encouraging and certainly doesn't make you feel like jumping back into your research, which would be a shame because you can find a lot of valuable information and research help online.

Chapter 2

Getting to Know You (And Your Ancestors)

. . . .

In This Chapter

▶ Getting information from kinfolk
▶ Gathering records you already have
▶ Using census records
▶ Finding help at societies

. . . .

You may not believe it when we tell you this, but one of the first things to do when researching your family history online doesn't involve a computer. That's right: You don't necessarily need to flip that switch on that computer to start your research. Start by collecting some basic information about your family the "old-fashioned" way — getting family stories from relatives, digging through trunks in the attic, and visiting some traditional places for records. Then you can use some of this basic information to guide your research and help you make decisions about the quality of the information you find online.

In addition to helping to determine whether online information is helpful to your particular research, you need a good grounding in traditional research because you can't complete your entire family history online. We want to make sure that your expectations of online research are appropriate. Although you can find a lot of records online and the number of original records available online increases every day, several sets of crucial records are still not available through the Internet. The best way to think of online genealogy is as one of many tools that you use to put together the pieces of your family puzzle.

In this chapter, we give an overview of several resources that you can rely on for information before you begin your online genealogical research and to which you're likely to return over and over again as you start researching additional family lines. We also provide some Web sites that can assist you in accessing these resources.

Helping Yourself to a Good Start

You are really excited about getting started finding information on your great-great-grandfather Absalom Looney. You fire up the computer, log on to your online service, and put good old Absalom's name into one of the many genealogical search sites. The Results Web page comes up, showing entries for 685 Absalom Looneys with the same name. Of course, the question is whether any of these people are the Absalom you're looking for and, if so, which is the magic one? Well, if you know a little bit about Absalom, you can make some decisions as to which record or site is likely to contain information about him.

At this point, you might be asking yourself how you find information that can confirm whether the Absalom on the screen is the one you're looking for. You're in luck because that's just what this section is all about. But before we go any further, we want to let you in on a little secret: Instead of starting your journey with Absalom, it's better to begin by finding information about someone you already know a little bit better — yourself.

Creating a biographical brag book

You already know more about yourself than anyone else knows about you. (Regardless of what your spouse thinks he knows, we are convinced that you're really the expert on you.) You probably know your birth date, place of birth, parents' names, and where you've lived. (We recognize that not everyone knows all this information; adoptions or other extenuating circumstances may require you to do the best you can with what you know until you can discover additional information about yourself.) So, sit down at that computer, open your word processor, and create an autobiographical sketch. (Of course, if you prefer, you can take out a piece of paper or spiral notebook and write down all those details instead.)

You can approach the sketch in several ways. Sometimes, the easiest method is to begin with current events and work back through your life. For instance, first note the basics: your current marital or family status, occupation, residence, and activities. Then move back to your last residence, occupation, and so on until you arrive at your birth date. Make sure that you include milestones like children's birth dates, marriage dates, military service dates, educational experience, religious affiliations, participation in organizations and sports, and other significant events in your life. If you prefer, you can cover your life by beginning with your birth and working forward to the present. Either way is fine, as long as all the important events are listed in the sketch.

Another method is to use index cards or a spreadsheet on

your computer to make notes about things that you recall over a certain period of time. Then you can arrange the cards or spreadsheet cells/fields to create a biographical sketch.

The biographical sketch that you create now may become an important research tool for one of your descendants who decides to conduct research about you in the future. So, when you have the time, we recommend that you turn that sketch into a full-blown autobiography. This way, your descendants not only know the facts about your life, but they also will have some insight as to why you chose the paths you did throughout your life.

Finding primary sources

If you're like most of us, you think you know a lot about yourself. If we ask you what your birthday is, you can tell us without batting an eye. But how do you know the birth date? You were obviously there, but probably you were not in a condition to be a reliable witness — given that you were just born and most likely not fully aware of what was going on. This is where primary sources come in handy. Most likely there were witnesses present who helped create a record of the event.

Primary sources are documents, oral accounts (if the account is made soon after the actual event and witnessed by the person who created the account), photographs, or any other items created at the time of a certain event's occurrence.

For example, a primary source for your birth date is your birth certificate. Typically, a birth certificate is prepared within a few days of the actual event and is signed by one or more actual witnesses to the birth. Because of the timeliness and involvement of direct witnesses, the information contained on the record (like the time, date, and parents' names) is usually a reliable firsthand account of the event. It's important to recognize that even if a record was prepared near the time of an event, such a unilateral account doesn't automatically mean that every fact provided on the record is correct. Cases arise where typographical errors occurred, or incorrect information was provided to the creator of the record. Often these errors are not caught when the certificate application is signed because new parents are preoccupied with things other than government paperwork during their stay at the hospital. So it's always a good idea to try to find other primary records that can corroborate the information found in any record.

Secondary sources are documents, oral accounts, and so on that are created some length of time after the event or for which information is supplied by someone who wasn't an eyewitness to the event. A secondary source can also be a person who was an eyewitness to the event but recalls it after a significant period of time passes.

Some records may be considered both primary and secondary sources. For example, a death certificate contains both primary and secondary source information. The primary source information includes the death date and cause of death. These facts are primary because the certificate was prepared around the time of death, and the information is usually provided by a medical professional who pronounced the person dead. The secondary source information on the death certificate includes the birth date and place of birth of the deceased individual. These details are secondary because the certificate was issued at a time significantly later than the birth (assuming that the birth and death dates are at least a few years apart). Secondary sources don't have the degree of reliability or surety of primary sources. Often secondary source information, such as that found on death certificates, is provided by an individual's children or descendants who may or may not know the exact date or place of birth and who may be providing information during a stressful situation. Given the lesser reliability of secondary sources, we recommend backing up your secondary sources with reliable primary sources whenever possible.

Although we've said that secondary sources are not as reliable as primary sources, that doesn't mean that secondary sources are always wrong or aren't useful. A good deal of the time, the information is correct, and such records provide valuable clues to locating primary source information. For example, in the case of a birth date and birthplace on a death certificate, the information provides a place and approximate time frame you can use as a starting point when you search for a birth record.

You can familiarize yourself with primary sources by collecting some information for your own biographical profile. Try to match up primary sources for each event in the sketch — for example, birth and marriage certificates, deeds, leases, diplomas or certificates of degree, military records, and tax records. There's more information on finding some of these types of documents later in this chapter. If you can't locate primary source documents for each event in your life, don't fret! Your biographical sketch can serve as a primary source document because you write it about yourself.

For additional information on primary sources, see The Historian's Sources page at the Library of Congress Web site at

lcweb2.loc.gov/ammem/ndlpedu/lessons/psources/pshome.html

For comparisons of primary, secondary, and *tertiary* sources and more examples of each, see James Cook University's overview of Primary, Secondary, and Tertiary Sources at

www.library.jcu.edu.au/LibraryGuides/primsrcs.shtml

or William Madison Randall Library's Identifying Primary, Secondary, and Tertiary Sources at

library.uncw.edu/web/research/topic/identifysources.html

Getting the 4-1-1 from Your Kinfolk

It is likely that you have some valuable but overlooked sources of genealogical gold. You are probably looking right through them as they hang around the food table at the family reunion, ask you embarrassing questions about your love life, and overstay their welcome in your home. Yes, they are your relatives.

Interviewing your relatives is an important step in the research process. They can provide family records and photographs, give you the dirt on other family members, and identify which other people would be beneficial to talk to about the family history. When talking with relatives, you want to collect the same type of information about their lives that you provided about your own when you wrote your biographical sketch.

Your parents, brothers, sisters, grandparents, aunts, uncles, and cousins are all good candidates for information sources about your family's most recent generations. Talking to relatives provides you with leads that you can use to find primary sources. (For more information on primary sources, see "Finding primary sources" in the preceding section.) You can complete family interviews in person or through a questionnaire — although we strongly recommend that you conduct them in person. For an example of a cover letter to send your family asking for an interview, go

to the Family Tree Maker Web site at

www.familytreemaker.com/00000059.html

There's no easy way to say this, so please excuse us for being blunt — you may want to begin interviewing some of your older relatives as soon as possible, depending on their ages and health. If a family member passes on before you have the chance to interview him or her, you may miss the opportunity of a lifetime to learn more about his or her personal experiences and knowledge of previous generations.

Here are a few tips to remember as you plan a family interview:

✔ **Prepare a list of questions that you want to ask:** Knowing what you want to achieve during the discussion helps you get started and keeps your interview focused. (See the sidebar "Good interviewing questions" in this chapter for some ideas.) However, you also need to be flexible enough to allow the interviewee to take the conversation where he or she wants to go. Often some of the best information comes from memories that occur while the interviewee is talking — rather than being generated strictly in response to a set of questions.

✔ **Bring a recorder to the interview:** Use a recorder of your choice whether it's your computer, an audiocassette recorder, or a video camera. Make sure that you get permission from each participant before you start recording. If the interviewee is agreeable and you have the equipment, we recommend you videotape the session. That way, you can see the expressions on his or her face as he or she talks.

- ✔ **Use photographs and documents to help your family members recall events:** Often photographs can have a dramatic effect on the stories that the interviewee remembers. If there is a lull in the interview, pulling out a photo album is an excellent way to jump-start things.

- ✔ **Try to limit your interviews to two hours or less:** You don't want to be overwhelmed with information, and you don't want the interviewee to get worn out by your visit. Within two hours, you can collect a lot of information to guide your research. And remember, you can always do another interview if you want more information from the family member. (Actually, we strongly encourage you to do subsequent interviews — often the first interview stimulates memories for the individual that you can cover during a later interview. Who knows? It might lead to a regularly scheduled lunch or tea time with a relative whom you genuinely enjoy visiting.)

- ✔ **Be grateful and respectful:** Remember that these are people who have agreed to give you time and answers. Treat them with respect by listening attentively and speaking politely to them. And by all means, be sure to thank them when you've completed the interview.

Treasure-Hunting in Your Closet, Basement, and Under the Bed

Are you, or have you ever been, accused of being a pack rat? You know what we mean: someone who keeps every little scrap of paper that he or she touches. Recently we heard that such people are not called pack rats anymore — it's not

Good interviewing questions

Before you conduct a family interview, pull together a set of questions to guide the discussion. A little planning on your part makes the difference between an interview in which the family member stays focused, or a question-and-answer session that invites bouncing from one unrelated topic to another. Here are examples of some questions that you may want to ask:

- ✔ What is your full name, and do you know why you were named that?

- ✔ Where were you born and when? Do you remember any stories that your parents told you about your birth?

- ✔ What do you remember about your childhood?

- ✔ Where did you go to school? Did you finish school? If not, why? (Remember to ask about all levels of schooling through college.)

- ✔ What were your brothers and sisters like?

- ✔ Where and when were your parents born? What did they look like? What were their occupations?

- ✔ Did your parents tell you how they met?

- ✔ Do you remember your grandparents? Do you recall any stories about them? What did they look like?

- ✔ Did you hear any stories about your great-grandparents? Did you ever meet your great-grandparents?

- ✔ When you were a child, who was the oldest person in your family?

- Did any relatives (other than your immediate family) live with you?

- Do you remember who your neighbors were when you were a child?

- Did your family have any traditions or celebrate any special holidays?

- Have any items (stories, traditions, or physical items) been handed down through several generations of the family?

- When did you leave home? Where did you live?

- Did you join the military? If so, what branch of service were you in? What units were you a part of? Did you serve overseas?

- What occupations have you had? Did you have any special training?

- How did you meet your spouse?

- When and where did you get married? Did you go on a honeymoon? Where?

- When were your children born? Do you have any stories about their births?

- Do you know who in the family originally immigrated to this country? Where did they come from? Why did they leave their native land?

You can probably think of more questions that are likely to draw responses from your family. If you want to see additional hints for conducting interviews, see the Capturing the Past Web site (www.byubroadcasting.org/capturingpast/).

politically correct or doesn't sound fancy enough or something. Apparently we're supposed to refer to people who keep everything as chronic hoarders. Regardless of what you call yourself, you know who you are. (And we know how to recognize you because — and here's a deep, dark confession — we're *both* pack rats of the serious variety!) If you are, you're well suited for genealogy. In fact, if you're lucky, you descended from a whole family of pack rats who saved all those scraps from the past in their attics or basements. You may be able to share in their treasures — digging to find things that can further your genealogical research. For example, pay a visit to grandma's attic, and you may discover an old suitcase or cigar box full of documents like driver's licenses, wartime ration cards, and letters. These items may contain information that you can use to reconstruct your ancestor's past.

When you go through old family treasures, look for things that can serve as primary sources for facts that you want to verify. For more information on primary sources, see "Finding primary sources," earlier in this chapter. Here's a list (although not an exhaustive one) of some specific things to look for:

- Family Bibles
- Legal documents (such as mortgages, titles, and deeds)
- Insurance policies
- Wills
- Family letters
- Obituaries and newspaper articles
- Diaries

- Naturalization records

- Baptismal certificates and other church records

- Copies of vital records (such as birth, marriage, and death certificates, and divorce decrees)

- Report cards from school

- Occupational or personnel records

- Membership cards

These gems that you find buried around the house contain all sorts of information: names and vital statistics of ancestors; names and addresses of friends of the family and neighbors; military units; religious affiliations; medical conditions and names of doctors or hospitals; work histories; and so many other things that will add color to your family history as well as give you place names and timeframes to guide you in your subsequent research.

For a list of other items to look for around the home, see the Treasures in the Attic page at

www.ancestry.com/library/view/ancmag/673.asp

Dusting Off the Old Photo Albums

A picture is worth a thousand words — so the saying goes. That's certainly true in genealogy. Photographs are among the most treasured documents for genealogists. Pictures show how your ancestors looked and what conditions they lived in. Sometimes the flip side of the photo is more important than the picture itself. On the back, you may find crucial information such as names, dates, and descriptions of places.

Photographs are also useful as memory-joggers for your family members. Pictures can help others recollect the past and bring up long-forgotten memories. Just be forewarned — sometimes the memories are good, and sometimes they're not so good! Although you may stimulate thoughts of some great moments long ago, you may also open a can of worms when you ask grandma about a particular person in a picture. On the plus side, in the end she may give you the lowdown on not only that person but every single individual in the family who has ever made her angry — this can provide lots of genealogical leads.

You may run into several different types of photographs in your research. Knowing when certain kinds of photographs were produced can help you associate a time frame with a picture. Here are some examples:

- **Daguerreotypes:** Daguerreotype photos were taken from 1839 to 1860. They required a long exposure time and were taken on silver-plated copper. The photographic image appears to change from a positive to a negative when tilted.

- **Ambrotypes:** Ambrotypes used a much shorter exposure time and were produced from 1858 to 1866. The image was made on thin glass and usually had a black backing.

- **Tintypes:** Tintypes were produced from 1858 to 1910. They were made on a metal sheet, and the image was often coated with a varnish. You can usually find them in a paper cover.

- **Cartes-de-visite:** Cartes-de-visite were small paper prints mounted on a card. They were often bound together into a photo album. They were produced between 1858 and 1891.

- ✔ **Cabinet cards:** Cabinet cards were larger versions of cartes-de-visite. They sometimes included dates on the borders of the cards. The pictures themselves were usually mounted on cardboard. They were manufactured primarily between 1865 and 1906.

- ✔ **Albumen prints:** These were produced on thin pieces of paper that were coated with albumen and silver nitrate. They were usually mounted on cardboard. These prints were used between 1858 and 1910 and were the types of photographs found in cartes-de-visite and cabinet cards.

- ✔ **Stereographic cards:** Stereographic cards were paired photographs that rendered a three-dimensional effect when used with a stereographic viewer. They were prevalent from 1850 to 1925.

- ✔ **Platinum prints:** Platinum prints have a matte surface that appears embedded in the paper. The images were often highlighted with artistic chalk. They were produced mainly between 1880 and 1930.

- ✔ **Glass-plate negatives:** Glass-plate negatives were used between 1848 and 1930. They were made from light-sensitive silver bromide immersed in gelatin.

When you deal with photographs, keep in mind that too much light or humidity can easily destroy them. For more information on preserving photographs, see Chapter 3. Also, some online resources can help you identify types of pictures. See the City Gallery Web site (www.city-gallery.com/learning/) for information about nineteenth-century photography, and visit the Everything You Ever Wanted to Know About Your Family Photographs page at for descriptions of several types of photographs.

Sifting Through Birth, Death, Marriage, and Divorce Records

Vital records are among the first sets of primary sources typically used by genealogists (for more on primary sources, see "Finding primary sources," earlier in this chapter). Vital records include birth, marriage, divorce, and death records. For the most part, local governments keep the originals (although some governments have microfilmed them and stored them centrally). These records contain key and usually reliable information because they were produced near the time that the event occurred, and a witness to the actual event provided the information. (Outside the United States, vital records are often called *civil registrations.*)

Vital records are usually maintained in the county or parish, or in some cases the town, where the event occurred. Normally, you must contact the county, parish, or town clerk to receive a copy of a record. Some states centrally collect or microfilm their vital records, and they're available for public use at the state archives or library. You can find an online list of centralized vital record repositories in each of the United States at the Vital Records Information site (vitalrec.com). For information on where to find vital record (and civil registration) information online, see Chapter 5.

Each state has different laws regarding the release of vital records. It's a good idea to check the policy of the governing agency before making the trip or ordering a vital record. In some cases, the agency may only release a record for a good cause or to a close relative.

Birth records

Birth records are good primary sources for verifying — at a minimum — the date of birth, birthplace, and names of an individual's parents. Depending on the information requirements for a particular birth certificate, you may also learn the birthplace of the parents, their ages, occupations, addresses at the time of the birth, whether the mother had given birth previously, date of marriage of the parents, and the names and ages of any previous children. Sometimes, instead of a birth certificate, you may find another record in the family's possession that verifies the existence of the birth record. For example, instead of having a certified copy of a birth certificate, Matthew's grandmother had a Certificate of Record of Birth. This certificate attests to the fact that the county has a certificate of birth and notes its location. These certificates were used primarily before photocopiers became commonplace, and it became easier to get a certified copy of the original record.

Birth records were less formal in earlier times. Before modern record-keeping, a simple handwritten entry in a book sufficed as an official record of an individual's birth. So be very specific when citing a birth record in your genealogical notes. Include any numbers you find on the record and where the record is located (including not only the physical location of the building, but also the book number and page number of the information, and even the record number if one is present).

Marriage records

Marriage records come in several forms. Early marriage records may include the following:

- **Marriage bonds:** Financial guarantees that a marriage was going to take place

70

- **Marriage banns:** Proclamations of the intent to marry someone in front of a church congregation

- **Marriage licenses:** Documents granting permission to marry

- **Marriage records or certificates:** Documents certifying the union of two people

These records usually contain — at a minimum — the groom's name, the bride's name, and the location of the ceremony. They may also contain occupation information, birthplaces of the bride and groom, parents' names and birthplaces, names of witnesses, and information on previous marriages.

Here's one thing to be careful about when using marriage records: Don't confuse the date of the marriage with the date of the marriage bond, bann, or license — it's easy to do. The latter records were often filed anywhere from a couple of days to several weeks *before* the actual marriage date. Also, do not assume that because you found a bond, bann, or license that a marriage actually took place. Some people got cold feet then (as they do today) and backed out of the marriage at the last minute.

If you have trouble finding a marriage record in the area where your ancestors lived, try looking in surrounding counties or parishes or possibly even states. Like today, it was not uncommon to marry in a nearby town in order to have the wedding at a particular relative's house or church. So if the record isn't in the location you expect, be sure to look in the areas where the parents of the ancestors lived.

Divorce records

Genealogists often overlook divorce records. Later generations may not be aware that an early ancestor was divorced,

71

and the records recounting the event can be difficult to find. However, divorce records can be quite valuable. They contain many important facts, including the age of the petitioners, birthplace, address, occupations, names and ages of children, property, and the grounds for the divorce.

Death records

Death records are excellent resources for verifying the date of death, but are less reliable for other data elements such as birth date and birthplace, because people who were not witnesses to the birth often supply that information. However, information on the death record can point you in the right direction for records to verify other events. More recent death records include the name of the individual, place of death, residence, parents' names, spouse's name, occupation, and cause of death. Early death records may only contain the date of death, cause, and residence.

Coming to Your Census

A lot of key dates in a person's life are recorded in vital records (see "Sifting Through Birth, Death, Marriage, and Divorce Records," earlier in this chapter, for more details). However, unless your ancestors were consistently encountering life-events that resulted in numerous vital records, there will still be some gaps to fill in your research. Census records are an excellent resource in the United States for filling in these gaps. *Census records* are periodic counts of a population by a government or organization. These counts can be regular (such as every ten years) or special one-time counts made for a specific reason. Some censuses contain just statistical information; others contain names and additional demographic information.

United States census schedules

Federal census records in the United States have been around since 1790. Censuses were conducted every ten years to count the population for a couple of reasons — to divide up the number of seats in the U.S. House of Representatives, and to assess federal taxes. Although census collections are still done to this day, privacy restrictions prevent the release of any detailed census information on individuals for 72 years. Currently, you can find federal census data only for the census years 1790 to 1930. However, practically all of the 1890 Census was destroyed due to actions taken after a fire in the Commerce building in 1921 — for more on this, see "First in the Path of the Firemen," The Fate of the 1890 Population Census, at

www.archives.gov/publications/prologue/1996/spring/1890
-census-1.html

Federal census records are valuable in that you can use them to take historical "snapshots" of your ancestors in ten-year increments. These snapshots enable you to track your ancestors as they moved from county to county or state to state, and to identify the names of parents and siblings of your ancestors that you may not have previously known.

Each census year contains a different amount of information, with more modern census returns (also called *schedules*) containing the most information. Schedules from 1790 to 1840 only list the head of household for each family, along with the number of people living in the household broken down by age classifications. Schedules from 1850 on have the names and ages of all members of the household.

The people who collected census details on individuals were called *enumerators.* Traveling door to door, these census-takers worked within an assigned district where they stopped at each residence to ask questions about the household. Being a census enumerator was not the most glamorous work. They were typically paid small amounts of money — usually barely enough to cover their expenses. Enumerators possessed differing levels of training and penmanship. These variations resulted in census returns that contained some readable information and some that had illegible entries and notes. Of course, on the plus side for genealogists, some enumerators went beyond the call of duty and made interesting notes on the families that they visited.

Using American Soundex to search United States census records

For the censuses conducted from 1880 to 1920, you can use microfilmed indices organized under the American Soundex system.

The *American Soundex* system is a method of indexing that groups together names that are pronounced in a similar way but are spelled differently. This indexing procedure allows you to find ancestors who may have changed the spelling of their names over the years. For example, you find names like Helm, Helme, Holm, and Holme grouped together in the American Soundex.

The American Soundex code for a name consists of a letter and then three numbers. (Double letters count for only one number, and if your surname is short or has a lot of vowels in it, you use zeros on the end to bring the total numbers to three.) To convert your surname to American Soundex, use the first letter of your surname as the first letter of the American Soundex code, and then substitute

74

numbers for the next three consonants according to the following table. (For example, the American Soundex code for the surname *Helm* is H450.)

1	B, P, F, V
2	C, S, K, G, J, Q, X, Z
3	D, T
4	L
5	M, N
6	R

We know that probably sounds confusing, so just follow these steps to convert your surname to an American Soundex code:

1. **Write down your surname on a piece of paper.**
   As an example, we convert the surname *Abell.*

2. **Keep the first letter of the surname and then cross out any remaining vowels (A, E, I, O, U) and the letters *W, Y,* and *H*.**
   If your surname begins with a vowel, keep the first vowel. If your surname does not begin with a vowel, cross out all the vowels in the surname. So, in the surname *Abell,* we keep the letters *A, B, L,* and *L.*

3. **If the surname has double letters, cross out the second letter.**
   For example, the surname Abell has a double *L,* so we cross out the second *L,* which leaves us with the letters *A, B,* and *L.*

4. **Convert your letters to the American Soundex code numbers according to the preceding chart.**
   We have the letters *A, B,* and *L* remaining. Because *A*

is the first letter of the surname, it remains an *A*. The *B* converts to the number 1 and the *L* to the number 4. That leaves us with A14.

5. **Cross out the second occurrence of any repeated numbers that are side by side, including a number that repeats the value that the letter at the beginning would have.**
   The remaining numbers of the Abell (A14) surname do not have the same numerical code next to each other. But it could happen with a name like Schaefer. Ordinarily, the name Schaefer would have the American Soundex code of S216. However, because the *S* and the *C* would both have the code of 2 and are side by side, you would eliminate the second 2 and come up with an American Soundex code of S160.

6. **If you do not have three numbers remaining, fill in the rest with zeros.**
   Only two numbers remain in the Abell surname after we cross out the vowels and double letters. Because the American Soundex system requires a total of three numbers to complete the code, we must fill in the remaining numerical spot with a zero. Thus, our result for Abell is A140.

If you're like us, you want the most efficient way to do things. Although figuring out an American Soundex is not overly complicated, it can be a little time-consuming if you have several names to calculate. Fortunately, there are some free online sites that calculate American Soundex codes. Here are a few:

✔ **Yet Another Soundex Converter:**

www.bradandkathy.com/genealogy/yasc.html

✔ Surname to Soundex Code:

resources.rootsweb.com/cgi-bin/soundexconverter

✔ Surname to Soundex Converter:

www.geocities.com/Heartland/Hills/3916/soundex
.html

American Soundex indexes are subject to human error and in some cases are incomplete — for example, the 1880 Federal Census American Soundex primarily focuses on indexing those households with children age 10 years or younger. And those who carried out the actual indexing did not always handle American Soundex codes correctly or consistently. So the indexer may have made a coding error or failed to include some information. Therefore, if you're relatively certain that an ancestor *should* show up in a particular county in a census that uses American Soundex, but the American Soundex microfilm doesn't reflect that person, you may want to go through the census microfilm for that county anyway and look line by line for your ancestor. This process may seem tedious but the results can be very worthwhile.

We should also mention that population schedules were not the only product of the federal censuses. There were also special schedules including returns of slaves, mortality, agriculture, manufacturing, and veterans. Each type of special schedule contains information pertaining to a specific group or occupation. In the case of slave schedules (used in the 1850 and 1860 censuses), slaves were listed under the names of the slaveowner, and information was provided on the age, gender, and race of the slave. If the slave was over 100 years of age, his or her name was listed on the schedules (although names may have been included for other slaves if the enumerator felt inclined to list them).

Soundex improvements

Many of you have heard of the Soundex System — especially if you've worked with the United States census in the past, or you live in a state that uses the Soundex as part of your driver's license number, or you're just a nut for indexing systems. However, you might not realize that there's more than one Soundex System. The American Soundex, which is the one used for the United States census and the one most widely recognized, is not the only one, nor was it the first system developed.

The ***Russell Soundex System***: Robert C. Russell patented the first Soundex system in 1918. The Russell Soundex System categorizes the alphabet phonetically and assigns numbers to the categories. There are eight categories and four other rules to follow. The odd-looking terms that refer to parts of the mouth are technical descriptions of how to make the sounds; just try making the sounds of the letters shown with each one, and you'll get the idea. Here's what they look (and sound) like:

Categories

1. Vowels or Oral Resonants: *a, e, i, o, u, y*
2. Labials and Labio-Dentals: *b, f, p, v*
3. Gutturals and Sibilants: *c, g, k, g, s, x, z*
4. Dental-Mutes: *d, t*
5. Palatal-Fricative: *l*
6. Labio-Nasal: *m*
7. Dento- or Lingua-Nasal: *n*
8. Dental-Fricative: *r*

Other Rules

✔ The code always begins with the first letter of the word.

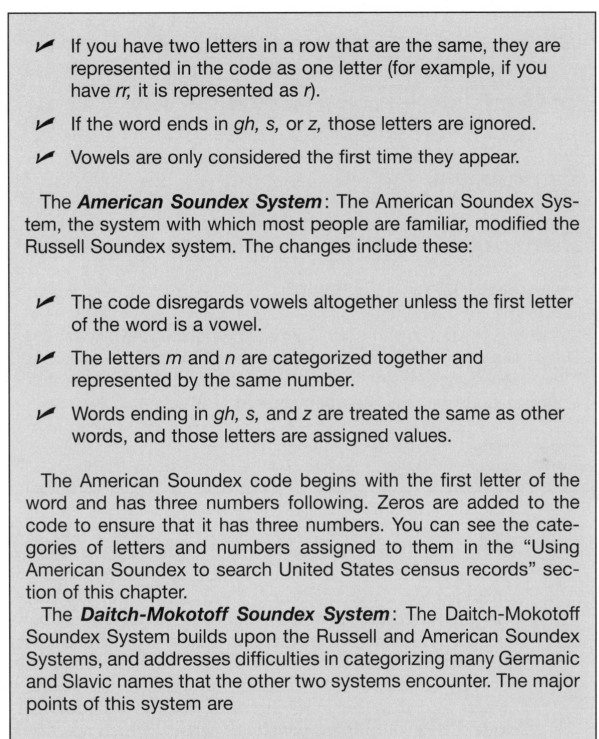

✔ If you have two letters in a row that are the same, they are represented in the code as one letter (for example, if you have *rr*, it is represented as *r*).

✔ If the word ends in *gh, s,* or *z,* those letters are ignored.

✔ Vowels are only considered the first time they appear.

The ***American Soundex System***: The American Soundex System, the system with which most people are familiar, modified the Russell Soundex system. The changes include these:

✔ The code disregards vowels altogether unless the first letter of the word is a vowel.

✔ The letters *m* and *n* are categorized together and represented by the same number.

✔ Words ending in *gh, s,* and *z* are treated the same as other words, and those letters are assigned values.

The American Soundex code begins with the first letter of the word and has three numbers following. Zeros are added to the code to ensure that it has three numbers. You can see the categories of letters and numbers assigned to them in the "Using American Soundex to search United States census records" section of this chapter.

The ***Daitch-Mokotoff Soundex System***: The Daitch-Mokotoff Soundex System builds upon the Russell and American Soundex Systems, and addresses difficulties in categorizing many Germanic and Slavic names that the other two systems encounter. The major points of this system are

✔ The code is made up of six numbers.

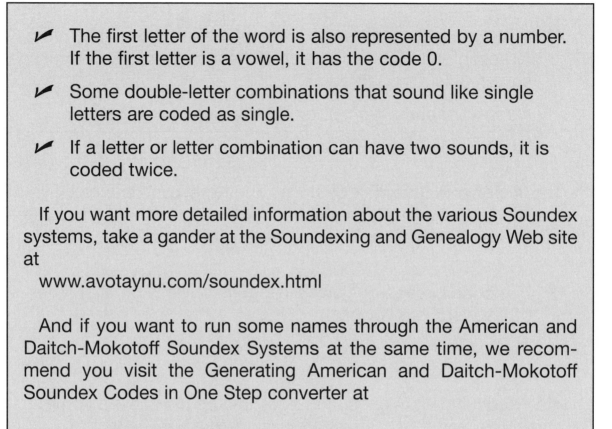

✔ The first letter of the word is also represented by a number. If the first letter is a vowel, it has the code 0.

✔ Some double-letter combinations that sound like single letters are coded as single.

✔ If a letter or letter combination can have two sounds, it is coded twice.

If you want more detailed information about the various Soundex systems, take a gander at the Soundexing and Genealogy Web site at
www.avotaynu.com/soundex.html

And if you want to run some names through the American and Daitch-Mokotoff Soundex Systems at the same time, we recommend you visit the Generating American and Daitch-Mokotoff Soundex Codes in One Step converter at

stevemorse.org/census/soundex.html

Mortality schedules (used in 1850, 1860, 1870, and 1880) include information on people who died in the 12 months previous to the start of the census. Agricultural schedules were used between 1840 and 1910. However, only the schedules from 1840 to 1880 survive. They contained detailed demographic and financial information on farm owners. Manufacturing schedules (taken infrequently between 1810 and 1880) contain information on business owners and their business interests. Veteran schedules include the Revolutionary pensioner census, which was taken as part of the 1840 Census, and the special census for Union veterans and their widows (taken in 1890).

Other census records in the United States

Federal census records are not the only population enumerations you'll find for ancestors in the United States. You may also find census records at the state, territorial, and local level for certain areas of the United States. For example, the state of Illinois has federal census records for 1810 (one county), 1820, 1830, 1840, 1850, 1860, 1870, 1880, 1890 (small fragment), 1900, 1910, and 1920. In addition to these, Illinois has two territorial censuses taken in 1810 and 1818 — and eight state censuses taken in 1820, 1825, 1830, 1835, 1840, 1845, 1855, and 1865. Some city-census enumerations were taken in the 1930s, and a military census was taken in 1862. Other states that have state or territorial census returns include Alabama, Alaska, Arizona, Arkansas, California, Colorado, Delaware, District of Columbia, Florida, Georgia, Hawaii, Indiana, Iowa, Kansas, Louisiana, Maine, Maryland, Massachusetts, Michigan, Minnesota, Mississippi, Missouri, Nebraska, Nevada, New Jersey, New Mexico, New York, North Carolina, North Dakota, Oklahoma, Oregon, Rhode Island, South Carolina, South Dakota, Tennessee, Texas, Utah, Virginia, Washington, Wisconsin, and Wyoming.

Non-federal census records can often help you piece together your ancestors' migration patterns or account for ancestors who may not have been enumerated in the federal censuses. Sometimes, these censuses can also provide more detail on your ancestors than the federal census schedules can.

Guides that offer information on census returns at the local and state level include *Ancestry's Red Book: American State, County and Town Sources,* Third Revised Edition, edited by Alice Eichholz (Ancestry Publishing), *Your Guide to the Federal Census: For Genealogists, Researchers, and Family Historians,* by Kathleen Hinckley (Betterway Books), and *State Census Records* by Ann Smith Lainhart (Genealogical Publishing Company).

Although state censuses and special schedules from the federal censuses are not readily available on the Internet, there are a few subscription databases online that have some of them. For more information on online subscription databases, flip over to Chapter 4.

Searching census records from other countries

The United States isn't the only country that has collected information on its population. Census counts have taken place in several countries throughout history. Here are examples of a few countries with census records.

Australia

Although Australia has taken a census every ten years since 1901, the first Australia-wide census was conducted in 1911. Now for some bad news — every return has been destroyed, in accordance with law. There are other records that you can substitute for census returns in the form of convict returns and musters and post office directories. These returns are available for some states for the years 1788, 1792, 1796, 1800, 1801, 1805, 1806, 1811, 1814, 1816, 1817, 1818, 1819, 1820, 1821, 1822, 1823, 1825, 1826, and 1837. Some of these records can be found at these locations:

✔ The New South Wales Government, Department of Commerce, State Records Authority of New South Wales site at

www.records.nsw.gov.au/archives/indexes_online_3357.asp

82

↙ The Archives Office of Tasmania at

portal.archives.tas.gov.au/menu.aspx?search=10

↙ The Public Records Office of Victoria at

www.prov.vic.gov.au

For more information on locating census returns, see the Census in Australia page at

www.jaunay.com/auscensus.html

Austria

Austrian censuses were taken in the years 1857, 1869, 1880, 1890, 1900, and 1910. The first census that listed individuals by name was the 1869 Census. These returns include surname, sex, year of birth, place of birth, district, religion, marital status, language, occupation, literacy, mental and physical defects, residence, and whether the household had farm animals.

Canada

Canadian census returns are available for the years 1851, 1861, 1871, 1881, 1891, and 1901. The returns from 1851 to 1891 contain the individual's name, age, sex, province or country of birth, religion, race, occupation, marital status, and education. The returns for 1901 also include birth date, year of immigration, and address. For more information on data elements in the 1901 Census, see the Description of Columns on the 1901 Census Schedule page at

freepages.genealogy.rootsweb.com/~wjmartin/census.htm

These returns are stored at the National Archives of Canada (www.archives.ca/).

If you're looking for online information on specific census records, see the Virtual Reference Library at

www.virtualreferencelibrary.ca/

Scroll down the Subject Directory and select Genealogy, then click on the Census Records link to get to a list of sites specifically about — you guessed it — census records. The list includes sites about the 1752 Laroque Census (Isle Royale and Isle St. Jean), 1872 Victoria Census, The First Census of New France (Quebec), and the 1901 and 1911 censuses for several provinces.

Denmark

The Danish Archives has census returns for the years 1787, 1801, 1834, and 1840, as well as other years up to 1916 at

ddd.dda.dk/kiplink_en.htm

The returns contain name, age, occupation, and relationship for each individual in the household. After 1845, census returns include information on the individual's place of birth. Census returns for Denmark are available after 80 years.

Germany

The German central government held censuses in 1871, 1880, 1885, 1890, 1895, 1900, 1905, 1910, 1919, 1925, 1933, and 1939. Unfortunately, these census returns do not have much genealogical value because they were statistical in nature.

Ireland

Countrywide census enumerations have been conducted every ten years since 1821. Unfortunately, the census returns from 1821 to 1851 were largely destroyed in a fire at the Public Record Office in 1922. Fragments of these census returns are available at the National Archives of Ireland, and an online transcription of the census fragments with more information is available at the Powell & Related Genealogy site at

home.iprimus.com.au/s_steffensen/1851IrelandCensus.htm

The government destroyed the returns from 1861 and 1871. Returns for 1901 and 1911 still survive and are available at the National Archives of Ireland. The 1911 Census for Dublin is available online at

www.nationalarchives.ie

The Public Records Office of Northern Ireland has information about census records for 1901 and the nineteenth century, as well as information about other resources that serve as substitutions for census records. If you are interested in Northern Ireland, see the Public Record Office of Northern Ireland site:

www.proni.gov.uk/records/records.htm

Italy

The Italian State Archives contains national censuses for the years 1861, 1871, 1881, 1891, and 1901. Its Web site is

www.archivi.beniculturali.it

Norway

The first census in Norway was conducted in 1769. A census by name was conducted for the first time in 1801, but was not repeated again until 1865. Each census after 1865 contained information such as name, sex, age, relationship to head of household, civil status, occupation, religion, and place of birth.

An online searchable index of the 1801, 1865, 1875, and 1900 censuses of Norway is available at

digitalarkivet.uib.no/cgi-win/WebFront.exe?slag=vis&tekst=meldingar&spraak=e

The 1865, 1875, and 1900 censuses of Norway are also available from the Norwegian Historical Data Centre. Here's the site:

www.rhd.uit.no/folketellinger/folketellinger_avansert_e.aspx

United Kingdom

Since 1801, censuses have been taken in the United Kingdom every ten years (except 1941). Most of the returns from 1801 to 1831 were statistical and did not contain names, making them useless for genealogists. Beginning in 1841, the administration of the census became the responsibility of the Registrar General and the Superintendent Registrars, who were responsible for recording civil registrations (vital records). This changed the focus of the census from the size of the population to details on individuals and families. The National Archives releases information in the census only after 100 years, and can be found at

www.nationalarchives.gov.uk/census/?homepage=fr-census

The censuses for Scotland from 1841 to 1901 are available at the ScotlandsPeople site maintained by the General Register Office for Scotland:

www.scotlandspeople.gov.uk

Land Ho! Researching Land Records

In the past, an individual's success could be measured by the ownership of land. The more land your ancestors possessed, the more powerful and wealthy they were. This concept often encouraged people to migrate to new countries in the search for land.

Land records may tell you where your ancestor lived prior to purchasing the land, spouse's name, and the names of children, grandchildren, parents, or siblings. To use land records effectively, however, you need to have a general idea of where your ancestors lived and possess a little background information on the history of the areas in which they lived. Land records are especially useful for tracking the migration of families in the United States before the 1790 Census.

Most land records are maintained at the local level — in the town, county, or parish where the property was located. These records can come in multiple forms that reflect various types of land records and the locations in which they exist.

Finding land records in the United States

Your ancestors may have received land in the early United States in several different ways. Knowing more about the ways in which people acquired land historically can aid you in your research.

Your ancestor may have purchased land or received a grant of land in the public domain — often called *bounty lands* — in exchange for military service or some other service for the country. Either way, the process probably started when your ancestor petitioned (or submitted an application) for the land. Your ancestor may have also laid claim to the land, rather than petitioning for it.

If the application was approved, your ancestor was given a *warrant* — a certificate that allowed him or her to receive an amount of land. (Sometimes a warrant was called a *right*.) After your ancestor presented the warrant to a land office, an individual was appointed to make a *survey* — or detailed drawing and legal description of the boundaries — of the land. The land office then recorded your ancestor's name and information from the survey into a *tract book* (a book describing the lots within a township or other geographic area) and on a *plat map* (a map of lots within a tract).

After the land was recorded, your ancestors may have been required to meet certain conditions, such as living on the land for a certain period of time or making payments on the land. After they met the requirements, they were eligible for a *patent* — a document that conveyed title of the land to the new owner.

If your ancestors received bounty lands in the United States, you might be in luck. The Bureau of Land Management, Eastern States Land Office holds land records for public domain land east of the Mississippi River. Here's its site:

www.glorecords.blm.gov

And the National Archives (www.archives.gov/research _room/federal_records_guide/bureau_of_land_managemen t_rg049.html) holds the land records for the Western states.

For secondary land transactions (those made after the original grant of land), you probably need to contact the recorder of deeds for the county in which the land was held.

Here are some Web sites with information on land records:

- **History and Use of Land Records:**

  hometown.aol.com/CookCooke/historyanduse.html

- **Legal Land Descriptions in the USA:**

  www.outfitters.com/genealogy/land/land.html

- **Illinois:** Illinois Public Domain Land Tract Sales

  www.sos.state.il.us/departments/archives/data_lan.html

- **Indiana:** Land Office Records at the Indiana State Archives

  www.in.gov/icpr/archives/databases/land/indiana_.html

- **Louisiana:** State Land Office Online Documents

  1webfn.doa.la.gov/slodocs/SLO/home.asp

- **Maryland:** Land Records in Maryland

  www.mdarchives.state.md.us/msa/refserv/genealogy/html/land.html

- **Ohio:** Introduction to Ohio Land History

  users.rcn.com/deeds/ohio.htm

- **Oklahoma:** Federal Tract Books of Oklahoma Territory

www.sirinet.net/~lgarris/swogs/tract.html

- ✔ **Oregon:** Oregon State Archives Land Records

  arcweb.sos.state.or.us/land.html

- ✔ **Texas:** Texas General Land Office Archives

  www.glo.state.tx.us/archives/archives.html

- ✔ **Virginia:** Introduction to Virginia Land History

  www.ultranet.com/~deeds/virg.htm

- ✔ **Wisconsin:** Wisconsin Public Land Survey Records: Original Field Notes and Plat Maps

  digicoll.library.wisc.edu/SurveyNotes/

Because the topic of land records is so expansive, many books have been devoted to the subject. When you're ready to tackle land records in more depth, you may want to look at William Thorndale's "Land and Tax Records" in *The Source: A Guidebook of American Genealogy,* edited by Loretto Dennis Szucs and Sandra Hargreaves Luebking (Ancestry).

Finding land records in other countries

Depending on the country that you research, you may find a number of ways that land transactions occurred. Unfortunately, online information about historical land records in other countries is scarce. Chapters 5 and 6 offer help, and these links can assist you in figuring out how to research land records if your ancestors were from Canada, England, or Ireland:

✔ **Canada:** Canadian Genealogy Centre — Land

> www.collectionscanada.ca/genealogy/022-912-e.html

✔ **England:** Land Conveyances: Enrolment of Deeds, and Registration of Title

> www.nationalarchives.gov.uk/catalogue/rdleaflet.asp?s LeafletID=148

✔ **Ireland:** Land Records

> scripts.ireland.com/ancestor/browse/records/land/index.htm

Trial and Error at the Courthouse

Do you have an ancestor who was on the wrong side of the law? If so, you may find some colorful information at the courthouse in the civil and criminal court records. Even if you don't have an ancestor with a law-breaking past, you can find valuable genealogical records at your local courthouse. Typical records you can find there include land deeds, birth and death certificates, divorce decrees, wills and probate records, tax records, and some military records (provided the ancestors who were veterans deposited their records locally). We discuss many of these types of records in more detail in Chapter 5.

It's a good idea to check online or call ahead to the courthouse to find out whether the record you're looking for is actually at that facility. Sometimes records are kept at storage facilities off-site; it might be a waste of time to hit the road and go to the courthouse. Also, the more information you can provide to the clerk or customer service representative, the easier it will be for him or her to retrieve the record. Useful information includes full name of the ancestor, approximate date of the record, and any record identification number that you might find in an index to the record set.

Visiting Libraries, Archives, and Historical Societies

Earlier in this chapter, we discuss getting information from living relatives. But your kinfolk aren't the only people who can help you advance your research. There are some "institutional" type resources you don't want to forget.

Inevitably a time will come when you need to visit public (and possibly private) libraries in the areas where your ancestor lived. Although local history sections are not generally targeted toward genealogists, the information you can find there is quite valuable. For example, public libraries often have city directories and phone books, past issues of newspapers (good for obituary hunting), and old map collections. Libraries may also have extensive collections of local history books that can give you a flavor of what life was like for your ancestor in that area. And, of course, some libraries do have genealogy sections that have all sorts of goodies to help you locate records and discover interesting stories about your family. For a list of libraries with online catalogs, see The Library Index site at www.libdex.com/.

Archives are another place to find good information. They exist at several different levels (national, state, and local) and have different owners (public or private). Each archive varies — some may have a large collection of certain types of documents, whereas others may just contain documents from a certain geographical area. To find archives, see the Repositories of Primary Sources page at

www.uidaho.edu/special-collections/Other.Repositories.html

A third place to find additional information is at a historical society. Generally, historical societies have nice collections of maps, documents, and local history books pertaining to the area in which the society is located. They are repositories for collections of papers of people who lived in the community. Often, you can find references to your ancestors in these collections, especially if the person whose personal documents are in the collection wrote a letter or transacted some business with your ancestor. You can find links to historical societies on the Yahoo! site at

dir.yahoo.com/arts/humanities/history/organizations/historical_societies/

Getting Involved with Genealogical Societies

There are times when dealing with all of the different record sets and methods of researching your family can be overwhelming. On such occasions it's nice to be able to sit down with people who have similar experiences or more knowledge than you and discuss your research problems. One place that you can find such a group is your local genealogical society. Genealogical societies hold periodic meetings that focus on particular research methods. Some also have weekend seminars where they bring in genealogical lecturers to address topics of interest to their members.

If you have research needs in other areas of the country (or foreign countries for that matter), you might consider joining a society in that area. Although you do not live there, you can still use the resources of the society to find answers to your questions, and you can contribute to the distant organization more than you realize by sharing your findings and experiences. Most societies have people who are well versed in the records that pertain to the area where the society is located. These individuals can be a great resource as you go through the research process.

To find a genealogical society in the United States, check out the Federation of Genealogical Societies Society Hall at

www.familyhistory.com/societyhall/main.asp

A general search engine (such as Google or AltaVista) can help you find societies in other countries.

We delve into genealogical societies a bit more and explore specific ways you can become active and benefit from them in Chapter 11.

Discovering Family History Centers

If you live in a smaller community, you may be surprised to discover that your hometown has a resource specifically for local genealogical research! Sponsored by the Church of Jesus Christ of Latter-day Saints (LDS), over 3,400 Family History Centers worldwide provide support for genealogical research. Access to microfilms containing images of records are among the important resources found in Family History Centers.

 You are not required to be a member of the LDS church to use a Family History Center; the resources contained within them are available to everyone. Keep in mind that the workers at a Family History Center cannot research your genealogy for you, although they're willing to point you in the right direction. To find a Family History Center, use the FamilySearch search interface, which you can find at

Of course, your local telephone directory will have the Family History Center listed if you have one in your area. However, it probably will not have the hours right there in the phonebook (like the Web site does) so it is a good idea to call ahead and get their hours so you don't show up on a day that they are closed.

Chapter 3

You Found It, Now Keep It

It's the nightmare of any family historian — you spend hours researching a person, find the perfect piece of evidence you need to make a connection to your research, and then you misplace the copy of the record. We admit it. It has happened to us. But, it doesn't have to happen to you, if you keep your documents organized and easily accessible. With a good system of organization and a method of preserving important family heirlooms, you can greatly simplify your research tasks and perhaps find some direction on where to research next. This chapter examines ways of organizing and preserving genealogical information and documents using traditional storage methods and preservation techniques. It also looks at how to use genealogical software to store and organize information about your ancestors, as well as digitized documents and photographs.

Organization, Genealogy Style

We bet that you have seen the stereotypical family researcher — the type who walks into the library while trying to balance a stack of binders and loose-leafed papers. This could be you! There is no way to get around it: If you get into genealogy, you are going to collect tons of paper and photographs. After all, it's a time-honored tradition of genealogists.

Until now, you've probably used any means possible to take notes while talking with relatives about your ancestors or looking up information in the local library — from notebook paper to receipts you have in your pocket or purse to stick-on notes and paper napkins. You may have used your camera to take pictures of headstones in the cemetery where some of your ancestors are buried, or of the old family homestead that's now abandoned and barely standing. And you've probably collected some original source documents; possibly the certified copy of your mother's birth certificate that grandma gave you, the family Bible from Aunt Lola, and the old photograph of your great-great-grandfather as a child that you found while digging through the attic. Now what are you supposed to do with all these treasures? Organize, organize, organize!

Even if you decide to use genealogical software to track your research progress, you're always going to have paper records and photographs you want to keep. The following sections offer some tips to help you become well organized (genealogically, anyway).

Establishing good organizational skills

You probably already discovered that taking notes on little scraps of paper works adequately at first, but the more notes you take, the harder the time you have sorting through them and making sense of the information on each. To avoid this situation, establish some good note-taking and organizational skills early by being consistent in how you take notes. Write the date, time, and place that you do your research, along with the names of the family members you interview, at the top of each page of your notes. Then place those notes into a binder, perhaps organized by family group. This information can help you later on when you return to your notes to look for a particular fact or when you try to make sense of conflicting information.

You want to be as detailed as possible when taking notes on particular events, persons, books, and so forth. Just like you were taught in grade school, you should include the who, what, where, when, why, and how. And most importantly, always cite the source of your information, keeping the following guidelines in mind:

✔ **Person:** If your source is a person, include that person's full name, relationship to you (if any), the information, contact data (address, phone number, e-mail address), and the date and time that you and this person communicated. As the individual is recounting memories and family stories, be sure to ask his or her age at the time of any events that are being recalled. Also be sure to get the person's age at the time of your interview or communication. This information might help you approximate timeframes when looking for documentation to support the story.

✔ **Record:** Include the name or type of record, record number, book number (if applicable), the name and location of the record-keeping agency, and any other pertinent information.

✔ **Book or magazine:** Include all bibliographic information, including the name of the publication, volume number, date of issue, the publisher's name, page number of the applicable article, and the repository where you found the work.

✔ **Microfilm or microfiche:** Include all bibliographic information and note the document media (microfilm roll, microfiche), document number, and repository name.

✔ **Web site or other Internet resource:** Include the name of the copyright holder for the site (or name of the site's creator and maintainer if no copyright notice appears on it), name of the site, address or Uniform Resource Locator (URL) of the site, the date the information was posted or copyrighted, and any notes with traditional contact information for the site's copyright holder or creator.

 It's a good idea to print or save a copy of a Web page using a screen capture utility. You can then place the paper copy in your research files or attach the screen capture image to your genealogical database. Some Web sites have a tendency to disappear over time, so it's best to get documentation of the site while it exists.

 There are many ways to cite sources and even we have a difficult time remembering how to cite each different type of source. Fortunately, Elizabeth Shown Mills has come to the rescue. If you need some help citing almost any kind of source, check out *Evidence Explained: Citing History Sources*

from Artifacts to Cyberspace published by the Genealogical Publishing Company (www.genealogical.com).

Understanding genealogical charts and forms

By the time that you have information on a few hundred people, it will become nearly impossible to keep all of those ancestors straight. To make life simple, family historians use charts and forms to organize research and make findings easier to understand and share. Some examples include Pedigree charts that show the relationships between family members, Descendant charts that list every person who descends from a particular ancestor, and census forms in which you can record information enumerated about your ancestor during particular years. Some of these charts and forms are available online at sites like Genealogy Today at

www.genealogytoday.com/genealogy/enoch/forms.html

The sooner you become familiar with the most common types of charts and how to read them, the sooner you can interpret a lot of the information you receive from other genealogists. (Chapter 2 examines some of these charts and forms in greater detail.)

Assigning unique numbers to family members

If you have ancestors who share the same name, or if you've collected a lot of information on several generations of ancestors, you may have trouble distinguishing one person from another. For example, Matthew has an ancestor Samuel Abell, who had a son and two grandsons also named Samuel Abell. To avoid confusion and the problems that can arise from it, you may want to use a commonly accepted numbering system to keep everyone straight. Now genealogical numbering systems can be a bit confusing (and talking about them can be a little boring) but we'll do our best to make it as simple as possible and to give you a few examples to make it a little clearer.

The ahnentafel (Sosa-Stradonitz) system

One well-known numbering system is called *ahnentafel*, which means "ancestor" (*ahnen*) and "table" (*tafel*) in German. You may also hear the ahnentafel system referred to as the *Sosa-Stradonitz* system (the names get easier, trust us) of numbering because it was first used by a Spanish genealogist named Jerome de Sosa in 1676, and was popularized in 1896 by Stephan Kekule von Stradonitz.

The ahnentafel system is a method of numbering that shows a mathematical relationship between parents and children. Ahnentafel numbering follows this pattern:

1. **The child is assigned a particular number: *y***
   Of course, we recognize that *y* isn't really a number — it's a letter. In our mathematical (that is, algebraic) example, *y* represents a unique number for that particular person.

2. **The father of that child is assigned the number that is double the child's number: 2y**

3. **The mother of that child is assigned a number that is double the child's number plus one: 2y + 1**

4. **The father's father is assigned a number that is double the father's number: 2(2y)**
   The father's mother is assigned the number that is

101

double the father's number plus one: $2(2y) + 1$

5. The mother's father is assigned a number that is double the mother's number: $2(2y + 1)$
The mother's mother is assigned a number that is double the mother's number plus one: $2(2y + 1) + 1$

6. Continue this pattern through the line of ancestors.

The mathematical relationship works the same way going forward through the generations — a child's number is one-half the father's number and one-half (minus any remainder) the mother's number.

In a list form, the ahnentafel for April's grandfather looks like the following list (see Figure 3-1 for the chart):

1   John Duff Sanders, b. 10 Mar 1914 in Benjamin, Knox Co., TX; d. 15 Mar 1996 in Seymour, Baylor Co., TX; ma. 24 Dec 1939 in Sherman, Grayson Co., TX.

2   John Sanders, b. 19 Oct 1872 in Cotton Plant, Tippah Co., MS; d. 2 Mar 1962 in Morton, Cochran Co., TX; ma. 28 Sep 1902 in Boxelder, Red River Co., TX.

3   Nannie Elizabeth Clifton, b. 1 Apr 1878 in Okolona, MS; d. 27 Apr 1936 in Morton, Cochran Co., TX.

4   Harris Sanders, b. 27 Mar 1824 in Montgomery Co., NC; d. 21 Feb 1917 in Tippah Co., MS; ma. 26 June 1853.

5   Emeline Crump, b. 20 Oct 1836; d. 21 Feb 1920 in Tippah Co., MS.

6   William Clifton, b. 5 Mar 1845 in SC; d. 9 Feb 1923 in Boxelder, Red River Co., TX; ma. 5 Nov

1872 in Birmingham, AL.

7   Martha Jane Looney, b. 8 Mar 1844; d. Boxelder, Red River Co., TX.

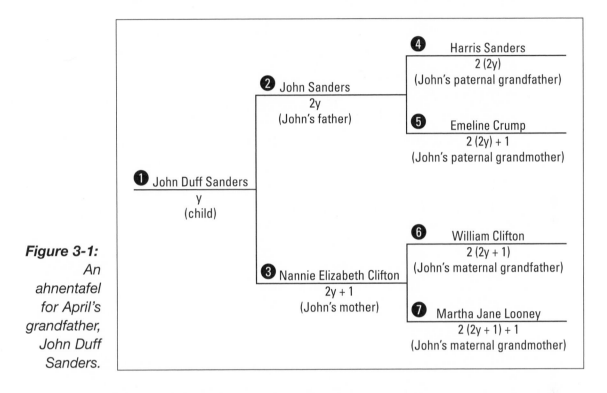

Figure 3-1:
An ahnentafel for April's grandfather, John Duff Sanders.

John Duff Sanders is number one because he's the base individual for the ahnentafel. His father (John Sanders) is number two (because 2 x 1 = 2), and his mother (Nannie Elizabeth Clifton) is number three (2 x 1 + 1 = 3). His father's father (Harris Sanders) is four (2 x 2 = 4), and his father's mother (Emeline Crump) is five (2 x 2 + 1 = 5). John Sanders' number (2) is one-half his father's number (4 ÷ 2 = 2), or one-half minus any remainder of his mother's number (5 ÷ 2 = 2.5; 2.5 minus remainder of .5 = 2) — well, you get the idea.

As you can imagine, after a while, you begin to tire from all these calculations — especially if you do them for ten or more generations of people. So, if your genealogy software supports it, we highly recommend that you run an ahnentafel report from it — saving you a lot of time and trouble.

The tiny tafel system

Some people confuse ahnentafel with *tiny tafel*, which is a compact way to show the relationships within a family database. Tiny tafel provides only the Soundex code for a surname, and the dates and locations where that surname may be found according to the database. (For more on Soundex codes and how they work, check out Chapter 2.) Computer programs sometimes use tiny tafels to match the same individual in two different genealogy databases. The following example shows a tiny tafel:

C413	1845	1936	Clifton\South Carolina/ Cochran Co. TX
C651	1836	1920	Crump/Mississippi
L500	1844		Looney/Red River Co. TX
S536	1824	1996	Sanders\Montgomery Co. NC/Baylor Co. TX

The Henry system

The *Henry* system is another well-known numbering system. This system assigns a particular number to the *progenitor*, or the ancestor farthest back (that you know about) in your family line. Then each of the progenitor's children is assigned a number in a sequence that starts with his number and adds the numbers one, two, three, and so forth through nine. (If the progenitor had more than nine children, the tenth child is assigned an X, the eleventh an A, the twelfth a B, and so on.) Then the children's children are assigned the parent's number plus a number in sequence (again one through nine, then X, A, B, and so on). For example, if progenitor number one (1) had 12 children, then

104

his children would be 11, 12, 13, . . . 1X, and 1A. The eleventh child's children would be assigned the numbers 1A1, 1A2, 1A3, and so forth.

For example, suppose that one of your ancestors, John Jones, had 12 children. The names of these children were Joseph, Ann, Mary, Jacob, Arthur, Charles, James, Maria, Esther, Harriett, Thomas, and Sophia. Joseph had one child named Gertrude and Thomas had three children named Lawrence, Joshua, and David. Under the standard Henry system, the children's children are numbered like this:

1	John Jones		
11	Joseph Jones		
111	Gertrude Jones		
	12	Ann Jones	
	13	Mary Jones	
	14	Jacob Jones	
	15	Arthur Jones	
	16	Charles Jones	
	17	James Jones	
	18	Maria Jones	
	19	Esther Jones	
	1X	Harriett Jones	
	1A	Thomas Jones	
		1A1	Lawrence Jones
		1A2	Joshua Jones
		1A3	David Jones
		1B	Sophia Jones

By no means are these systems the only genealogical numbering systems in existence. Ahnentafel and Henry are just two of the easier systems to learn. Several others have been designed to display genealogies in book form, such as the Register system (based on the style of the New England

Historical and Genealogical Register) and the National Genealogical Society Quarterly system. If you're curious about some of these systems, take a look at the Numbering Systems in Genealogy page at www.saintclair.org/numbers/. There you can find descriptions of each major numbering system and variations of these systems.

If you decide to use a numbering system, you can place the corresponding unique number for each individual on the file that you set up for that person in your paper record-keeping system, as well as in your genealogical software.

Making copies of source documents

You don't want to carry original records with you when you're out and about researching. The chances of misplacing or forgetting a document are too great. You have a few options:

- You can enter the information into a database and take a notebook computer with you.

- You can copy data from your desktop computer to a personal digital assistant (PDA).

- You can copy data from your computer to a CD, DVD, or flash drive (see Chapter 14 for more information about flash drives).

- You can print out your data.

- You can make photocopies of data that you must have with you for your research.

- You can scan the documents and store them on your laptop or notebook computer. (We talk more about using computers for your notes later in this chapter.)

Then use your notes and copies out in the field. Place the

original documents in the safest place you can think of that is available to you — a lockbox, fireproof file cabinet or safe, or a safety-deposit box.

Deciding on a storage method

How are you going to store all that information? A filing system is in order! You can set up a good filing system in many ways, and no one system is right or wrong. Just use one that's comfortable for you.

If you're at a loss as to how to start a system, here's one we like: We prefer to have both electronic and physical components to our filing system. To establish an electronic system, enter your ancestors' names into your database. Most genealogical programs enable you to enter numbers for each individual. Use the numbers that you create in the electronic system on file folders for paper documents that you collect on each individual. Although we like to scan all our paper documents, sometimes we get behind, so we set up temporary folders in which we can store the documents until we can scan them. After we scan the documents, we transfer them to permanent folders that we keep in a fireproof container. You may consider saving your scanned images to a notebook computer's hard drive, an external hard disk, or a writable CD-ROM/DVD-ROM so you can easily transport the images when you go on research trips.

 Make backup copies of all your electronic documents as a safety precaution and store these backups in a location that is off-site from where the originals are stored.

Preserving Your Family Treasures

Time is going to take its toll on every artifact in your possession — whether it is a photograph or an original document. The longer you want your records and pictures to last, the better care you need to take of them now. The following sections discuss some tips for preserving your family treasures so you can pass them down to future generations in the best possible shape.

Storing vital records under the right conditions

Place birth certificates, marriage licenses, and other records between sheets of acid-free paper in albums. Keep these albums in a dark, dry, and temperature-consistent place. Ideally, store these documents in a place that is 65 to 70 degrees Fahrenheit year-round, with a relative humidity of less than 50 percent. You may consider placing these albums in a steel file cabinet (but make sure it's rust-free). Also, try to avoid using ink, staples, paper clips, glue, and tape around your documents (unless you use archival products specifically designed for document repair).

For your precious documents (original birth certificates and family papers), rent a safety-deposit box or find another form of secure off-site storage. Of course, one of the best ways to ensure the success of your preservation effort is to make electronic copies of your documents using a scanner, and then keep disk backups at a fire-safe, off-site location (again, a safety-deposit box is a good choice).

Protecting your photographs

Fight the urge to put all your photos of every ancestor on display, because light can damage them over time. A better option is to scan the photographs and make copies or printouts of them to hang on the wall. Keep your most-prized pictures in a dark, dry, and temperature-consistent place. If you use a photo album for storage, make sure that it has acid-free paper or chemically safe plastic pockets, and that you affix the pictures to the pages using a safe adhesive. Other storage options include acid-free storage boxes and steel file cabinets. Store the photographs in a place that stays around 65 to 70 degrees Fahrenheit year-round, with a relative humidity of less than 50 percent. Avoid prolonged exposure of photographs to direct sunlight and fluorescent lights. And, by all means, have negatives made of those rare family photos and store them in clearly marked, acid-free envelopes (the kind without gumming or glue!).

You can preserve photographs a couple of other ways. First, you can convert photographs from an earlier time to a newer and safer kind of film. A local photograph shop that specializes in preservation can do this for you. Because color photographs fade more quickly than their black-and-white counterparts, you may want to make black-and-white negatives of your color photographs. Also, as with documents, you can always preserve your photographs electronically by scanning them into your computer or by having a photo CD made by your photographic developer.

 An electronic version isn't a real substitute for an original. Don't throw away the photos you scan (but you already knew that).

Here are a few Web sites that provide more detailed tips on preserving your family treasures:

- **Just Black and White's Tips for Preserving Your Photographs and Documents** by David Mishkin: www.maine.com/photos/tip.htm

- **Guidelines for Preserving Your Photographic Heritage** by Ralph McKnight: www.geocities.com/Heartland/6662/photopre.htm

- **Document and Photo Preservation FAQ** by Linda Beyea: loricase.com/faq.html

And when you're looking for some of the chemically safe archival materials that we've described here (including albums, paper, boxes, adhesives, etc.), head on over to

- ✔ **Archival Products** at www.archival.com/
- ✔ **Light Impressions** at http://www.lightimpressions direct.com/servlet/OnlineShopping

Even though you want to preserve everything to the best of your ability, don't be afraid to pull out your albums to show visiting relatives and friends if you want to do so. On the other hand, don't be embarrassed to ask these guests to use caution when looking through your albums. Depending on the age and rarity of some of your documents, you may even want to ask guests to wear latex gloves when handling the albums so the oil from their hands doesn't get on your treasures. Upon realizing how important these treasures are to you, most guests won't mind using caution.

Let's Talk Hardware: Is Your Computer Equipped?

After organizing your paper records and photographs, put your computer to work storing and manipulating your family history. We think that a computer may be your best friend when it comes to storing, organizing, and publishing your genealogical information.

As you grow more accustomed to using the information you store in your computer, you may want to consider adding other hardware and peripheral equipment to your system to enhance your genealogy research and the reports that you generate. You may want to start including electronic images of some of the photographs and original documents that you have in your paper filing system. You may think about adding audio of your grandmother reminiscing, or video of your grandchild greeting people at the family reunion. As you find additional documents, you may want to add images of them to your main database as well. So what kind of computer hardware or other equipment do you need in order to include images and other enhancements with your genealogical information?

You should consider several pieces of equipment as you prepare to enhance your genealogy with audio and video. These include writable CD-ROM or DVD drives, sound cards, video-capture boards, scanners, digital cameras, and external hard drives.

Writable CD-ROM or DVD drives

If you're looking to solve both the space needs of files and mobility issues when you'd like to take your database on the road, you may want to consider getting a writable CD-ROM/DVD drive. With it, you can cut your own data CDs or DVDs — filling them with family photos (which typically take up a lot of space on your computer) or family files that you want to share at the family reunion — or some of both. Writable CD-ROM/DVD drives are available in internal and external varieties. A writable CD-ROM can hold around 650–700 megabytes of information and DVDs can hold around 4.7 *gigabytes.*

Sound cards

A *sound card* is an internal device that is a standard feature on most computers today. It allows you to hear any audio that comes on software (particularly games) or audio files that you download off the Internet. In most cases, the card also enables you to record your own audio from your stereo, radio, video camera, or microphone — but you must have software that supports recordings. If your sound card is capable of recording and you have adequate software, you simply plug the sound source into the microphone jack (or the sound-in jack on the back of your computer), set your software to record, and go for it. After you make the recording, you can import it into your genealogical software if your genealogical software supports audio.

Video-capture devices

Similar to a sound card, a *video-capture board* enables you to grab images from your video camera or VCR. You can use moving images or still pictures, depending on the type of your video-capture board and the accompanying software. Video-capture boards aren't usually a standard feature on computers. They have varying system requirements depending on the manufacturer and the software that's included. Be sure that your computer system can handle a particular video-capture board and software before making your purchase. Or, if you don't want to mess with putting a board inside of your computer, there are several external video-capture products on the market that plug into the USB port on your computer.

Scanners

Scanners remain one of the most popular computer peripherals for genealogists. Everyone wants to include some family photos with their genealogy or preserve precious documents electronically. With the cost of scanners decreasing — and the availability of bundled software that allows you to use a scanner not only as a scanner, but also as a fax machine and copier — adding a scanner to your equipment collection makes a lot of sense. It can make your genealogical research more colorful and more efficient without making a big dent in your wallet.

A variety of scanners are available. The most common types are snapshot, sheet-fed, flatbed, and, at the high end, microfilm scanners. Although they're harder to find, a few hand-held scanners are still around. The system requirements for scanners vary greatly, so read the packaging of any scanner you're considering very carefully. Additionally, each scanner requires software to make it work, so carefully check the software's system requirements and capabilities as well. Here's a quick rundown of the major types of scanners:

- **Photo scanners:** Useful for creating electronic images of photographs that measure 5 x 7 inches or smaller because they're designed to work primarily with that size of photograph. Photo scanners (also called snapshot scanners) are compact and come in external and internal varieties. You feed the photograph into the scanner, and then the scanner captures an image before sending the photo back out. Some photo scanners have a removable top that you can use as a hand-held scanner when you want to capture images larger than 5 x 7 inches. One caution with photo scanners: You may not want to use these with old, fragile photographs. The scanner can damage the photograph as it's fed through the scanner.

- **Film scanners:** Check out a film scanner if you'd like to produce your own photographs directly from negatives. These compact scanners can capture images in color or black and white. You manually feed the negative into the scanner. Some film scanners have optional slide feeders.

- **Document scanners:** Document scanners are also sometimes called sheet-fed scanners because they are typically a little wider than a regular sheet of paper (8.5 inches across). They're still rather compact as far as scanners go, but all are external. You feed the photograph or document into the feeder on the scanner, and the scanner captures an image as the document goes through. As do some photo scanners, some document scanners have a removable top that you can use as a hand-held scanner to capture images larger than 8.5 inches across. Use caution when using these scanners with fragile photographs.

- **Flatbed scanners:** These scanners used to be large and bulky but are now incredibly light and compact. You lift the top of the scanner and place your document or photograph on the bed, close the lid, and tell the scanner (through software) to capture the image. Flatbed scanners are somewhat safer for photographs and old paper records than are other types of scanners. That's because photos are laid on the scanner's glass plate, not fed through the device.

- **Hand-held scanners:** Although these are great for genealogy because of their flexibility and mobility, they're also more difficult to find these days. You can use them not only for scanning photographs and paper documents but also for scanning books. Hand-held scanners are external and compact. They're the perfect size to carry with you when you go on-site for your genealogical research. You scan photos and other objects by holding the scanner and slowly moving it over the object while holding down a button.

- **Microfilm scanners:** In the past, microfilm scanners were so costly that they were used only by companies. Now, there are a few companies that are producing microfilm scanners at a more "modest" cost. However, the cost of these scanners is still significantly more than flatbed or document scanners.

Digital cameras

Digital cameras have become an indispensable tool for genealogists as well as the general public. The ability to take all your photographs with a camera that downloads the images directly to your computer is very appealing. And the fact that you can easily attach digital photos to your genealogical database (or import them in) is definitely exciting. Some digital cameras even come with a document setting, so you don't need both a scanner and a digital camera. This feature is extremely convenient when you're on the road researching your ancestors — you can use your digital camera to capture images from cemetery visits, pictures of long-lost cousins at reunions, and copies of rare documents at the local courthouse.

As with every other computer peripheral, if you're considering purchasing a digital camera, carefully read the package and software requirements to make sure that your computer system can support the equipment.

Finding a Research Mate (Of the Software Variety)

You may think you already have the perfect research mate — that special person who accompanies you to every library, cemetery, and courthouse as you research, right? Wrong! The research mate we're referring to comes on CD-ROMs or is downloadable from the Internet; you install it on your computer and then let it perform all sorts of amazing tasks for you.

Coordinate your research via phone and GPS

You already know a couple of good reasons to carry your cellular phone with you on research trips, right? It enables you to call relatives in the town you're visiting, and allows you to call ahead to ensure that a record exists in a location before traveling there. It also gives you reassurance that you can reach help if something goes wrong while you're away from home. But there's another wonderful reason to carry certain types of cellular phones on genealogical jaunts. That's because several cellular phones now have Global Positioning System (GPS) receivers built in. The GPS is a satellite system that receives and sends signals to a receiver, enabling the person controlling the receiver to determine her exact geographical coordinates. This is a handy system to employ when recording the locations of family markers, such as burial plots and old homesteads. After all, natural markers (such as rocks and trees) and man-made markers (such as buildings) may move or disappear entirely after years and years, but the latitude and longitude of a location will remain the same. For more information about using GPS for genealogical purposes, check out Chapter 7.

Several software programs can store and manipulate your genealogical information. They all have some standard features in common; for instance, most serve as databases for family facts and stories, have reporting functions to generate pre-designed charts and forms, and have export capabilities so you can share your data with others. Each software program also has a few unique features (for example, the capability to take information out of the software and generate online reports at the click of a button) that make it stand out from the others. Here's a list of the features you want to look for when evaluating different software packages:

- ✔ **How easy is the software to use?** Is it reasonably intuitive graphics-wise so that you can see how and where to enter particular facts about an ancestor?

- ✔ **Does the software generate the reports you need?** For instance, if you're partial to Family Group Sheets, does this software support them?

- ✔ **Does the software allow you to export and/or import a GEDCOM file?** *GEDCOM* is a file format that's widely used for genealogical research. For more info about GEDCOM, see the "GEDCOM: The genealogist's standard" sidebar later in this chapter.

- ✔ **How many names can this software hold?** Make sure that the software can hold an adequate number of names (and accompanying data) to accommodate all the ancestors about whom you have information.

  Keep in mind that your genealogy continues to grow over time.

- ✔ **Can your current computer system support this software?** If the requirements of the software cause your computer to crash every time you use it, you won't get very far in your genealogical research.

- ✔ **Does this software provide fields for citing your sources and keeping notes?** Including information about the sources you use to gather your data — with the actual facts, if possible — is a sound genealogical practice. Take a look at Chapter 12 for more information about the importance of citing sources and how to do so.

GEDCOM: The genealogist's standard

As you probably have already discovered, genealogy is full of acronyms. One such acronym that you hear and see repeatedly is *GEDCOM (GEnealogical Data COMmunication).* GEDCOM has become the standard for individuals and software manufacturers for exporting and importing information to or from genealogical databases. Simply put, GEDCOM is a file format intended to make data transferable between different software programs so people can share their family information easily.

The Church of Jesus Christ of Latter-day Saints first developed and introduced GEDCOM in 1987. The first two versions of GEDCOM were released for public discussion only and not meant to serve as the standard. With the introduction of Version 5.*x* and later, however, GEDCOM was accepted as the standard.

Having a standard for formatting files is beneficial to you as a researcher because you can share the information that you collect with others who are interested in some (or all) of your ancestors. It also enables you to import GEDCOM files from other researchers who have information about family lines and ancestors in whom you're interested. And you don't even have to use the same software as the other researchers! You can use Reunion for Macintosh and someone with whom you want to share information can use Family Tree Maker; having GEDCOM as the standard in both software programs enables each of you to create and exchange GEDCOM files.

To convert the data in your genealogical database to a GEDCOM file, follow the instructions provided in your software's manual or Help menu. You can create the GEDCOM file relatively easily; most software programs guide you through the process with a series of dialog boxes.

In addition to creating GEDCOM files to exchange one-on-one with other researchers, you can generate GEDCOM files to submit to larger cooperatives that make the data from many GEDCOM files available to thousands of researchers worldwide.

You can also convert your GEDCOM file to HTML so that you can place the data directly on the World Wide Web for others to access. Software utilities are available (such as GED2HTML) that make it a snap to convert your GEDCOM file to HTML. (For more information on generating Web pages using GED2HTML, see Chapter 13.)

Entering Information into RootsMagic

To help you get a better idea of how software can help you organize your records and research, and to help you figure out what features to look for in particular software packages, this section examines how to use RootsMagic, a popular genealogy software program.

When you open RootsMagic for the very first time, you see a screen that contains four buttons at the top. To begin your family tree, follow these steps:

1. **Click New.**
    A box appears on the screen asking for a new file name.

2. **Type the new file name in the box next to File Name and click Save.**
    In our case, we are starting a family tree for the Abell family, so we enter Abell as the file name and click Save. The database is created and the New Database Options box appears.

3. **Select your preferred settings for the database and click OK.**
    You can set the date format using the drop-down box, choose whether to have a reference number

displayed after the name, display surnames in all capital letters, or allow LDS support (this setting opens some additional fields for members of the Church of Jesus Christ of Latter-day Saints). In our case, we set the date format to "10 Jan 1959," choose not to include reference numbers, select to display surnames in uppercase, and turn off the LDS support functionality.

After you set the preferences, a Pedigree chart appears where you can enter information about yourself (presuming you choose to start with yourself) and five generations of your ancestors. Figure 3-2 shows the pedigree page within RootsMagic.

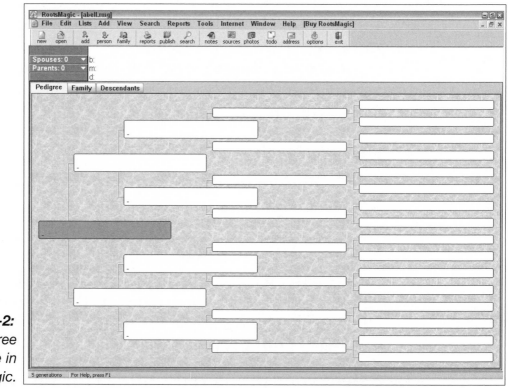

Figure 3-2:
The pedigree page in RootsMagic.

Completing the pedigree page

Usually, it's easiest to enter information about yourself, your spouse, and children, and then work backward through your parents, grandparents, great-grandparents, and so forth. After you complete your direct lines back as far as you can, come back and enter information about each of your siblings, nieces and nephews, cousins, and other relatives. Always enter as much information as you can in each of the fields in the Add Person dialog boxes. Follow these steps to fill in the pedigree page:

1. **Click Add at the top of the page, and then select Individual from the drop-down menu.**
   The Add Person dialog box appears, where you can fill in details about yourself or an ancestor.

2. **Complete the Add Person box and click OK.**
   Type your first and middle names in the Given name(s) field and your last name in the Surname field. Then complete the remaining fields to the extent that you know the data that belongs in them. Remember to use your maiden name if you're female — regardless of your marital status. Of course, we want to set a good example in this book when it comes to privacy for living relatives, so rather than type in information about one of us, we type in Matthew's great-great-grandfather **Samuel Clayton Abell, Jr**.
   After you click OK, the Edit Person dialog box appears.

3. **Complete the Edit Person dialog box and click OK.**
   You can add more facts about yourself or an ancestor by completing the fields in each of the six

tabs — General, Notes, Sources, Multimedia, Address, and To Do. After you finish adding the details, click OK.

Make sure that you use the four-digit year any time that you enter dates into RootsMagic. If you inadvertently use only two numerals for the year, the software accepts the year as is, leaving it ambiguous for anyone who references your database in the future.

After you have entered your first person, you can use the Add button to enter information for people related to the individual such as spouse, children, and parents. You can keep track of family units by clicking on the Family tab (see Figure 3-3).

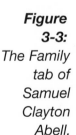

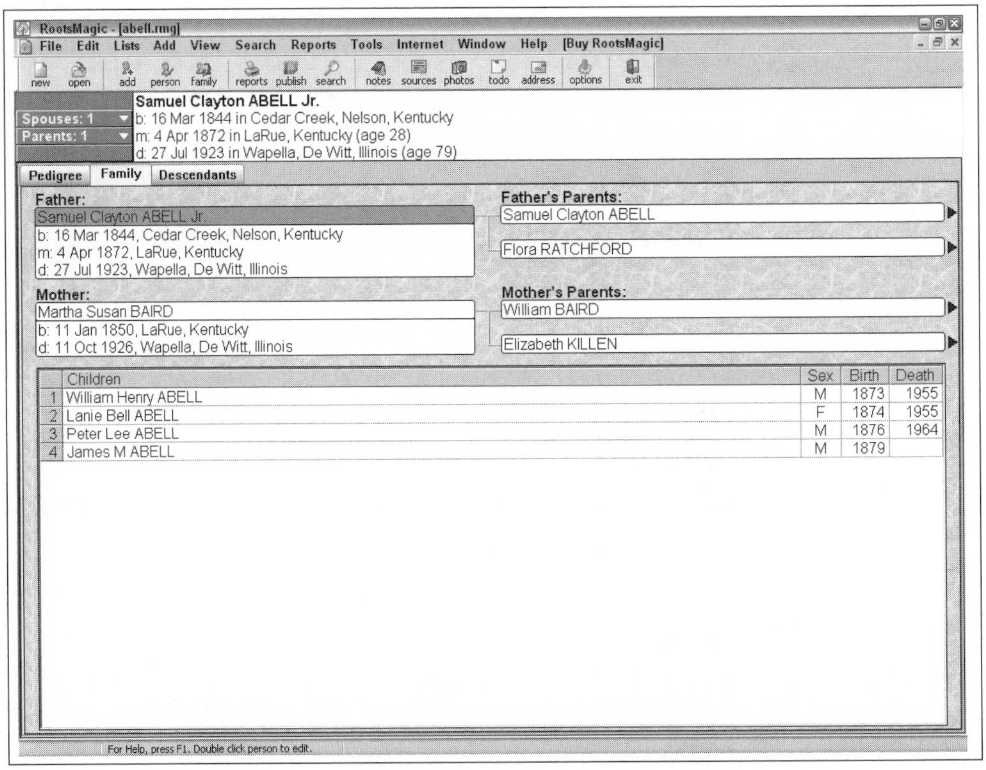

Figure 3-3:
The Family tab of Samuel Clayton Abell.

Sourcing your information

As you enter information about people, it is critical that you cite your data sources. Most genealogical software programs, including RootsMagic, allow you to enter source information. For specific instructions on how to enter info in your particular software, see the Help file or user's manual that comes with the software. In RootsMagic, you add sources through the Edit Person box.

To add a source for your information, try the following:

1. **From the Pedigree chart view, double-click on the person that the source references.**
   We have the source documents for the marriage of Samuel and Martha — so for this example, we double-click on Samuel Abell, Jr. This launches the Edit Person box.

2. **Double-click on the fact or event that you wish to source.**
   We double-click on the marriage fact, which launches the Edit Fact dialog box.

3. **Click on the Sources tab.**
   You see a Sources list box and buttons on the side.

4. **Select Add New Source.**
   The Edit Source box appears (see Figure 3-4). Give the source a descriptive name in the Picklist name field. This allows you to find the source in case you want to use the source for another person. In our case, we put **Abell, Samuel C. and Martha S. Beard Marriage License**. At this point, you can choose to annotate the source from this screen, or use the SourceWizard to format the source.

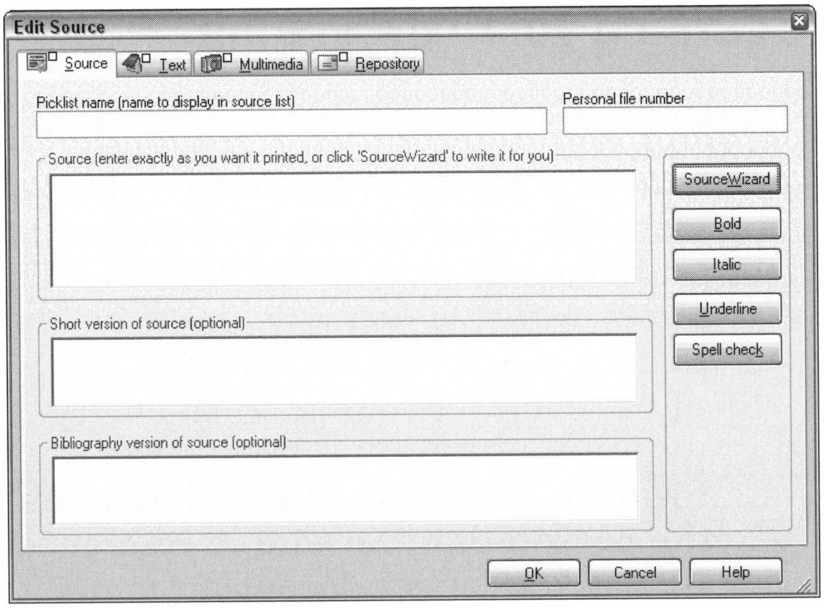

Figure 3-4:
The Edit Source dialog box.

5. **Choose SourceWizard.**

   The SourceWizard dialog box appears. Choose the type of source you are adding from the drop-down box. We have a copy of the marriage license for Samuel and Martha. So, we select Marriage License from the drop-down box. The SourceWizard box changes to include fields unique to the source type that you select. In the Names field, we put **Samuel C. Abell** and **Martha S. Beard**. The record does not have a license number, so we leave it blank. In the Year field, we put **4 April 1872**. In the repository, we put **LaRue County Clerk (Kentucky)**. In the location field, we type **LaRue County, Kentucky**. Click OK to return to the Edit Source screen.

6. **Add a digitized copy of the document.**

   We always like to store a copy of the source document with the source. To do this, select the Multimedia tab on the Edit Source dialog box. Select the Add button which launches the Edit

Scrapbook dialog box. Choose the Browse button next to the File Name field to find the image of the document and then click OK. A thumbnail of the image should show in the Multimedia area.

7. **Click OK.**
   You should now see the source icon next to the field on the Family View.

You may have already noticed that there's another way to get to the Edit Person box to add Sources. You can highlight the individual's name box on the Pedigree chart, and then select the Person Sources link from the drop-down menu that you access through the Sources icon on the toolbar. This enables you to add a source that is not necessarily tied to one specific event in that person's life. If your ancestor kept a diary or memoirs of sorts, you might prefer to use this type of citing sources. Similarly, there is functionality to add sources that pertain to more than one person (called Family Sources in the drop-down list accessible from the Sources icon).

Part II
Focusing on Your Ancestor

The 5th Wave

By Rich Tennant

"Well, she now claims she's a descendant of the royal Egyptian line of cats, but I'm not buying that just yet."

In this part . . .

This part covers how to locate resources that provide information on your ancestors by name. You can also find search strategies for using a variety of government documents online to substantiate your ancestor's life.

Chapter 4

What's in a Name?

....

In This Chapter

▶ Using search engines to find your ancestors
▶ Making the most out of online databases
▶ Using mailing lists
▶ Posting queries
▶ Contacting fellow researchers

....

As a genealogist, you may experience sleepless nights trying to figure out all the important things in life — the maiden name of your great-great-grandmother, whether great-grandpa was really the scoundrel that other relatives say he was, and just how you're related to Daniel Boone. (Well, isn't everyone?) Okay, so you may not have sleepless nights, but you undoubtedly spend a significant amount of time thinking about and trying to find resources that can give you answers to these crucial questions.

In the past, finding information on individual ancestors online was compared with finding a needle in a haystack. You browsed through long lists of links in hopes of finding a site that contained a nugget of information to aid your search. But looking for your ancestors online has become easier than ever. Instead of merely browsing links, you can use search engines and online databases to pinpoint information on your ancestors.

This chapter covers the basics of searching for an ancestor by name, presents some good surname resource sites, and shows you how to combine several different Internet resources to successfully find information on your family.

Finding the Site That's Best for You

Your dream as an online genealogist is to find a Web site that contains all the information that you ever wanted to know about your family. Unfortunately, these sites simply don't exist. However, during your search you may discover a variety of sites that vary greatly in the amount and quality of genealogical information. Before you get too deep into your research, it's a good idea to look at the type of sites that you are likely to encounter.

Personal genealogical sites

The majority of sites that you encounter on the Internet are personal genealogical sites. Individuals and families who have specific research interests establish these pages and they usually contain information on the site maintainer's ancestry or on particular branches of several different families rather than on a surname as a whole. That doesn't mean valuable information isn't present on these sites — it's just that they have a more personal focus.

You can find a wide variety of information on personal genealogical sites. Some pages list only a few surnames that the maintainer is researching; others contain extensive online genealogical databases and narratives. A site's content depends on the amount of research, time, and computer skills the maintainer possesses. Some common items that you see on most sites include a list of surnames, an online genealogical database, Pedigree and Descendant charts (for information on these charts, see Chapter 3), family photographs, and the obligatory list of the maintainer's favorite genealogical Internet links.

Personal genealogical sites vary not only in content, but also in presentation. Some sites are neatly constructed and use plain backgrounds and aesthetically pleasing colors. Other sites, however, require you to bring out your sunglasses to tone down the fluorescent colors, or they use lots of moving graphics and banner advertisements that take up valuable space and make it difficult to navigate through the site. You should also be aware that the JavaScript, music players, and animated icons that some personal sites use can significantly increase your download times.

An example of a personal genealogical site is the Baker Genealogy — Western North Carolina site by Marty Grant (www.martygrant.com/gen/baker.htm). This is just one part of Grant's Web site; the other parts deal with other families he is researching. The site includes census transcriptions, a narrative of Grant's findings on his Baker lines, a list of researchers interested in the same Baker families, and other sections that have personal information about Grant. The site is neat and clean, and it is very easy to navigate. (See Figure 4-1.) Another example is Janet and Richards Genealogy Homepage (freepages.genealogy. rootsweb.com/~shebra/). In addition to the family charts, census transcriptions, and maps that we expect to find on personal genealogical sites, this site contains lots of interesting resources. It has digitized booklets, transcribed vital records for certain areas in which the site maintainers are researching, old postcards showing what towns looked like historically, and transcriptions of old city directories.

After you find a site that contains useful information, write down the maintainer's name and e-mail address and contact him or her as soon as possible if you have any questions or want to exchange information. Personal genealogical sites have a way of disappearing without a trace as individuals frequently switch Internet service providers or stop maintaining sites.

Figure 4-1:
The Baker
genealogy:
Western
North
Carolina Site
is an example
of a personal
genealogical
site.

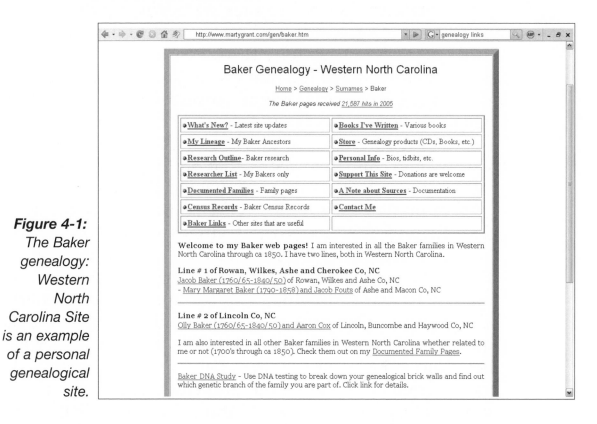

One-name study sites

If you're looking for a wide range of information on one particular surname, a one-name study site may be worth your while. These sites usually focus on one surname regardless of the geographic location where the surname appears. In other words, they welcome information about people with the surname worldwide. These sites are quite helpful because they contain all sorts of information about the surname, even if they don't have specific information about your branch of a family with that surname. Frequently they have information on the variations in spelling, origins, history, and heraldry of the surname. One-name studies have some of the same resources you find in personal genealogical sites, including online genealogy databases and narratives.

Although one-name study sites welcome all surname information regardless of geographic location, the information presented at one-name study sites is often organized around geographic lines. For example, a one-name study site may categorize all the information about people with the surname by continent or country — such as Helms in the United States, England, Canada, Europe, and Africa. Or the site may be even more specific and categorize information by state, province, county, or parish. So, you're better off if you have a general idea of where your family originated or migrated from. But if you don't know, browsing through the site may lead to some useful information.

The Iseli Family World Wide Web site (www.iseli.org/) is a one-name study site with an international focus. From the home page (see Figure 4-2), you can choose to change the language in which you view the site; your options are German or English. The main menu offers Topics, News, FAQs, Family Tree, and a Gallery. Each of these sections has information and resources broken down a bit further. For example, if you visit the Topics part of the site, you can get more specific information about the variations in surname spelling, family branches, notable Iselis, family heraldry, and links to Iseli researchers' Web sites.

The maintainers of one-name study sites welcome any information you have on the surname. These sites are often a good place to join research groups that can be instrumental in assisting your personal genealogical effort.

It gives you just a sampling, though. To find one-name study sites pertaining to the surnames you're researching, you have to go elsewhere. Where, you say? One site that can help you determine whether any one-name study sites are devoted to surnames you're researching is the Guild of One-Name Studies (www.one-name.org).

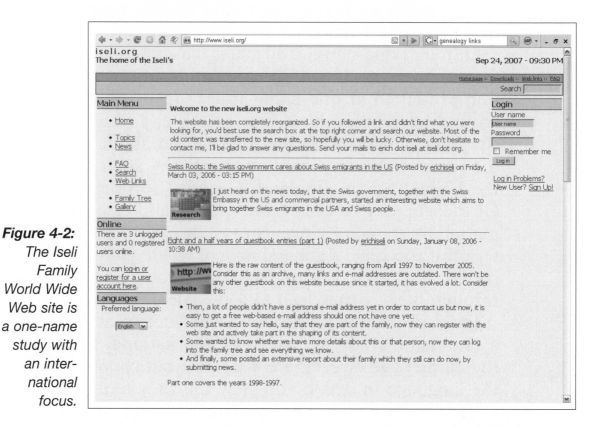

Figure 4-2:
The Iseli Family World Wide Web site is a one-name study with an international focus.

Gee, we bet you can't figure out what the Guild of One-Name Studies is! It's exactly as it sounds — an online organization of registered sites, each of which focuses on one particular surname. The Guild has information about more than 7,000 surnames. Follow these steps to find out whether any of the Guild's members focus on the surname of the person you're researching:

1. **Open your Web browser and go to** www.one-name.org.

2. **Select the Registered Names link from the navigation menu at the top of the page.**

3. **Choose the letter that corresponds to the first letter of the surname.**
   The resulting page contains a list of names. Those with a link contain more information about the study.

Family associations and organizations

Family association sites are similar to one-name study sites in terms of content, but they usually have an organizational structure (such as a formal association, society, or club) backing them. The association may focus on the surname as a whole or just one branch of a family. The goals for the family association site may differ from those for a one-name study. The maintainers may be creating a family history in book form or a database of all individuals descended from a particular person. Some sites may require you to join the association before you can fully participate in their activities, but this is usually at a minimal cost or free.

The Wingfield Family Society site (www.wingfield.org), shown in Figure 4-3, has several items that are common to family association sites. The site's contents include a family history, newsletter subscription details, a membership form, queries, mailing list information, results of a DNA project, and a directory of the society's members who are online. Some of the resources at the Wingfield Family Society site require you to be a member of the society in order to access them.

Another family association site to check out is The

McKusick Family Association at www.mckusick.org. They have information about the organization, genealogical findings on the descendants of John McKusick and Mary Barker, information about the clan tartan, and reunion facts.

To find a family association Web site, your best bet is to use a search engine or a comprehensive genealogical index. For more on search engines see the sections "Focusing on genealogically focused search engines" and "Browsing Comprehensive Genealogical Indexes" later in this chapter.

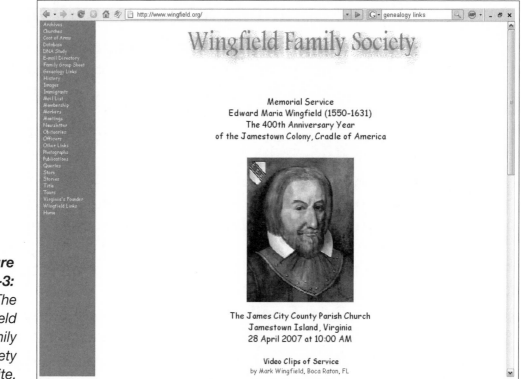

Figure 4-3:
The Wingfield Family Society site.

Surnames connected to events or places

Another place where you may discover surnames is a site that has a collection of names connected with a particular event or geographic location. The level of information avail-

What about blogs?

Since previous editions of this book were published, the Internet has been inundated by blogging, or Web logging. A *blog* (also known as Web log) is an online, personal journal of sorts — a site where an individual or even a group of people with a common interest can record their daily, weekly, monthly, or whatever-timed-interval thoughts and experiences. The field of genealogy is no exception! There are many genealogy blogs now available and they cannot be categorized under just one of the groupings we've covered so far in this chapter. In other words, they don't all fit into personal genealogical sites, nor do they all fit into family associations or organizations.

One example of a blog that is genealogical and geographic in nature is the Texas History and Genealogy Blog (texashistoryblog.blogspot.com/). As you might imagine, it covers a wide range of topics relating to Texas. At irregular intervals, the host of the blog posts various types of information ranging from cemetery transcriptions, to information about upcoming conferences, to historical markers, to things to see when driving through Texas, to other Web sites or articles that she thinks will interest readers.

A couple of other blogs that are more like personal genealogical sites are Mike's Genealogy Blog (mikegen48.wordpress.com/) and Bob and Reb's Genealogy Blog (www.orrellfamily.com/blog/). Both of these blogs have research findings of the blog hosts.

When you are ready to share your knowledge with the world, you might consider setting up your own genealogical blog. We provide the specific steps for doing so in Chapter 13.

able on these sites varies greatly among sites and among surnames on the same site. Often, the maintainers of such sites include more information on their personal research interests than other surnames, simply because they have more information on their own lines.

Typically, you need to know events that your ancestors were involved in or geographic areas where they lived to use these sites effectively. Also, you benefit from the site simply because you have a general, historical interest in the particular event or location even if the Web site contains nothing on your surname. Finding Web sites about events is easiest if you use a search engine, a comprehensive Web site, or a subscription database. Because we devote an entire chapter to researching geographic locations (Chapter 7), we won't delve into that here.

Taking the Plunge

After you've decided on a particular person to research (for more on selecting a good research candidate, see Chapter 2), it's time to research online. As we've mentioned frequently in this book, it's a good idea to arm yourself with some facts about the individual before venturing online.

Let's say that Matthew wants to research his paternal grandfather's line. His grandfather was Herschel Helm who lived in Macon County, Illinois. From memory and supported by a copy of a death certificate for Herschel, Matthew knows that his grandfather died in 1985 — information that can be used to distinguish him from another Herschel Helm found online.

Due to privacy laws, the amount of information online on people in the United States after 1930 is pretty limited. However, one source that does provide information on deceased individuals during this time period is the Social Security Death Index (SSDI), also called the Social Security Death Master file — a good place to get your feet wet.

As of 2007, the SSDI contained more than 80 million records of deaths of individuals having a Social Security Number. The vast majority of these records deal with individuals who died after 1962 — although a few scattered records pre-date that year. Each entry includes the following:

- ✔ Name of deceased
- ✔ Birth date
- ✔ Death date
- ✔ Last residence
- ✔ Last benefit received
- ✔ Social Security Number
- ✔ State where person lived when Social Security card was issued

Several places exist online where the SSDI can be searched. The most up-to-date version is found at the GenealogyBank.com site at

www.genealogybank.com/gbnk/ssdi.html

However, a subscription is required for access. For free access to the SSDI, try ssdi.genealogy.rootsweb.com.

To search the SSDI, try the following:

1. **Point your browser to ssdi.genealogy.rootsweb.com.**
   The Social Security Death Index Interactive Search page at Rootsweb.com appears with a search form near the bottom of the page.

2. **Type in the last name and first name of the individual and click Submit.**
   You can search for an exact match on the surname,

or use a Soundex or metaphone (a phonetic code algorithm that is similar to Soundex) equivalent for the search. (For more information about Soundex, flip back to Chapter 2.) These sound-based equivalents can be used to find names that are not spelled exactly as you expect them to be. In our case, we type "helm" in the last name and "herschel" in the first name fields.

3. **Browse the results page for the appropriate individual.**
   The results are presented in a table with nine columns. Our search yielded four results, and only one of those has the last residence of Macon County and a death date of 1985.

Whenever you use this database and find someone for whom you're searching, you have the opportunity to generate a letter to order the original Social Security application (Form SS-5) from the Social Security Administration.

Family Trees Ripe for the Picking: Finding Compiled Resources

Using online databases to pick pieces of genealogical fruit is wonderful. But you want more, right? Not satisfied with just having Social Security information on his grandfather, Matthew is eager to know more — in particular, he'd like to know who Herschel's grandfather was. There are a couple of research tactics to explore at this point. Perhaps the first is to see if someone has already completed some research on Herschel and his ancestors.

 When someone publishes his or her genealogical findings (whether online or in print), the resulting work is called a *compiled genealogy.*

140

Compiled genealogies can give you a lot of information about your ancestors in a nice, neat format. When you find one with information relevant to your family, you get this overwhelming feeling of instantaneous gratification. Wait! Don't get too excited yet! When you use compiled genealogies, it's very important to remember that you need to verify any information in them that you're adding to your own findings. Even when sources are cited, it's wise to get your own copies of the actual sources to ensure that the author's interpretation of the sources was correct and that no other errors occurred in the publication of the compiled genealogy.

Compiled genealogies take two shapes online. One is the traditional narrative format — the kind of thing that you typically see in a book at the library. The second is in the form of information exported from an individual's genealogical database and posted online in a lineage-linked format (lineage-linked means that the database is organized by the relationships between people).

Narrative compiled genealogies

Narrative compiled genealogies usually have more substance than their exported database counterparts. Authors sometimes add color to the narratives by including local history and other text and facts that can help researchers get an idea of the time in which the ancestor lived. An excellent example of a narrative genealogy is found at The Carpenters of Carpenter's Station, Kentucky at

freepages.genealogy.rootsweb.com/~carpenter/

The site maintainer, Kathleen Carpenter, has posted a copy of her mother's historical manuscript on the Carpenter family, as well as some photos and a map of Carpenter's

Station. You can view the documents directly through the Web, or you can download PDF copies.

To locate narrative genealogies, try using a search engine or comprehensive genealogical index. (For more information on using these resources, see the sections later in this chapter.) Often, compiled genealogies are part of a personal or family association Web site.

Compiled genealogical databases

Although many people don't think of lineage-linked, online genealogical databases as compiled genealogies, these databases serve the same role as narrative compiled genealogies — they show the results of someone's research in a neatly organized, printed format.

For example, the Simpson History site (simpsonhistory.com/_main_page.html) is a personal site that contains a compiled genealogical database providing information on John "The Scotsman" Simpson and his descendants. There are descendant charts and family group sheets that you can navigate through, clicking on particular individuals to access more information about them. (Descendant charts and family group sheets are two different ways to present genealogical information about a person. For more information about them, check out Chapter 12.)

Finding information in compiled genealogical databases can sometimes be tough. There isn't a grand database that indexes all the individual databases available online. Although general Internet search engines have indexed quite a few, some very large collections are still only accessible through a database search — something that general Internet search engines don't normally do.

In the previous section, we conducted a search on Matthew's grandfather, Herschel Helm. Now we want to find out more about his ancestry. We can jump start our research by using a lineage-linked database in hopes of finding some information compiled from other researchers that can help us learn who his ancestors were (perhaps even several generations' worth). From documents such as his birth and death certificates, we learn that Herschel's father was named Emanuel Helm. And from interviews with family members, we also learn that Emanuel was born in Fayette County, Illinois, in the early 1860s. Armed with this information, we can search a compiled genealogical database.

The FamilySearch Internet Genealogy Service (www.familysearch.org) is the official research site for the Church of Jesus Christ of Latter-day Saints (LDS). This free Web site allows you to search several LDS databases including the Ancestral File, International Genealogical Index, Pedigree Resource File, vital records index, census records, and a collection of abstracted Web sites — all of which are free. The two resources that function much like lineage-linked databases are the Ancestral File and the Pedigree Resource File. Fortunately, you don't have to search each of these resources separately. A master search is available that allows you to search all seven resources on the site at once.

To search the FamilySearch site, do the following:

1. **Open your Web browser and go to** www.familysearch.org.

2. **In the Search For Your Ancestors section (near the top, left of the main Web page), type the first and last name of the ancestor you're researching into the fields marked** First Name **and** Last Name.
   If you're researching a common name and know more information about the individual, you might want to click the Advanced Search link. This takes

you to a page showing several additional fields, including names for father, mother, and spouse. It also enables you to restrict your search by state and to use the exact spelling that you provide of the ancestor's name. If you decide to use the Advanced Search and include information on the spouse or mother or father and you don't receive adequate results, try doing the search on only the name of the ancestor.

Back to our explanation for the general search interface that you encounter on the main FamilySearch.org page — in addition to the first and last name fields, you can complete optional fields such as Life Event, Year, Year Range, or Country. (Keep in mind that filling in any of these fields may reduce the overall number of results you receive.) We type in **Emanuel** in the first name box and **Helm** in the last name box.

3. **After you select the search options, click Search.**

   The Results page contains links (with descriptions) to the resources that met your search criteria. For example, our search for Emanuel Helm yields 51 results. These results come from eight different resources on the site. The far-right column, Sources Searched, provides a breakdown of the number of results you received from each FamilySearch resource, as shown in Figure 4-4.

4. **Click the link of any result to see more information.**

   A few results jump out at us. The second record is an Emanuel Helm born about 1863 in Fayette, Illinois. Looking for other records from Illinois, we find Manuel Helm in the 1870 U.S. Census and an

Emanuel Helm born about 1863 in Fayette, Illinois, in the International Genealogical Index. As it turns out, all of these are the same person — in the 1870 Census, his name was misspelled as *Manuel*.

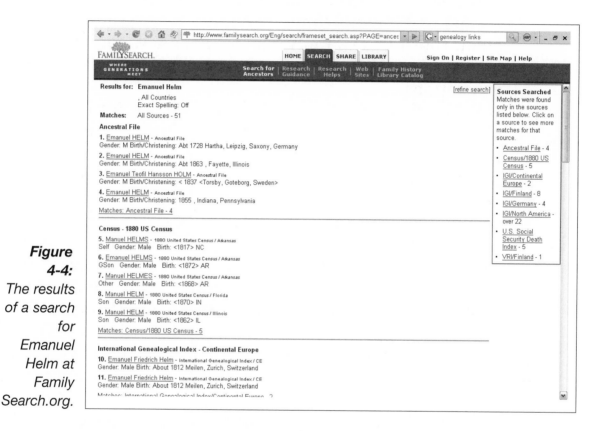

Figure 4-4: *The results of a search for Emanuel Helm at Family Search.org.*

If we select the Ancestral File entry for Emanuel Helm, we are taken to the Individual record page. This page shows the sex of the individual, the event prompting the record, the parent names (if known), and information on the submitter of the record. From this record, we see that someone submitted a record showing Emanuel's parents as Uriah Helm and Rebecca Norris. The source information for this is not here, so it would be worthwhile to contact the submitter to locate the source. The other links on the page allow us to generate a Pedigree chart of Emanuel's ancestors or a Family Group Sheet of his immediate family. Looking at the Family Group Sheet, the submission shows that Uriah and Rebecca had six children and that Uriah's parents' names were William Helm and Elizabeth Guffey. Clicking the Pedigree link generates a chart that shows ancestors of Emanuel going back five generations to George Helm (born in 1723 in Virginia). Matthew can use this information to look for primary records to document these generations.

WARNING!

Although the LDS Church is well known for its large genealogical collection, don't expect to find the complete collection online — the vast majority of LDS resources reside in its library and Family History Centers. Also, you need to verify with the help of the *original* records — any information that you do find online. Much of the information currently on the site was contributed by other family-history researchers, who may or may not have been careful in researching and diligent in documenting their family history.

We should also mention that there is another search site for the Pedigree Resource File component of the LDS site at www.findyourfamilytree.com. This site allows you to directly order the CD-ROM that contains the results of your search.

There are several other lineage-linked collections that may contain useful information, including WorldConnect (worldconnect.rootsweb.com), OneGreatFamily.com (www.onegreatfamily.com), and MyTrees.com (www.mytrees.com). The following list gives you details on some of the better-known collections:

✔ **Ancestry Family Trees:** The Ancestry.com site (www.ancestry.com/ search/rectype/default.aspx?rt=42) contains a free area where researchers can contribute GEDCOM files from their individual databases, as well as search through the files of other researchers.

- ✔ **WorldConnect:** The WorldConnect Project (world connect.rootsweb.com) is part of the RootsWeb.com site. The Project has more than 480 million names in its database.

- ✔ **MyTrees.com:** MyTrees.com (www.mytrees.com) is a site maintained by Kindred Konnections. The site has a lineage-linked database numbering 238 million records. The site is available only by subscription.

- ✔ **OneGreatFamily.com:** OneGreatFamily.com (www.onegreatfamily.com) hosts a subscription-based lineage-linked database. The database contains 190 million unique names contributed by users in 170 countries.

- ✔ **GenCircles:** GenCircles (www.gencircles.com) is a free, lineage-linked database site with a twist: Its SmartMatching feature compares individuals from different files and attempts to match them together. Thus a researcher who contributes to GenCircles can get in contact with another who may be working on the same family lines. The database currently has more than 60 million names.

Letting Your Computer Do the Walking: Using Search Engines

Imagine spending several hours clicking from link to link and not finding anything that relates to your research. Wouldn't it be nice to be able to just type in your ancestor's name and see if there are any sites that contain that name? That's exactly what search engines allow you to do.

Search engines are programs that examine huge indexes

of information generated by robots. *Robots* are programs that travel throughout the Internet and collect information on the sites and resources that they run across. You can access the information contained in search engines through an interface, usually through a form on a Web page.

The real strength of search engines is that they allow you to search the full text of Web pages instead of just the title or a brief abstract of the site. For example, say that we're looking for information on one of Matthew's ancestors whom we found by using a lineage-linked database: George Helm, who lived around the turn of the nineteenth century in Frederick County, Virginia. We could start by consulting a comprehensive genealogical index site (for more on comprehensive genealogical indexes, see "Browsing Comprehensive Genealogical Indexes," later in this chapter). There we could look for a Web site with *George Helm* in the title, or find an abstract of the site. Even if the comprehensive index contains tens of thousands of links, the chances of a Web site having *George Helm* in its title or its abstract is relatively small.

Different kinds of search engines are available to aid your search. These include genealogically focused search engines, general Internet search engines, and general Internet meta-search engines. We'll explore a couple in the next section.

Focusing on genealogically focused search engines

Your first stop on a search for a particular ancestor should be a search engine that's intended just for that purpose.

Genealogically focused search engines are sites that dispatch robots that index the full text of only those sites that contain information of interest to genealogists. By indexing only these types of sites, you receive fewer extraneous results when you type in your ancestor's name as a search term. An example of a genealogy focused search engine is TreEZy.com.

The TreEZy.com search interface allows free-form text (your entry doesn't have to be a name) and Boolean searching. (*Boolean* searches involve using the terms *and, or,* or *not* to narrow your results.)

1. **Using your browser, go to** www.treezy.com.

2. **Type your search term in the field labeled Enter Your Keywords located in the center of the screen and click Search.**
   For example, we type **George Helm** and click Search. The Results page appeared with 657 results. (See Figure 4-5.)

3. **Click a link that interests you.**
   The Results page shows the title of the page and an abstract of the site.

Using general Internet search engines

General search engines send out robots to catalog the Internet as a whole, regardless of the subject(s) of the site's content. Therefore, on any given search you're likely to receive a lot of hits, perhaps only a few of which hold any genealogical value — that is, unless you refine your search terms to give you a better chance at receiving relevant results.

You can conduct several different types of searches with most search engines. Looking at the <u>Help</u> link for any search engine to see the most effective way to search is always a good idea. Also, search engines often have two search interfaces — a simple search and an advanced search. With the *simple search,* you normally just type your query and click the Submit button. With an *advanced search,* you can use a variety of options to refine your search. The best way to become familiar with using a search engine is to experiment on a couple of searches and see what kinds of results you get.

One search engine that has proven successful for us when we search for genealogical data is Google (www.google.com). To conduct a search on Google, do the following:

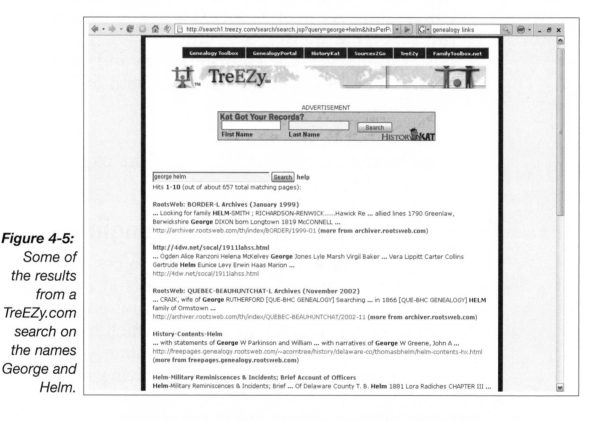

Figure 4-5:
Some of the results from a TreEZy.com search on the names George and Helm.

1. **Point your Web browser to** www.google.com.
   The Google home page is simple. It consists of a

field where you can enter search terms and two buttons marked *Google Search* and *I'm Feeling Lucky.*

2. **Type your ancestor's name into the search field and click Google Search. (We type "Uriah Helm".)**

   We use the quotation marks around Uriah Helm's name as a way of instructing Google to look for those two names next to each other and in that order. This helps reduce the number of hits when using a general Internet search engine.

   The Results page appears with a list of URLs and an abstract of the site, showing the search term bolded. (See Figure 4-6.) In our case, the search results in 34 pages.

3. **Click a search result that looks like it relates to your ancestor.**

 If you're looking for additional leads, Google allows you to view other pages that are similar to results that you receive from your original search. For more search hints, you can click the Search Tips link available at the bottom of the Results page.

Of course, Google is not the only general search engine available. Some others include Alta Vista (www.altavista .com) and Ask.com (www.ask.com).

Web   Images   Video   News   Maps   Gmail   more ▾   Sign in

Google   "uriah helm"   Search   Advanced Search   Preferences

New! View and manage your web history

Web   Results **1 - 10** of about 34 for "**uriah helm**". (0.10 seconds)

RootsWeb: ILFAYETT-L Re: [ILFAYETT-L] Rebecca Norris
in the 1850s except for my direct line (William Helm - **Uriah Helm** - Wesley ... married **Uriah
Helm** in Fayette County on 5 March 1854. Uriah was the son ...
archiver.rootsweb.com/th/read/ILFAYETT/2000-07/0963006559 - 12k - Cached - Similar pages

RootsWeb: ILFAYETT-L [ILFAYETT-L] Rebecca Norris
married **Uriah Helm** in Fayette County on 5 March 1854. Uriah was the son of William Helm
and Elizabeth Guffy/Guffey. This thread: ...
archiver.rootsweb.com/th/read/ILFAYETT/2000-07/0962985650 - 9k - Cached - Similar pages
[More results from archiver.rootsweb.com]

RootsWeb's WorldConnect Project: York's Fentress County Tennessee
Uriah Helm was born 5 Sep 1833 in , Roane, Tennessee, and died 20 Feb 1911 in Avena,
Fayette, Illinois. ... Children of Rebecca Norris and **Uriah Helm** are: ...
wc.rootsweb.com/cgi-bin/igm.cgi?op=AHN&db=bruceyork&id=I13005 - 14k -
Cached - Similar pages

I1694: Wilbur HARRIS (-   )
Father: **Uriah HELM** Family 1 : Henry Stephen HEUSTIS. MARRIAGE:. Ernest Loren
HEUSTIS; Lester La Salle HEUSTIS; Clyde HEUSTIS; Goldie HEUSTIS ...
www.three-systems.com/Gen/heustis/d0000/g0000044.html - 28k - Cached - Similar pages

Pensioners Ending The Week Of Oct. 24, 1890
Uriah HELM, Loogootee. Stephen F. MITCHELL, Mitchellville. Edward DAY, Illiopolis. Michael
WICK, Mattoon. Asbury MORSE, Bloomington. Jos. S. LUTZ, Chicago ...
www.iltrails.org/oct241890.htm - 12k - Cached - Similar pages

Newsletter
If you want information on **Uriah Helm**, for example, would you think to click on a site entitled
John Smith's Genealogy Page on a link-based index? ...
www.rootsweb.com/~kylgs/nlnov04.html - 10k - Cached - Similar pages

Genealogy Software
Help Ô Research Services Ô Shareware Ô Software Ô Speakers Ô Special Interest Groups ...
... **uriah helm**" Visit the online store on Helm's Genealogy Toolbox ...
genealogykingdom.com/copx/ - 9k - Cached - Similar pages

*Figure
4-6:*
*Search
results
from
Google.*

Looking at general Internet meta-search engines

Wouldn't it be nice if we never had to visit multiple sites to search the Internet? This burning question led directly to the creation of *meta-search engines,* which use a single interface (or form) to execute searches using several different search engines. They then return the results of all the individual search engines back to a single page that you can use to view the results. The number of results from meta-search engines can be overwhelming, so it's important for you to have a good search term and to know something substantial about the person you're researching. That way, you can quickly determine whether a result is relevant to your search. You also need to have patience because you may have to trudge through several sets of results before you find something useful. Some general Internet meta-search engines include the following:

- ✔ **Vivisimo:** vivisimo.com
- ✔ **Ixquick:** ixquick.com
- ✔ **Dogpile:** www.dogpile.com
- ✔ **MetaCrawler:** www.metacrawler.com
- ✔ **Search.com:** www.search.com

Online Subscription Databases: Goldmines of Genealogy?

Some of your ancestors may have been prospectors. You know the type — they roamed from place to place in search of the mother lode. Often, they may have found a small nugget here or there, but they never seemed to locate that one mine that provided a lifetime supply of gold. When searching on the Internet, you become the prospector. You pan through results from search engines only to find small nuggets of information here and there. However, don't lose hope. There may be some goldmines waiting for you if you can only stumble upon the right site to dig — and the right site may be in the form of an online subscription database.

Online subscription databases are repositories of information that you can retrieve by paying a monthly, quarterly, or yearly fee. Most online subscription databases are searchable and allow you to type in your ancestor's name and execute a search to determine whether any information stored in the database relates to that particular name. Databases can be large or small; they can focus on a small geographic area or have a broad scope that encompasses many different areas. Each database may also have its own unique search method and present information in its own format. The online subscription database sites vary in the types of content they offer and the amounts and quality of background or historical information they provide about each of the databases within their collections.

You can find online subscription databases in many ways. You can find references to them through search engines (see the section "Letting Your Computer Do the Walking: Using Search Engines" earlier in this chapter), comprehensive genealogical indexes (see "Browsing Comprehensive Genealogical Indexes" later in this chapter), and links that appear on personal and geographic-specific Web sites. To give you a flavor of the type of goldmines that are available, we take a look at some of the larger online subscription databases.

Ancestry.com

Ancestry.com (www.ancestry.com) is a commercial site that contains information on billions of names and adds new databases daily. The site has some free content in its Learning Center section, including articles and tips for researching. But to access the text of the databases, you must be a member. Ancestry.com does allow you the opportunity to test drive the subscription service in the form of a two-week free trial. The extensive collections at the Ancestry.com site are sorted into various categories including census, military, immigration, newspapers, and directories.

Footnote.com

Footnote.com (www.footnote.com) is a subscription database site that has over 18 million documents online, falling into 12 categories including timeframes in United States history, naturalization records, town news and records, and photos. They offer a seven-day free trial that enables you to access their entire collection for that limited time and they make some databases available for free each week.

HistoryKat.com

HistoryKat.com (www.historykat.com) is a commercial endeavor that targets smaller, underrepresented types of records of interest to genealogists. Currently all of the databases available are assigned to one of four categories: U.S. Military Collection, U.S. Postal Records, State and Territorial Censuses, and U.S. Government Employee Records.

WorldVitalRecords.com

Worldvitalrecords.com (www.worldvitalrecords.com) contains subscription databases including census, vital records, military, immigration, directories, court, and parish registers. The site also features content from Quintin Publications, Find-a-Grave, Accessible Archives, and Newspaper-Archive.com.

Browsing Comprehensive Genealogical Indexes

 If you're unable to find information on your ancestor through a search engine or online database, or you are looking for additional information, another resource to try is a comprehensive genealogical index. A comprehensive genealogical index is a site that contains a categorized listing of links to online resources for family history research. Comprehensive genealogical indexes can be organized in a variety of ways, including by subject, alphabetically, or by resource type. No matter how the links are organized, they usually appear hierarchically — you click your way down from category to subcategory until you find the link you're looking for.

Some examples of comprehensive genealogical indexes include the following:

- **Cyndi's List of Genealogy Sites on the Internet:** www.cyndislist.com

- **Genealogy Home Page:** www.genealogyhomepage.com

- **Helm's Genealogy Toolbox:** www.genealogytoolbox.com

- **Linkpendium:** www.linkpendium.com

To give you an idea of how comprehensive genealogical indexes work, try the following example:

1. **Fire up your browser and go to Cyndi's List (www.cyndislist.com).**
   This launches the home page for Cyndi's List.

2. **Scroll down to the portion of the main page labeled Cyndi's List Main Category Index.**

3. **Select a category, such as Surnames, Family Associations & Family Newsletters.**
   For example, we're looking for a page that may contain information on our ancestors. We can select to restrict the number of links by General Surname Sites or Surname DNA Studies and Projects, or we can click directly on the first letter of the surname we're looking for.

4. **Select the letter that begins the surname you're researching.**

Say we're interested in finding some information on the Helm family. We select the <u>H</u> link and we're taken to the appropriate subcategory page. We then scroll down to the section titled Surname Specific Sites and Resources and look for Helm resources. (See Figure 4-7.) We find one possible resource; however, it's on the Helms — not Helm — family.

5. **Click a promising link.**

Of course, one drawback to comprehensive genealogical indexes is that they can be time-consuming to browse. It sometimes takes several clicks to get down to the area where you believe links that interest you may be located. And, after several clicks, you may find that no relevant links are in that area. This may be because the maintainer of the site has not yet indexed a relevant site, or the site may be listed somewhere else in the index.

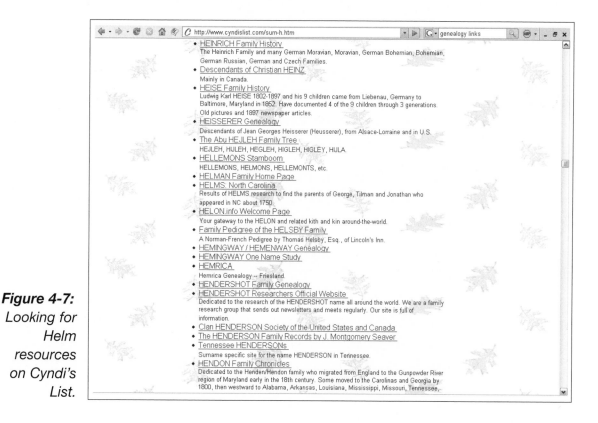

Figure 4-7:
Looking for
Helm
resources
on Cyndi's
List.

Integrated Genealogical Search Sites

Clearly, search engines and comprehensive genealogical indexes can help you find information online about your ancestors. Wouldn't it be nice, though, if you could use both resources at the same time? We're proud to say that one Web site does integrate full-text searching of genealogical Web sites with a comprehensive genealogical index. The site is, drum roll please, Helm's Genealogy Toolbox (www.genealogytoolbox.com).

Helm's Genealogy Toolbox is one of the oldest genealogical Web sites — growing out of a list of links first placed on the Web in September 1994. The site currently contains links to sites of interest to genealogists along with a search engine that indexes the full text of online genealogical sites. The directory of links is divided into three sections: People, Places, and Topics.

Searching Helm's Genealogy Toolbox is easy. Here's what you do:

1. **Launch your Web browser and type in the address for Helm's Genealogy Toolbox (www.genealogytoolbox.com).**
   The home page for the site appears.

2. **Scroll down a bit to find the Enter Your Keywords field in the Search for Genealogical and Local History Web Sites section.**

3. **Type your ancestor's name into the field and click Search.**
   The Results page returns a list of links that met your search criteria. These links include resources from the categorized list of links, the full-text search engines, queries from other researchers, and names from digitized records.

4. Click a link that may relate to your ancestor.

To browse links on Helm's Genealogy Toolbox site, complete the following steps:

1. Launch your Web browser and type in the address for Helm's Genealogy Toolbox (www.genealogytoolbox.com).
The Site Categories are accessible through the list of links in the Contents box or you can scroll down the page to find the listing.

2. Click the <u>People</u> link or scroll down the page.
The link takes you to a section containing links to surname subcategories arranged by letter of the alphabet. (The letter of the alphabet corresponds to the first letter of the surname that's the subject of the Web site.)

3. Choose a link to a surname subcategory or select a link that looks interesting.
On some pages, you may encounter further subcategories that break down the letters of the alphabet into smaller sections. Other pages merely contain links to other Web sites.

Query for One: Seeking Answers to Your Surname Questions

Even if you can't find any surname-specific sites on your particular family, you still have hope! This hope comes in the form of queries. *Queries* are research questions that you post to a particular Web site, mailing list, or newsgroup so other researchers can help you solve your research problems. Other researchers may have information that they haven't yet made available about a family, or they may have seen some information on your family, even though it isn't a branch that they're actively researching.

Web queries

One of the quickest ways of reaching a wide audience with your query is through a query site on the Web. For an example of a query site, try GenForum:

1. **Open your Web browser and go to** www.genforum.com.

2. **In the field under Forum Finder, type the surname you're looking for and click Find.**
   In our case, we enter **Helm**. But feel free to enter a surname that interests you. If you feel like browsing the forums, you can also select a letter beneath the word *Surnames.*

   Don't worry if your surname doesn't have a forum. The GenForum section is constantly growing and adding surnames, so you should check back every so often to see if one's been added, or you may consider requesting that a new forum be added for your surname. (Look for the little link called Add Forum near the bottom of the GenForum pages.)

   You may also want to search other forums to see if the name is included in a variant spelling or if someone else mentioned the name in a passing reference in another forum. (See the next section for details.)

3. **After you find a forum, read a message by clicking its link.**
   As soon as your browser loads the message board page, you should see a list of bulleted messages to

160

choose from. You can also navigate to other pages of the message board if the messages don't all fit on a single page. If you don't want to read all messages, you have the option to see only the latest messages, only today's messages, or any messages posted in the last seven days. These options are available at the top of the list of posted messages.

4. **To post a new query, click Post New Message at the top of the list of posted messages.**
   If you're not already a registered user of GenForum, you get a page with instructions on registering.

   If you're already a registered user or after you become one, a page containing the fields that generate your message pops up. This page includes the name of the forum to which you're posting, your name and e-mail, the subject of the posting, and a free-form text field where you can enter your message, as shown in Figure 4-8.

5. **Fill out the appropriate fields and then click Preview Message.**
   Make sure that your message contains enough information for other researchers to determine if they can assist you. Include full names, birth and death dates and places (if known), and geographic locations where your ancestors lived (if known).

   Clicking the Preview Message button is an important step because you can see how the message will look when it's posted. This option can prevent you from posting an embarrassing message — you know, one filled with those embarrassing typos.

6. **If you're satisfied with the way the message looks, click Post Message.**

Mailing-list queries

When you think of mailing lists, you may have nightmares of the endless stream of junk mail that you receive every day as a result of some company selling your name to a mailing list. Well, fear no more. The type of mailing list we refer to delivers mail that you request. Such lists also provide a way you can post queries and messages about your surnames and genealogical research in general.

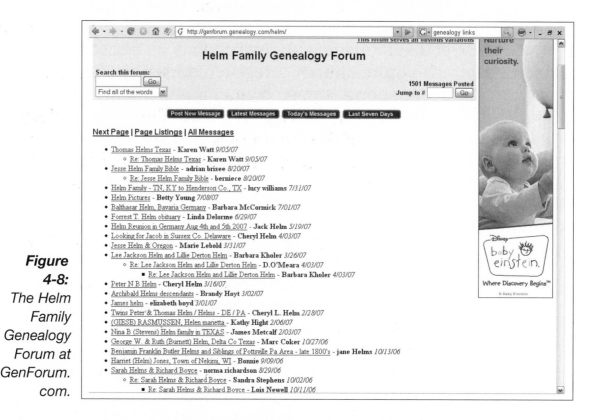

Figure 4-8:

The Helm Family Genealogy Forum at GenForum. com.

Mailing lists are formed by groups of people who share common interests, whether those interests are surnames, specific geographic areas, particular topics, or ethnic groups. A list consists of the e-mail addresses of every person who joins (subscribes to) the group. When you want to send a message to the entire group, you send it to a single e-mail address that in turn forwards the message to everyone on the list. To join a mailing list, you send an e-mail to a designated address with a subscription message. You should then receive a confirmation e-mail that lets you know you're subscribed to the list and tells you where to send an e-mail if you want to send a message to everyone on the list.

Okay, even when you're hip to what a mailing list is, how do you find one of interest to you? One way is to consult the comprehensive list of mailing lists found on the Genealogy Resources on the Internet site (www.rootsweb.com/~jfuller/gen_mail.html). The site breaks down the mailing lists into various categories including Countries other than USA, USA, Adoption, Computing/Internet Resources, DNA Studies/Testing, Emigration/Migration Ships and Trails, General Information/Discussion, and Uncategorized.

Here's how you can find and join a mailing list for your surname:

1. **Point your Web browser to www.rootsweb.com/~jfuller/gen_mail.html.**

2. **Scroll down the list to the Surnames section and select the first letter of a surname you're interested in.**
   The letters appear near the bottom of the page. We select Hel-Hem because we're looking for a mailing list on the surname Helm. A list of surnames with mailing lists pops up.

3. **Scroll through the list and click one of the surname links on the page.**
   By scrolling through the list, you can see if your surname is represented. We scroll through until we find our surname (see Figure 4-9) and click that link. It takes us to a page that has information on a

163

mailing list pertaining to Helm.

4. **Follow the subscription instructions for your mailing list.**

   The instructions for the Helm mailing list tell us to send an e-mail message with the word *subscribe* as the only text in the message body to one of two addresses.

   Typically, you can receive mailing lists in one of two ways. The first way, mail mode, simply forwards e-mail messages to you every time someone posts to the mailing list. Although this practice is fine for small mailing lists, you probably don't want hundreds of messages coming in individually — unless you like to have lots of e-mail sitting in your inbox. To avoid this, try the second way of receiving the mailing list — digest mode. This mode groups several messages together and then sends them out as one large message. Instead of receiving 30 messages a day, you may receive only two messages, with the text of 15 messages in each.

5. **Start your e-mail program and subscribe to the mailing list.**

   We decide to subscribe to the digest mode of the Helm mailing list. To do this, we start our e-mail program, create a new message with only the word *subscribe* in the body, and send the message to the digest address — helm-d-request@rootsweb.com. (See Figure 4-10.) Within a couple of minutes, we receive a confirmation message welcoming us to the mailing list.

6. **Read the messages without responding or posting your own messages for a while. Begin posting your own queries and responses to**

others' messages when you feel comfortable.
Reading messages but not posting your own
messages is called *lurking.* You may want to lurk on
the mailing list to see what other messages look like
and to become familiar with the general culture of
the list. After you get a feel for the structure and
attitude of the messages, jump in and begin sending
your own queries and messages!

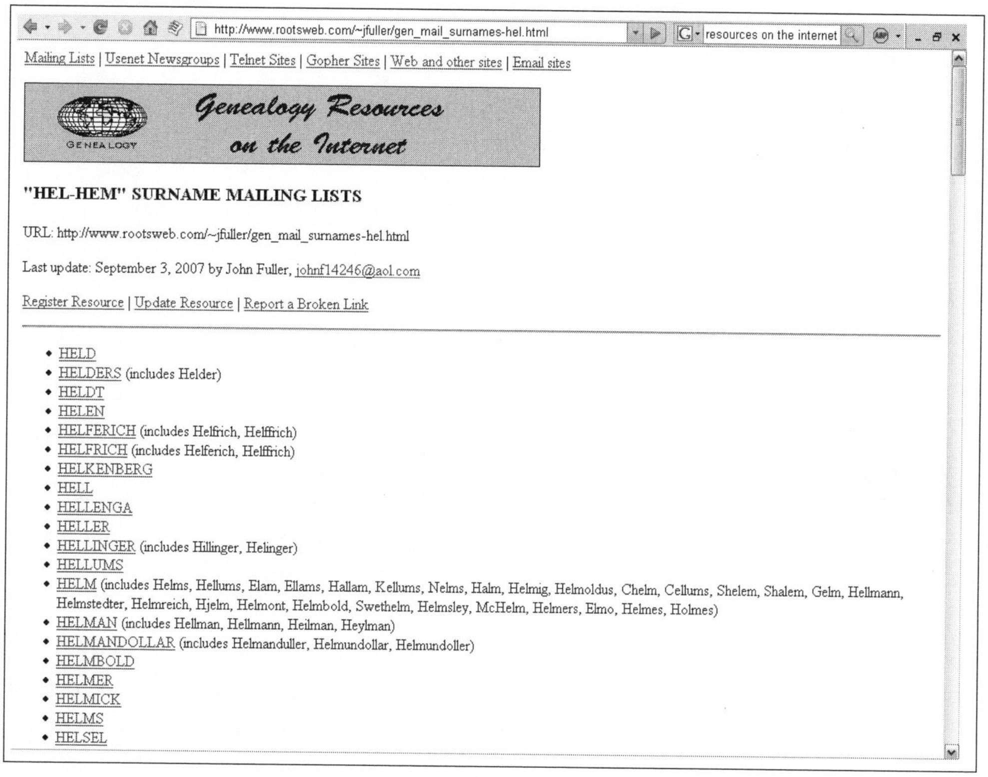

Figure 4-9: Identifying mailing lists at the Genealogy Resources on the Internet site.

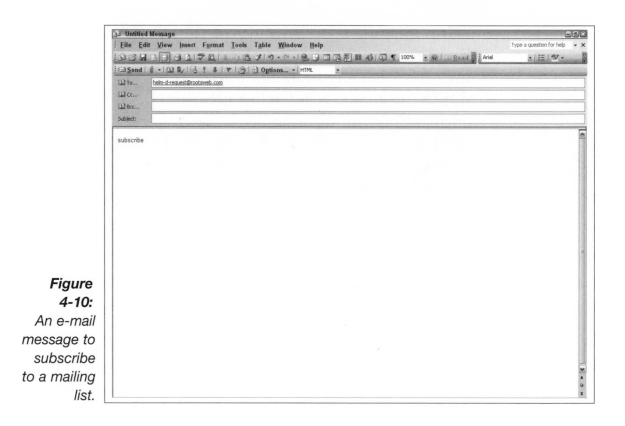

Figure 4-10:

An e-mail message to subscribe to a mailing list.

Using E-Mail to Get Help

In the section "Query for One: Seeking Answers to Your Surname Questions" earlier in this chapter, we discuss a couple of ways to research surnames through e-mail by using queries. You can also use e-mail to directly contact other researchers of your surname. You just need to know where to find them.

Identifying potential e-mail pals by using online directories to find everyone with the surname you're researching, getting their e-mail addresses, and then mass e-mailing all of them about your research and questions is a bad idea. Although mass e-mailing everyone you can find with a particular surname generates return e-mail for you, we can almost guarantee that the responses will be hateful, not

166

helpful. Sticking with genealogical sites (such as those we identify in a moment) when you're looking for other researchers interested in the same surnames is a better way to go about it.

One of the oldest of the Internet genealogy resources is the Roots Surname List at rsl.rootsweb.com/. The Roots Surname List (RSL) is simply a list of surnames (and their associated dates and locations) accompanied by contact information for the person who placed the surname on the list. So if you want to contact other submitters about particular surnames, all you have to do is look at the contact information and send them e-mail messages or letters in the mail detailing your interest in the surnames.

You start by searching the RSL Database for messages about the surname(s) you're researching. Simply follow these steps:

1. **Go to rsl.rootsweb.com/cgi-bin/rslsql.cgi#.**

2. **Click the link titled Search the RSL Database.**

3. **Type the Surname you're researching in the Surname field.**
   We type Helm in the field.

4. **If you desire, enter the Location, select the type of search (Surname, Soundex, or Metaphone are your options), and select whether you wish to restrict the timeframe in which the messages were posted.**
   We don't wish to restrict the search, so we leave all of these fields and radio buttons they way they were.

5. **Click Submit.**

The list of postings related to that surname appears. You can scroll through the list to see if there are any of interest to you. The format for the list looks like this:

Surname	From	To
	Migration	Submitter
	Comments	
Helm	1723	Now
	FrederickCo,VA>FentressCo, TN>FayetteCo, IL,USAmhelm	

The line contains the surname, earliest date for which you have information on the surname, most recent date that you have for the surname, locations through which your family passed showing migration patterns (using a list of standard abbreviations), and a name tag for the submitter.

If you click on the submitter name tag, you get status information for that person. It includes whether he or she is currently active, as well as provides his or her username (mhelm in the case above), his or her real name, and an email address.

You can submit surnames to the RSL through e-mail or with a form on the Web. Before you submit something for the first time, take a few minutes to read the RSL instructions (helpdesk.rootsweb.com/help/rsl6.html).

Verifying Your Information: Don't Believe Everything You Read!

We have one last piece of advice for you when you're researching — surnames or otherwise. *Don't believe everything you read.* Well, actually a pure genealogist would say, "Don't believe *anything* that you read." Either way, the point is the same — always verify any information that you find online with primary records. (For more on primary

168

records, see Chapter 2.) If you can't prove it through a vital record, census record, or some other authoritative record, the information simply may not be as valuable as you think. However, just because you can't *immediately* prove it doesn't mean that you shouldn't hold on to the information and continue to try to prove or disprove it with a primary document. At some time in the future, you may run across a record that does indeed prove the accuracy of the information; in the meantime, it might give you some leads of where to look for more about that person.

Chapter 5

Bureaucracy At Its Best: Using Government Sources

....

In This Chapter

▶ Finding census images online
▶ Vital-records sources on the Internet
▶ Immigration databases
▶ Electronic military records
▶ Online land- and tax-record sources

....

As we all know, governments love paper. Sometimes it seems government workers can't do anything without a form. Luckily for genealogists, governments have been this way for a number of years — otherwise, it might be next to impossible to conduct family history research. In fact, the number of useful government records available online has exploded in the past few years. Not only have government entities been placing records and indexes online — private companies have also put great effort into digitizing and indexing government records for online use.

In this chapter, we show you what kinds of records are currently available and some of the major projects that you can use as keys for unlocking government treasure chests of genealogical information.

Counting on the Census

Census records are one of the most valuable tools to a genealogist, at least in the United States. Many countries periodically count and gather information about their populations, although most didn't conduct nationwide censuses regularly until the nineteenth century.

Census records are valuable for tying a person to a place and for discovering relationships between individuals. For example, suppose you have a great-great-great-grandfather by the name of Nimrod Sanders. You're not sure who his father was, but you do know that he was born in North Carolina. By using a census index, you may be able to find a Nimrod Sanders listed in a North Carolina census index as a child of someone else. If Nimrod's age, location, and siblings' names fit, you may have found one more generation to add to your genealogy.

Often a census includes information such as a person's age, sex, occupation, birthplace, and relationship to the head of the household. Sometimes the *enumerators* (the people who conduct the census) added comments to the census record (such as a comment on the physical condition of an individual or an indication of his wealth) that may give you further insight into the person's life. For additional information about the value and format of censuses, see Chapter 2.

Getting the lowdown on censuses

Before using census records, it's a good idea to get some background knowledge on why they were created. We provide a high-level overview of census records in Chapter 2.

If you need more information, one site to look at is Census Records History and How to Use Them at home pages.rootsweb.com/~haas/learningcenter/censusrecords .html. The site contains a brief history of the census, information on where to locate the records, a primer on the accuracy of census entries, and an introduction to finding aids. For the official view of the census, see the Availability of Census Records About Individuals from the United States Census Bureau at www.census.gov/prod/2000pubs/ cff-2.pdf.

For a summary of the contents of each United States census return and advice on how to use the censuses, see *The Census Book* by William Dollarhide (Heritage Quest). Also, a key to using census records is to know what county your ancestors lived in during any given year. A good guide for this is the *Map Guide to the U.S. Federal Censuses, 1790-1920* by William Thorndale and William Dollarhide (Genealogical Publishing Company). If you run into abbreviations in censuses that you don't understand, take a look at the Abbreviations Found in Genealogy page at www.rootsweb.com/~rigenweb/abbrev.html.

Finding your ancestors in census records

Imagine that you're ready to look for your ancestors in census records. You hop in the car and drive to the nearest library, archives, or Family History Center. On arrival, you find the microfilm roll for the area where you believe your ancestors lived. You then go into a dimly lit room, insert the microfilm into the reader, and begin your search. After a couple hours of rolling the microfilm, the back pain begins to set in, cramping in your hands becomes more severe, and the handwritten census documents become blurry as your eyes strain from reading each entry line by line. You come to the end of the roll and still haven't found your elusive ancestor. At this point, you begin to wonder if a better way exists.

Fortunately, a better way *does* exist for a lot of census records: census indexes. A *census index* contains a listing of the people who are included in particular census records, along with references indicating where you can find the actual census record. Traditionally, these indexes come in book form, but you can now find these indexes online.

Although no single World Wide Web site contains indexes of all available census records for all countries (at least not yet), some sites contain substantial collections of census indexes.

So how do you find these online indexes? Well, there are a few ways, depending upon whether you want to use a free site or a subscription site. First, you can check a comprehensive index site, search engine, or a site listing links to census indexes to find an index that was placed on a free site by an individual or group project.

If you don't want to pay a fee to access census indexes online, you can find some census indexes under the USGen-Web Archives Census Project at www.rootsweb.com/ ~usgenweb/census/.

The Census Project is a volunteer effort to index the United States censuses and provide them online for free. If you can't find an index there, try a site dedicated to providing links to online census resources, such as Census Online (www.census-online.com) or CensusLinks (www .censuslinks.com), or a geographic-specific site, such as the county-level pages in the USGenWeb Project (www.usgenweb.org). Also, a number of independent sites have census indexes; typically you can find them by using a search engine such as Google (www.google.com).

 Say you want to find Samuel Abell, who lived in St. Mary's County, Maryland, in 1790. Your first step is to see if an index is available for that county during the 1790

Census. To do this, try the following:

1. **Fire up your Web browser and go to Census Online (www.census-online.com).**

2. **Click Links to Online Census Records.**
   This page contains a number of links represented by a state or province (depending on whether it's a state in the United States or province in Canada).

3. **Click the Maryland link.**
   A page appears, showing a column (on the left) with state-wide links to censuses and the names of counties for the state, and a second column containing a map of the state.

4. **Select a county from the left column or from the map.**
   In this case, St. Mary's County has eight links.

5. **Click the Index to 1790 Federal Census link.**
   This takes you to a text file on the USGenWeb Census project containing the index. The sixteenth person on the list is Samuel Abell (see Figure 5-1).

Another free index that you may want to take a look at is the 1880 U.S. Census index at FamilySearch. This index contains more than 50 million names. Here's how:

1. **Point your Web browser to www.familysearch.org.**
   At the top of the page your will see four tabs — labeled Home, Search, Share, and Library.

2. **Click the tab marked Search.**
   In the left column (colored tan), there is a list of resources to refine the search.

3. Select the Census link.

At the top left of the search page is a Census link. You can select from all censuses, 1880 United States Census, 1881 British Isles Census, or the 1881 Canadian Census.

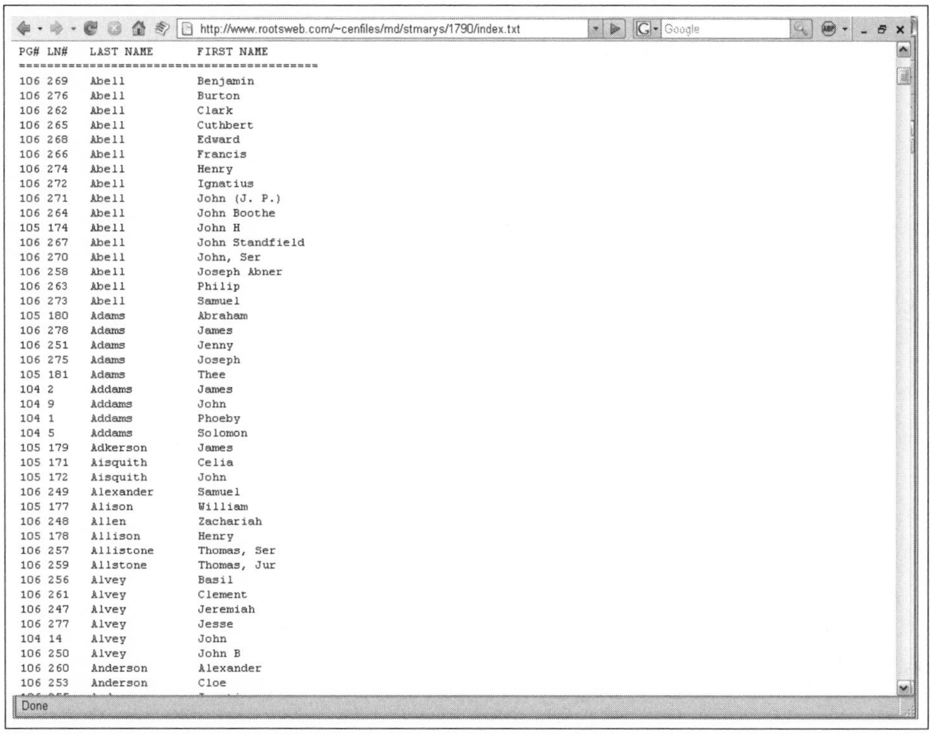

Figure 5-1:
Samuel Abell in the 1790 Census Index for St. Mary's County.

4. Use the Census drop-down box to select the 1880 Census.

The screen should refresh and new search criteria are displayed.

5. Type your search criteria into the appropriate fields and click Search.

We decided to search for Rutherford B. Hayes — the president during 1880. We typed **Rutherford** in the First Name field and **Hayes** in the Last Name field. To further refine the search, we selected District of

Columbia in the Census State drop-down box.

The search results show two Rutherford Hayes in the District of Columbia in the 1880 Census. We select the second one, because he was born in Ohio. Figure 5-2 shows the record for Rutherford B. Hayes, along with a link to the digital image of the census at Ancestry.com. To see the actual image, you must be a subscriber to Ancestry.com.

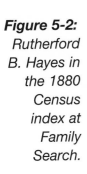

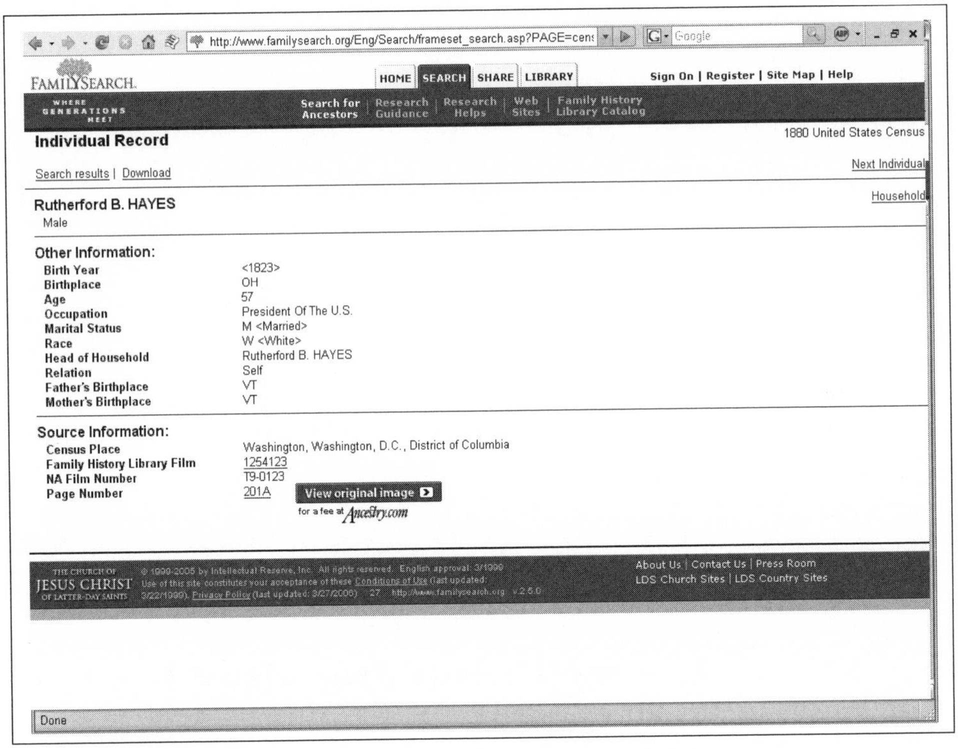

Figure 5-2:
Rutherford B. Hayes in the 1880 Census index at Family Search.

Finding individuals in subscription indexes

Currently, the largest United States Census population schedule index collections are found on the subscription-based Ancestry.com (available to individuals, libraries, and other institutions) and HeritageQuest Online (available only to libraries and other institutions). Ancestry.com (www.ancestry.com) has census indexes for the years 1790 through 1870, generated from print indexes. Ancestry.com also has re-indexed population schedules from 1790 to 1870 and from 1900 to 1930. They use the 1880 index produced by the Church of Jesus Christ of Latter-day Saints and have indexed the census fragment for 1890. Heritage-Quest Online has re-indexed census entries for the years 1790 through 1930.

We should mention that you need to be careful about using these indexes. First of all, not all indexes include every person in the census. Some are merely head-of-household indexes. So, it's a good idea to read the description that comes with the index to see how complete it is. Also, the same quality control may not be there for every census year even within the same index-producing company. If you do not find your ancestor in one of these indexes, don't automatically assume that he or she is not in the census. Another point to remember is that a lot of these indexes were created outside of the United States by people who were not native English speakers and who were under time constraints. It is quite possible that the indexer was incorrect in indexing a particular entry — possibly the person you are searching for.

One of the benefits of using a subscription census index is the value-added features that are built into the search mechanism. For example, if we do a search for the same Samuel Abell as we did in the last section on Ancestry.com, we see some of the additional features of the search engine. Figure 5-3 shows the search results for Samuel Abell limiting the search to the 1790 Census. The first column is the Match Quality, which is a visual representation of how close the search result is to the search terms. In this case, Samuel Abell ranks first based upon his name and his location in St. Mary's County, Maryland. From this same search results page, you can view a textual record of the individual, as well as a link to see a digital image of the census record. In addition to presenting results based on your search criteria, this search mechanism also displays other results that are similar — such as individuals with the same last name or people who have a name that sounds similar to the search criteria.

If you widen the search criteria to more than 1790 (such as in Figure 5-4), you can not only see entries for Samuel in the 1790 Census, but you can also see entries for him in the 1800 and 1810 censuses along with some rent roll records.

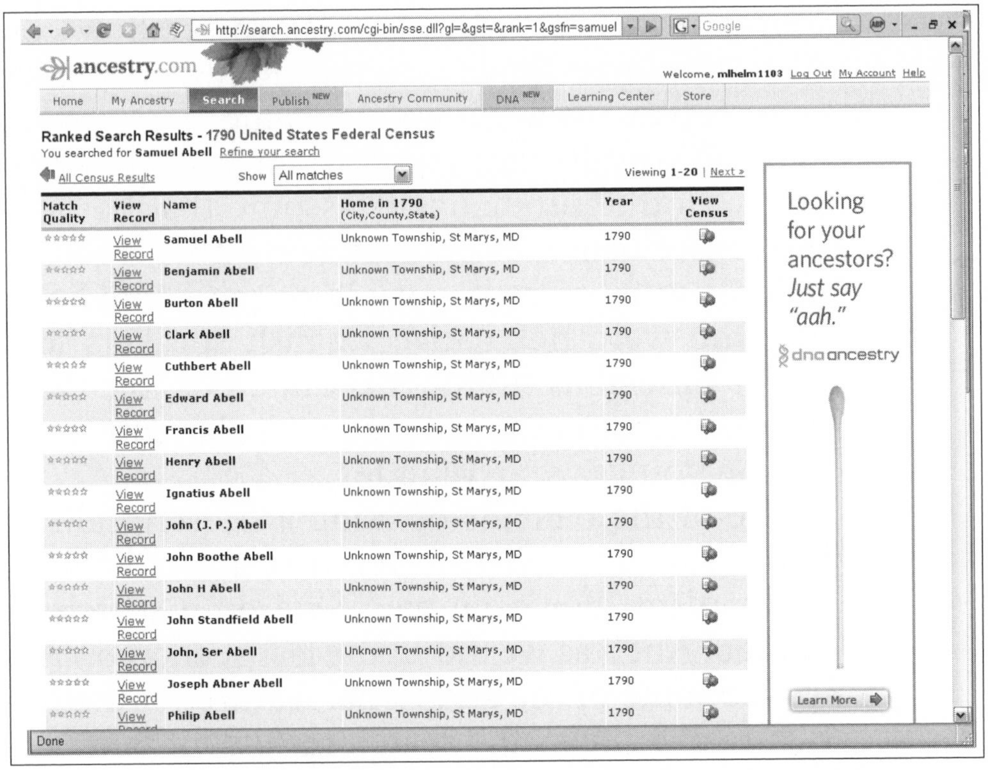

Figure 5-3:

Index results for Samuel Abell from Ancestry. com.

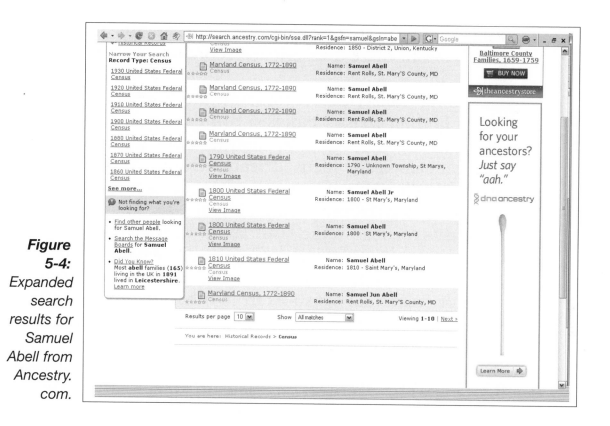

Figure 5-4: Expanded search results for Samuel Abell from Ancestry. com.

Using a transcribed online census

Although finding census indexes is a start, they don't show you enough to let you determine whether that record is of the person you're looking for. Often you need additional information such as the age of the individual or the number of people in the individual's household. That's where census transcriptions come in. Most of the free online transcriptions cover only a portion of a census area dealing with a particular family, or are complete transcriptions for a county.

As with any transcribed record, you should always verify your findings with either a digitized or microfilm copy of the original record. Often, census records are difficult to read because of their age, the quality of the handwriting,

179

and so on — so mistakes do occur in the transcription process. But these transcribed records are better than nothing at all.

Finding transcribed records on the Internet is very similar to finding census indexes. You can try one of the comprehensive genealogical sites under a geographical category or a genealogically focused search engine. To see a step-by-step walk-through of a search using a comprehensive site or genealogically focused search engine, see Chapter 4.

Census records in the United States are a mainstay of genealogists, so most transcribed censuses that you see on the Internet come from the United States (although that doesn't mean that censuses from other countries aren't online — as we explain in the next chapter). There are a couple of projects undertaken by USGenWeb volunteers to systematically transcribe census records. You can find the USGenWeb Archives Census Project at www.roots web.com/~usgenweb/census/ and the USGenWeb Census Project On-Line Inventory of Transcribed Censuses at www.us-census.org/inventory/inventory.htm. Individuals simply transcribed those censuses in which they are interested, or those associated with a geographical area they are researching. This fact doesn't diminish the importance of these efforts; it only explains why you may see a census record for one county but not for the county right next to it.

Here's a sample search on the USGenWeb Archives Census Project site:

1. **Go to the USGenWeb Archives Census Project site** (www.rootsweb.com/~census/states.htm).
   You see a page with a map and list of states and territories for which census transcriptions are available.

2. **Select a state for your search by clicking the state on the map or its link in the list.**
   For our example, we're looking for census information on an Isaac Metcalf who lived in Baylor County, Texas, around 1880, so we select Texas. A list of available census schedules for the state appears at the top of the screen.

3. **Click a year or type of schedule that interests you.**
   We select 1880. The resulting page contains a table listing the location, roll number, status of the project, and transcriber's name.

4. **Click the status button for an available census.**
   We choose the transcription for Baylor County by clicking the status button marked Images, which takes us to a page of transcribed census entries where we can scroll down to an individual named Isaac Metcalf. You can also use your browser's Find in Page option to find the name you're looking for.

The transcriptions you can use at this site are the works of volunteers; it's possible that you may find errors here and there. Typographical errors may crop up, some censuses may not be indexed, or the status of the project for a particular county may be incorrect.

The most plentiful type of transcribed census records you're likely to encounter is what we refer to as the *plain-text census,* which is a Web page or text file that's simply a transcription of the actual census record without any kind of search function. You either have to skim the page or use your Web browser's Find in Page option to find the person you're looking for. The 1870 Census for Penn Township, Stark County, Illinois, at members.aol.com/ZCyberCat/private/castleton.html, is an example of this type of census return (see Figure 5-5). For each individual, the record includes the house number of the household, last name, first name, age, sex, race, occupation, real-estate value, personal-property value, and birthplace. This site is also typical of smaller census sites in its focus on the records on one county (actually, one township in one county).

Some sites contain collections of several census returns for a specific geographic area (over an extended period of time). A good example of this type of site is the Transcribed Census Records for Vernon County, Missouri, at freepages.genealogy.rootsweb.com/~jrbakerjr/census/census1.htm, which has several transcribed census returns for the county from 1860 to 1930.

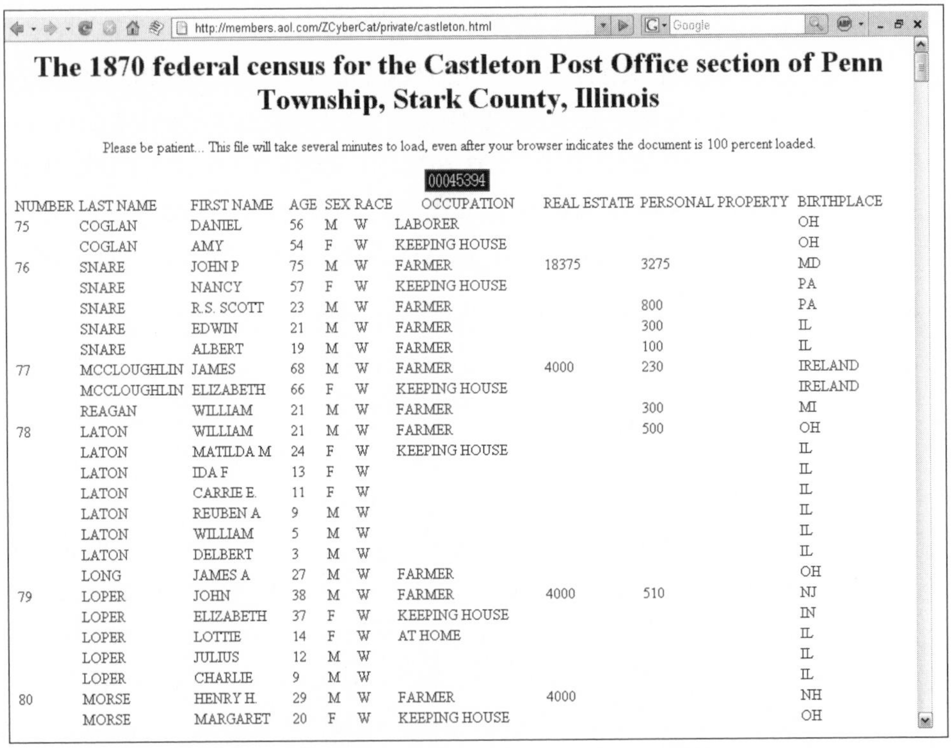
http://members.aol.com/ZCyberCat/private/castleton.html

The 1870 federal census for the Castleton Post Office section of Penn Township, Stark County, Illinois

Please be patient... This file will take several minutes to load, even after your browser indicates the document is 100 percent loaded.

00045394

NUMBER	LAST NAME	FIRST NAME	AGE	SEX	RACE	OCCUPATION	REAL ESTATE	PERSONAL PROPERTY	BIRTHPLACE
75	COGLAN	DANIEL	56	M	W	LABORER			OH
	COGLAN	AMY	54	F	W	KEEPING HOUSE			OH
76	SNARE	JOHN P	75	M	W	FARMER	18375	3275	MD
	SNARE	NANCY	57	F	W	KEEPING HOUSE			PA
	SNARE	R.S. SCOTT	23	M	W	FARMER		800	PA
	SNARE	EDWIN	21	M	W	FARMER		300	IL
	SNARE	ALBERT	19	M	W	FARMER		100	IL
77	MCCLOUGHLIN	JAMES	68	M	W	FARMER	4000	230	IRELAND
	MCCLOUGHLIN	ELIZABETH	66	F	W	KEEPING HOUSE			IRELAND
	REAGAN	WILLIAM	21	M	W	FARMER		300	MI
78	LATON	WILLIAM	21	M	W	FARMER		500	OH
	LATON	MATILDA M	24	F	W	KEEPING HOUSE			IL
	LATON	IDA F	13	F	W				IL
	LATON	CARRIE E.	11	F	W				IL
	LATON	REUBEN A	9	M	W				IL
	LATON	WILLIAM	5	M	W				IL
	LATON	DELBERT	3	M	W				IL
	LONG	JAMES A	27	M	W	FARMER			OH
79	LOPER	JOHN	38	M	W	FARMER	4000	510	NJ
	LOPER	ELIZABETH	37	F	W	KEEPING HOUSE			IN
	LOPER	LOTTIE	14	F	W	AT HOME			IL
	LOPER	JULIUS	12	M	W				IL
	LOPER	CHARLIE	9	M	W				IL
80	MORSE	HENRY H.	29	M	W	FARMER	4000		NH
	MORSE	MARGARET	20	F	W	KEEPING HOUSE			OH

Figure 5-5: *An online transcription of the 1870 Census for Penn Township, Stark County, Illinois.*

The Holy Grail of online censuses: Digitized images

Many genealogists are no longer satisfied with using transcribed information. After all, even if you find useful information, you must take a second step to confirm the information through a copy of the primary record. To avoid this two-step process, subscription sites have been focused on digitizing the complete population schedules of the United States census. The largest of these collections are found at the following sites.

HeritageQuest Online

HeritageQuest Online (www.heritagequestonline.com), a fee-based site produced by ProQuest, LLC, houses digitized images of United States census population schedules from 1790 to 1930. The collection numbers more than 10 million images taken from 12,555 rolls of microfilm. These images are bitonal (black and white) and require a TIFF viewer plug-in for your Web browser. Indexes for the images are included for 1790 to 1820, 1860 to 1870, and 1890 to 1930. In the case of the 1870 index, only selected individuals are indexed. If you're looking for individuals in other censuses, you must browse the images much as you would when using microfilm. A unique feature of the site is a sticky-note feature that enables you to annotate the census images. For example, if you have a correction or more information on a census entry, you can post a sticky note mentioning that fact. You can also use the feature to tell others that you're researching that family so they can share information with you.

U.S. census images and indexes

Ancestry.com currently offers the largest collection of U.S. census images at www.ancestry.com/search/rectype/census/

usfedcen/main.htm?o_iid=3717.

This resource contains the 1790 to 1930 census population schedules, an 1890 Census fragment, 1890 Veteran's Census Schedules, Slave Schedules from 1850 and 1860, Mortality Schedules from 1850 to1880, and the 1930 Merchant Seaman census. The images are 256-color grayscale, which typically makes them clearer than bitonal images. The site offers a plug-in viewer that displays the images in your Web browser. Also, these censuses contain indexes of every name to speed your search along. There are also some tools to assist you in your experience with the censuses. You can use a magnify feature that increases the size of the image in particular areas, and you can also save and print the images. Figure 5-6 shows the census enumeration of Abraham Lincoln in 1860 in Springfield, Illinois. Abraham is a lawyer with an estate worth $5,000. He is living with his wife Mary and sons Robert, Willie, and Thomas. Above the image are icons for the tools such as Drag, In, and Out that help users manipulate the image.

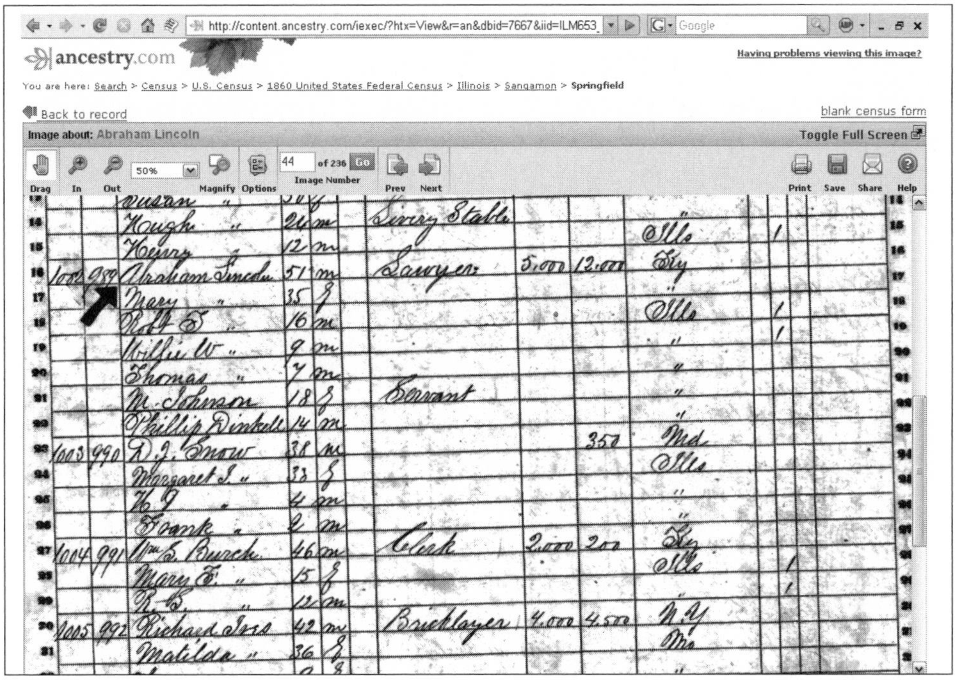

Figure 5-6:
Digital image of the 1860 Census enumeration for Abraham Lincoln at Ancestry.com.

Some noncommercial efforts also provide digitized census images. The primary source for these is the USGenWeb site. Its census images are available at www.rootsweb .com/~usgenweb/cen_img.htm.

The images are of various qualities and, in some cases, are difficult to read. You can't zoom in on these images (as you can with some commercial offerings), but they're available to researchers free of charge. Figure 5-7 shows an example 1860 Census image of Brevard County, Florida from the USGenWeb census project.

State, territorial, and other census images

Images of United States censuses are not the only census images available. State and territorial censuses are becoming available online. At the time of this writing, Ancestry.com has state and territorial censuses for Colorado (1885), Florida (1885), Iowa (1836-1925), Kansas (1855-1915), Minnesota (1849-1905), Mississippi

(1792-1866), New York (1880, 1892, 1905), Washington (1857-1892), and Wisconsin (1895, 1905). It also has images of the U.S. Indian Census schedules from 1885 to 1940.

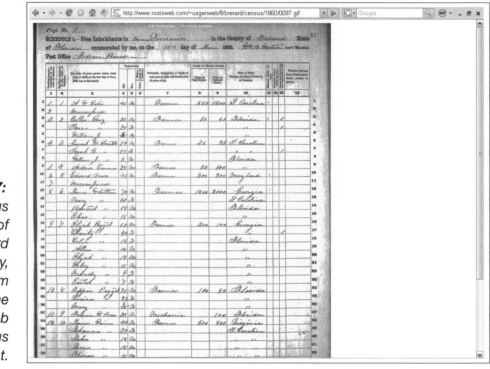

Figure 5-7:
1860 Census image of Brevard County, Florida from the USGenWeb census project.

Another source for state and territorial census images is at HistoryKat (www.historykat.com). HistoryKat has images for Colorado (1885), Florida (1885), Illinois (1820-1865), Iowa (1836), Minnesota (1857), New Mexico (1885), Oklahoma (1890, 1907), and Wisconsin (1836-1847). Figure 5-8 shows an image from the 1840 Illinois State Census for Calhoun County.

These Records Are Vital

It seems that some kind of government record accompanies every major event in our lives. One is generated when we are born, another when we get married (as well as get divorced), another when we have a child, and still another when we pass on. *Vital records* is the collective name for records of these events. Traditionally, these records have been kept at the local level. Some states have only recently made an effort to collect and centralize their holdings of vital records. In a similar manner, the record holders have just recently begun to expand the number of vital record indexes available online. You're likely to encounter four types of vital record sites: *general information sites, vital record indexes, transcribed vital records,* and *digital image collections.*

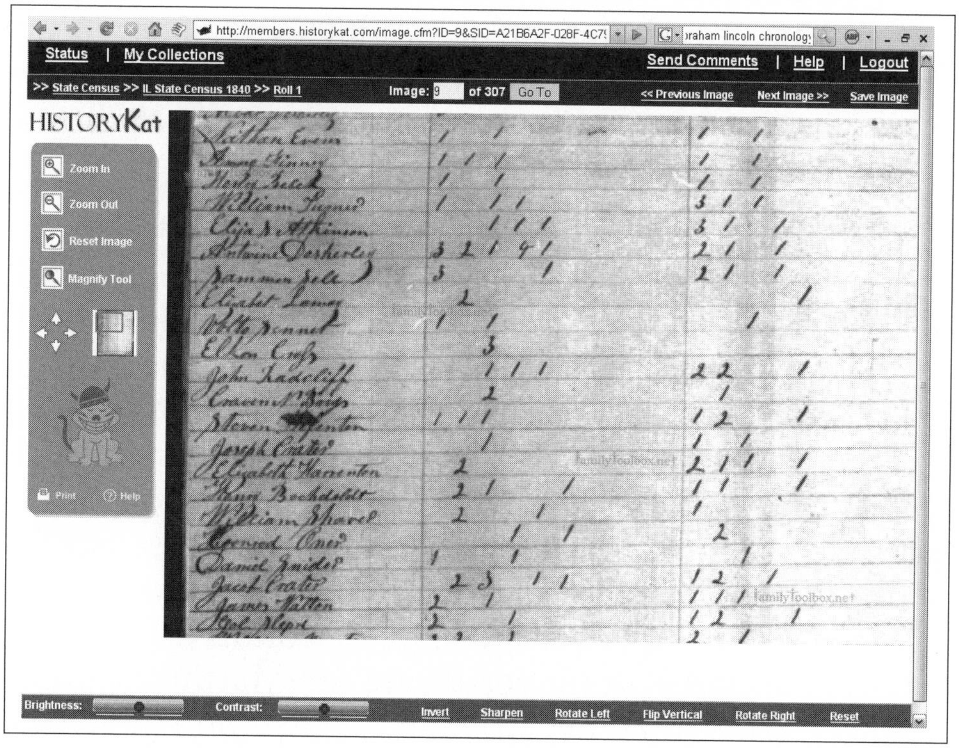

Figure 5-8:
1840 Illinois State Census image for Calhoun County at HistoryKat. com.

General information sites

If you're looking for information on how to order vital records within the United States, you can choose among a few sites. Vital Records Information — United States (vital rec.com/index.html) is probably the most comprehensive site. A page for each state lists the type of record, its cost, the address to which you should send requests, and additional remarks, such as the time period during which records were kept and to whom to make the check payable. You also can find information on obtaining vital records for foreign or high-sea births and deaths of United States citizens.

Although the Vital Records Information site doesn't contain any online indexes or records, using it is a good way to become familiar with where each state stores its vital records. Later on, as you locate records on more ancestors, you can use this site as a quick reference for getting mailing addresses for your many records requests.

Vital record indexes

Vital record indexes serve much the same purpose as census indexes: They point to the locations of original records. You can use indexes to confirm that an ancestor's vital records are available prior to submitting a request for the record. And knowing the exact location of the record can often make retrieval of the record a lot easier.

Another approach to finding vital statistics (civil registrations) is to go to the USGenWeb (www.usgenweb.org) site for the appropriate state or country. For example, we want to find a death certificate for Matthew's great-grandfather, William Henry Abell of Larue County, Kentucky. To do so, we go through the following steps:

1. **Go to the USGenWeb site (www.usgenweb.org).**
   You see a page with three columns on it.

2. **In the left column, click the link for a state that interests you.**

In our case, we select Kentucky because we're looking for someone who died in the state of Kentucky.

As a shortcut, you can always access any USGenWeb state page by typing www.usgenweb.org and the two-letter postal code for the state. For example, for Kentucky, you can type www.usgenweb.org/ky.

3. **At the USGenWeb state page for the state that you choose, look for a link to vital records information or research links.**
    We choose the Vital Statistics link in the table under the Welcome to Kentucky heading on the Kentucky USGenWeb page. This takes you to a page with search interfaces for the Kentucky Death Index, Birth Index, and Marriage Index.

4. **Scroll down to the appropriate section and type the name that you want to search in the text box and then click Submit Query.**
    Sticking with the example, we go to the Kentucky Death Index for 1911–2000 section, type **Abell** and **William H.**, and click **Search**. We then wait for the results to return.

5. **Scan the results of your query.**
    In our case, the results page contains two individuals named William H. Abell. One died in Larue County and the other in Jefferson County. The location seems right for the William from Larue County. We check the death date, September 7, 1955, and the age, 82, both of which are consistent with what we've heard from interviews with family members. The database also supplies us with the record volume number and certificate number, which we can use to obtain a copy of the certificate.

The following are some free sites containing state-wide vital records indexes:

- ✔ **California:** Death Records 1940-1997

  vitals.rootsweb.com/ca/death/search.cgi

- ✔ **California:** Pre-1905 CA Death Index Project

  www.rootsweb.com/~cabf1905/

- ✔ **Idaho:** Death Index 1911-1956

  www.rootsweb.com/~idgenweb/deaths/search.htm

- ✔ **Illinois:** Death Index 1916-1950

  www.cyberdriveillinois.com/departments/archives/idph
  deathindex.html

- ✔ **Kentucky:** Death Index 1911-2000

  vitals.rootsweb.com/ky/death/search.cgi

- ✔ **Maine:** Death Index 1960-1996

  portalx.bisoex.state.me.us/pls/archives_mhsf/archdev
  .death_archive.search_form

- ✔ **Maryland:** Death Index 1898-1951

  mdvitalrec.net/cfm/dsp_search.cfm

- ✔ **Massachusetts:** Vital Records 1600-1849

  www.ma-vitalrecords.org

- ✔ **Michigan:** Genealogical Death Indexing System 1867-1897

  www.mdch.state.mi.us/pha/osr/gendisx/search2.htm

- **Minnesota:** Death Certificates Index 1904-2001

  people.mnhs.org/dci/Search.cfm?bhcp=1

- **Missouri:** Death Certificates, 1910-1956

  www.sos.mo.gov/archives/resources/deathcertificates/

- **Montana:** Death Registry Index Pre-1954 and 1954-2002

  www.rootsweb.com/~mtmsgs/death_records.htm

- **New Mexico:** Death Index Project (1899-1940)

  www.rootsweb.com/~usgenweb/nm/nmdi.htm

- **North Dakota:** Public Death Index Project (1881-present)

  secure.apps.state.nd.us/doh/certificates/deathCertSearch.htm

- **Ohio:** Death Certificate Index, 1913-1944

  www.ohiohistory.org/dindex/

- **Oregon:** Death Index, 1903-1930

  www.heritagetrailpress.com/Death_Index/

- **South Carolina:** Death Indexes, 1915-1956

  www.scdhec.net/administration/vr/vrdi.htm

- **South Dakota:** Birth Record Search Site for South Dakota Birth Records with Birth Dates Over 100 Years

  apps.sd.gov/applications/PH14Over100BirthRec/index.asp

- **Tennessee:** Index to Tennessee Death Records

1908-1912

www.tennessee.gov/tsla/history/vital/death2.htm

✔ **Tennessee:** Index to Tennessee Death Records 1914-1922

www.tennessee.gov/tsla/history/vital/tndeath.htm

✔ **Tennessee:** Partial Index to Tennessee Death Records 1914-1925

www.tennessee.gov/tsla/history/vital/death.htm

✔ **Texas:** Texas Death Records 1964-1998

vitals.rootsweb.com/tx/death/search.cgi

✔ **Virginia:** Death Records Index 1853-1896

ajax.lva.lib.va.us/F/?func=file&file_name=find-b-clas29&local_base=clas29

✔ **Wisconsin:** Wisconsin Genealogy Index (pre-1907 birth, death, and marriage records)

www.wisconsinhistory.org/vitalrecords

There are also free sites with smaller collections of vital records — such as birth records for a particular county. To find these, use a genealogically focused search engine or your favorite general search engine.

Vital records indexes are available on subscription sites. At the time this book was written, Ancestry.com had vital record indexes for the states of Alabama, Arkansas, California, Connecticut, Delaware, District of Columbia, Florida, Georgia, Idaho, Indiana, Kentucky, Louisiana, Maine, Massachusetts, Michigan, Minnesota, Missouri, Montana, North Carolina, Ohio, Oregon, Rhode Island, South Carolina, South Dakota, Texas, Utah, Washington, and Wisconsin. WorldVitalRecords.com had vital record indexes for Connecticut, Kentucky, Maine, Rhode Island, Tennessee, Texas, and Virginia. Both sites also contain vital records collections for specific localities (such as a city or a county).

Transcribed vital records

If you aren't lucky enough to have a copy of your great-grandfather's marriage certificate, you need a way to discover the information that the document contains. The best way to find this information is to order a copy of the certificate from the appropriate government source. (For more information on this strategy, see "Vital record information sites," earlier in this chapter.) But before you spend the money to get a copy, you want to find out whether the record is really of interest to you — this is where transcribed vital records come in handy.

Transcribed records can come in several forms. A researcher may have transcribed a series of records of a particular county, a state may have established a database of records, or a commercial company may have created or bought a transcription. Either way, these sites can be helpful in determining whether the record you're looking for is useful.

To find a transcribed record, you could use a *meta-search engine* (a site that groups together the results from several search engines). When using meta-search engines, you tend to find links to commercial databases as well as to free databases — so be sure to check several results before subscribing to a commercial site just to get access to its database. For example, we can use Dogpile (www.dogpile.com) to search for a transcribed marriage record for Jacob Gardner, who was married sometime around 1850. Just follow these steps:

1. **Go to Dogpile (www.dogpile.com).**
   The page loads with the Web Search tab open and a search box displayed.

2. **Enter your search terms into the search box and click Go Fetch!**
   In our example, we type **Indiana marriage index**. We use the word *index,* rather than *transcribed record,* because the transcribed records are more likely to be accessed as part of a larger index — especially when held by a governmental institution. Also, with older records, there are so few items to index that often the contents of the whole record are indexed.

3. **Click a link that looks promising.**
   We receive multiple results. Scrolling through the list, we look for a promising link — finding one in the Indiana State Library marriage index, which offers free access.

4. **On the new site, follow the instructions to view the transcribed record.**
   We choose a link to the marriage database with last name E-F-G. This leads us to a search form, where we type **Jacob Gardner** and click Start Search. The result page we get lists a marriage between Jacob Gardner and Harriet Simmons in Jefferson County on November 2, 1848.

We could have taken a similar path to locate the same information with a commercial site, such as Ancestry.com (www.ancestry.com) or World VitalRecords.com (www.worldvitalrecords.com).

Digital images of vital records

One of the newest areas in the digitization of primary sources has been in the area of vital records. In the past, archives that house vital records have been reluctant to digitize them due to privacy concerns. However, as more and more requests come in for vital records, these archives have begun to place those records that fall outside of the provisions of the privacy act online. Here are a list of some of the vital records now available online:

- **Arizona:** Arizona Genealogy Birth and Death Certificates (births 1887-1931; deaths 1878-1956)

  genealogy.az.gov

- **Colorado:** Arapahoe County (Includes City of Denver) Marriages 1861-1868

  www.colorado.gov/dpa/doit/archives/DenMarriage/denver_and_arapahoe_county_marri.htm

- **Florida:** Hillsborough County Marriage Records

  www.lib.usf.edu/public/index.cfm?Pg=Hillsborough CountyMarriageRecords

- **Georgia:** Death Certificates, 1919-1927

  content.sos.state.ga.us/cdm4/gadeaths.php

- **Kentucky:** Death Certificates, 1911-1953 (subscription site)

  content.ancestry.com/iexec/?htx=List&dbid=1222&offerid =0%3a7858%3a0

- **Utah:** Death Certificates from 1905 to 1956

  historyresearch.utah.gov/indexes/

✔ **West Virginia:** Birth, Death, and Marriage Certificates

www.wvculture.org/vrr/va_select.aspx

Investigating Immigration and Naturalization Records

You may have heard the old stories about your great-great-grandparents who left their homeland in search of a new life. Some of these stories may include details about where they were born and how they arrived at their new home. Although these are great stories, as a genealogist, you want to verify this information with documentation.

Often the document you're looking for is an immigration or naturalization record. *Immigration records* are documents that show when a person moved to a particular country to reside; *naturalization records* are documents showing that a person became a citizen of a particular country without being born in that country. Sometimes these documents can prove difficult to find, especially if you don't know where to begin looking. Unless you have some evidence in your attic or have a reliable family account of the immigration, you may need a record or something else to point you in the right direction. Census records are one useful set of records. (For more information about census records, see "Counting on the Census," earlier in this chapter.) Depending on the year your ancestors immigrated, census records may contain the location of birth and tell you the year of immigration and the year of naturalization of your immigrant ancestor.

Emigration records — documents that reflect when a person moved out of a particular country to take up residence elsewhere — are also useful to researchers. You find these records in the country your ancestor left; they can often help when you can't find immigration or naturalization records in the new country.

To find more information on research using immigration records, see the Immigration and Ships Passenger Lists Research Guide at home.att.net/~arnielang/shipgide.html. For the types of immigration records held by the National Archives, see the Immigration Records page at www.archives.gov/genealogy/immigration/passenger-ar rival.html.

You can also check out Chapter 13, "Immigration: Finding Important Immigrant Origins," written by Kory L. Meyerink and Loretto Dennis Szucs, in *The Source: A Guidebook of American Genealogy,* edited by Szucs and Sandra Hargreaves Luebking (Ancestry, Inc.). Other sources to refer to include *They Became Americans,* written by Loretto Dennis Szucs (Ancestry Publishing), and *They Came in Ships,* Third Edition, written by John Philip Colletta (Ancestry Publishing). Both provide more information about immigration and naturalization within the United States.

Locating immigration, emigration, and naturalization records online can be challenging. But some good news is that the common types of records that genealogists use to locate immigrants — passenger lists, immigration papers, emigration records — have increased in availability on the Internet over the past few years and will likely continue to increase in numbers. A good starting point for determining an ancestor's homeland is to look at census records. (For more information about census records, see "Counting on the Census," earlier in this chapter.) Because a great deal of early immigration and naturalization processing occurred at the local level, census records may give you an indication of where to look for immigration records.

Some examples of online records include the following:

✔ **Immigration/Naturalization Records:** McLean County, Illinois, Immigration Records (www.co.mclean.il.us/CircuitClerk/imgrecs/imgrecs .html)

✔ **Passenger Lists:** *Mayflower* Passenger List (members.aol.com/calebj/passengers2.html)

If you don't have a lot of details on when your ancestor may have immigrated but have a general idea of the time or place of immigration, you may want to consider looking for information on a comprehensive genealogical index. As you look at comprehensive genealogy sites, you're likely to find these types of records categorized under immigration, naturalization, passenger lists, or by geographical area. If you know more details, try using a genealogically focused search engine or a general Internet search engine.

Passenger lists

Most of the immigration records that you will find on the Web are in the form of passenger lists. Passenger lists were manifests of who was on a particular ship. You can use passenger lists not only to see who immigrated on a particular ship, but you can also see citizens of the United States who were merely traveling on a particular ship (perhaps coming back from vacation in Europe).

To find passenger lists, you can try using a general search engine or a genealogically focused search engine. This is a particularly good strategy if you don't know what the name of the ship was or the year that they immigrated. If you do know the name of the ship, a comprehensive genealogical index may be more appropriate.

As an example, suppose that you have a family legend that Martin Saunders immigrated to America on a ship called *Planter* sometime in the first part of the seventeenth century. The following steps show you how to search for a passenger list to confirm the legend:

1. **Go to the Ask.com search engine (www.ask.com).**
   On the home page, the search box is located at the top of the page.

2. **Type your search terms into the Search the Web field and click Search.**
   For this example, we type **martin saunders on the ship planter**.

3. **Click a promising link from the list of results.**
   The results page shows the first 10 links of over 2,700 links found for these search terms. One of the top links goes to a transcription of the passengers on the *Planter,* which sailed on April 6, 1635 — the first on the list being "Martin Saunders, aged 40 years." Another link on the Results page reads <u>Ships Passenger List — PLANTER of London for Boston Massachusetts</u>. In the abstract that you access by clicking the link, you see that a Martin Saunders, age 40, sailed on the *Planter.*

Another source for passenger lists is the Immigrant Ships Transcribers Guild passenger-list transcription project (www.immigrantships.net). Currently, the Guild has transcribed over 8,000 passenger manifests. The passenger lists are organized by date, ship's name, port of departure, port of arrival, passenger's surname, and captain's name. You can also search the site to find the person or ship that interests you. Other pages containing links to passenger lists include

✔ Passenger Lists at

userdb.rootsweb.com/passenger/

✔ Olive Tree Genealogy at
olivetreegenealogy.com/ships/index.shtml

✔ Passenger Lists on the Internet at
members.aol.com/rprost/passenger.html

✔ Emigration & Immigration Records & Links at
home.att.net/~wee-monster/ei.html

✔ Castle Garden (the precursor to Ellis Island) at
www.castlegarden.org

✔ Famine Irish Passenger Record Data File
aad.archives.gov/aad/fielded-search.jsp?dt=180&tf=F&cat=
SB302&bc=sb,sl

✔ Ship Passenger List Index for New Netherlands
www.rootsweb.com/~nycoloni/nnimmdex.html

✔ Boston Passenger Manifests (1848-1891)
www.sec.state.ma.us/arc/arcsrch/PassengerManifest
SearchContents.html

✔ Maine Passenger Lists
www.mainegenealogy.net/passenger_search.asp

✔ The Great Migration: Ships to New England
1633-1635
www.winthropsociety.org/ships.php

✔ Partial Transcription of Inward Slave Manifests

www.afrigeneas.com/slavedata/manifests.html

✔ Maritime Heritage Project: San Francisco

www.maritimeheritage.org/log.htm

✔ Galveston Immigration Database

www.galvestonhistory.org/Galveston_Immigration_
Database.asp

There are also some significant commercial database collections of immigration records. Ancestry.com's U.S. Immigration Collection contains information on over 22 million names and immigration records from more than 100 countries. Highlights of the collection include

✔ New York passenger lists

✔ Passenger and immigration list indexes (1500s to 1900s)

✔ Passenger lists from Boston, Philadelphia, Baltimore, and New Orleans

✔ Naturalization records (1700s to 1900s)

✔ California passenger and crew lists (1893-1957)

If your family came through Ellis Island, your first stop should be the Ellis Island Foundation site. The site contains a collection of 25 million passengers, along with ship manifests, and images of certain ships.

To illustrate how the Ellis Island Foundation site works, look for Harry Houdini, who passed through the port a few times:

1. Go to the Ellis Island site at

www.ellisislandrecords.org/default.asp.
The search box is located just under the main header in a tan box.

2. **Type the passenger's name into the search boxes and click Start Search.**
You should see a results box with the name of the passenger, residence (if stated), arrival year, age, and some links to the passenger record, ship manifest, and the ship's image (if available).

3. **Click on the ship manifest link.**
Figure 5-9 shows the manifest for the ship Imperator that sailed from Southampton on 3 July 1920 and arrived on 11 July 1920. You can see from the manifest that Harry was traveling with his wife.

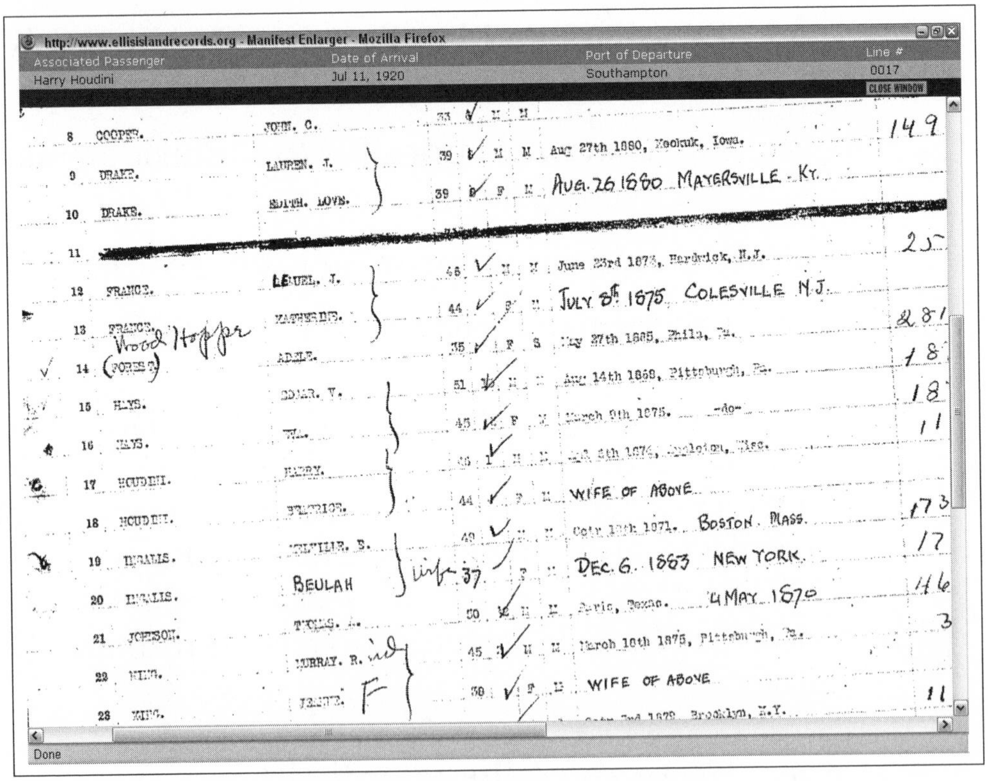

Figure 5-9: Harry Houdini's entry on a passenger list at the Ellis Island site.

Naturalization records

The road to citizenship was paved with paper. In this case, this is a good thing for researchers. A relatively new site, Footnote.com, has begun to place naturalization records housed in the National Archives online. Figure 5-10 shows a naturalization record from Footnote.com.

At the time this book was written, it offered the following record sets:

- Naturalization Petitions for the Southern District of California, 1887-1940

- Records of the U.S. Circuit Court for the Eastern District of Louisiana, New Orleans Division: Petitions, 1838-1861

- Petitions and Records of Naturalizations of the U.S. District and Circuit Courts of the District of Massachusetts, 1906-1929

- Naturalization Petitions of the U.S. District Court for the District of Maryland, 1906-1930

- Naturalization Petitions for the Eastern District of Pennsylvania, 1795-1930

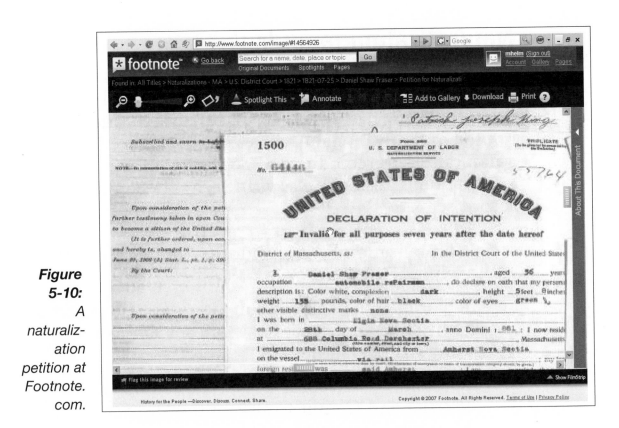

Figure 5-10: A naturalization petition at Footnote.com.

✔ Naturalization Petitions of the U.S. Circuit and District Courts for the Middle District of Pennsylvania, 1906-1930

✔ Naturalization Petitions of the U.S. District Court, 1820-1930, and Circuit Court, 1820-1911, for the Western District of Pennsylvania

✔ Index to Naturalizations of World War I Soldiers, 1918

You can also find some database indexes of naturalizations online. Here are some examples:

✔ **Arkansas:** Arkansas Naturalization Records Index 1809-1906 naturalizationrecords.com/usa/ar_natrecind-a.shtml

✔ **California:** Index to Naturalization Records in Sonoma County, California, 1841-1906

www.rootsweb.com/~cascgs/nat.htm

✔ **California:** Index to Naturalization Records in Sonoma County, California, Volume II, 1906-1930

rootsweb.com/~cascgs/nat2.htm

✔ **California:** Santa Barbara County Naturalized Citizens Index

www.cagenweb.com/santabarbara/sbcgs/natcitintro.htm

✔ **Colorado:** Colorado State Archives Naturalization Records

www.colorado.gov/dpa/doit/archives/natural.html

✔ **Delaware:** Naturalization Records Database

archives.delaware.gov/collections/natrlzndb/nat-index.shtml

✔ **Indiana:** Indiana Commission on Public Records Naturalization Index

www.state.in.us/serv/icpr_naturalization

✔ **Kansas:** Index of the Petitions for Naturalization at the Osage County Courthouse

skyways.lib.ks.us/towns/Lyndon/genealogy/natindex1.htm

✔ **Missouri:** Naturalization Records, 1816-1955

www.sos.mo.gov/archives/naturalization/

- **New York:** Albany County Clerk's Office Naturalization Index

  www.albanycounty.com/departments/achor/naturalization indexes.asp?id=856&SearchType=ExactPhrase&terms =naturalization%20records

- **New York:** Eastern District Court of New York Naturalization Project

  www.italiangen.org/EDN.stm

- **New York:** Kings County Clerk's Office Index to Naturalization Records

  www.jgsny.org/kingsintro1.htm

- **New York:** Queens County Naturalization Project

  www.italiangen.org/QueensNat.stm

- **North Dakota:** North Dakota Naturalization Records Index

  www.lib.ndsu.nodak.edu/ndirs/databases/naturalrec.php

- **Ohio:** Miami County Naturalization Papers, 1860-1872

  www.tdn-net.com/genealogy/m-county/natural.htm

- **Pennsylvania:** Centre County Naturalization Records, 1802-1929 (includes images of the records)

  www.co.centre.pa.us/hrip/natrecs/default.asp

- **Washington:** Digital Archives

  www.digitalarchives.wa.gov/default.aspx

Surveying Land Lovers

Land records are among the most plentiful sources of information on your ancestors. Although a census would have occurred only once every ten years, land transactions may have taken place two or three times a year, depending on how much land your ancestor possessed. These records don't always contain a great deal of demographic information, but they do place your ancestor in a time and location, and sometimes in a historical context as well. For example, you may discover that your ancestors were granted military bounty lands. This discovery may tell you where and when your ancestors acquired the land, as well as what war they fought in. You may also find out how litigious your ancestors were by the number of lawsuits they filed or had filed against them as a result of land claims.

 Getting a foundation in the history of land records prior to conducting a lot of research is probably a good idea, as the practices of land transfers differed by location and time period. A good place to begin your research is at the Land Record Reference page at www.directlinesoftware.com/landref.htm. This page contains links to articles on patents and grants, bounty lands, the Homestead Act, property description methods, and how land transactions were conducted. For a more general treatment of land records, see "Research in Land and Tax Records," by Sandra Hargreaves Luebking, in *The Source: A Guidebook of American Genealogy,* edited by Loretto Dennis Szucs and Luebking (Ancestry, Inc.).

There are several sites online that contain indexes to land transactions within the United States. Some of these are free and other broader collections require a subscription. The easiest way to find these sites is to consult a comprehensive genealogical index site and look under the appropriate geographical area. What you are likely to encounter in a land index is the name of the purchaser or warrantee, the name of the buyer (if applicable), the location of the land, number of acres, and the date of the land transfer. In some cases, you may see the residence of the person who acquired the land. Figure 5-11 shows an example of a land entry in the index to Texas Land Grants at wwwdb.glo.state.tx.us/central/LandGrants/LandGrants Search.cfm.

Here are some examples of land indexes available online:

- ✔ **Arkansas:** Land Records

  searches.rootsweb.com/cgi-bin/arkland/arkland.pl

- ✔ **California:** Early Sonoma County, California, Land Grants, 1846-1850

  www.rootsweb.com/~cascgs/intro.htm

- ✔ **Colorado:** Kit Carson County Land Registration Receipts 1913-1919

  www.colorado.gov/dpa/doit/archives/land/kit_carson_ land_index.html

- ✔ **Florida:** Spanish Land Grant Claims

  www.floridamemory.com/Collections/SpanishLandGrants/

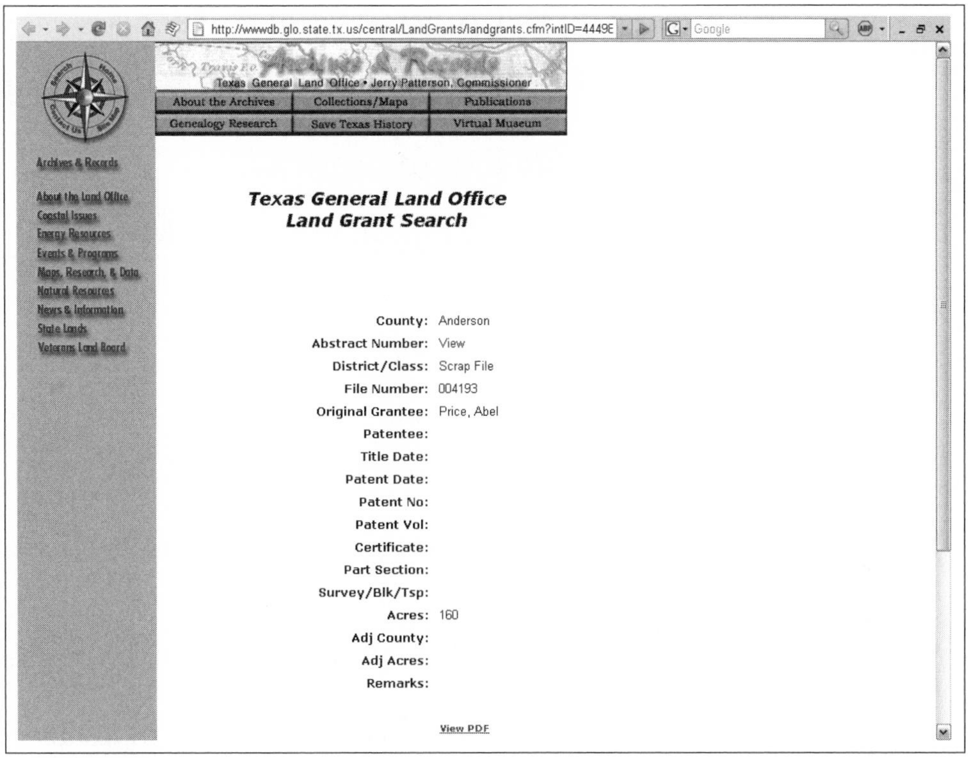

Figure 5-11: An entry from the Texas Land Grant index.

✔ **Georgia:** Chatham County Deed Books, 1785-1806

content.sos.state.ga.us/cdm4/chathamdeed.php

✔ **Illinois:** Illinois Public Domain Land Tract Sales

www.sos.state.il.us/departments/archives/data_lan.html

✔ **Indiana:** Land Records

www.in.gov/icpr/archives/databases/land/landindx.html

✔ **Kentucky:** Kentucky Land Office

sos.ky.gov/land/

✔ **Louisiana:** Acadian Memorial Archive Land Grants

www.acadianmemorial.org/ensemble_encore/landgrants
.htm

- **Louisiana:** Louisiana Land Records

  searches.rootsweb.com/cgi-bin/laland/laland.pl

- **Maryland:** Patents Index

  www.msa.md.gov/msa/stagser/s1400/s1426/html/index54
  .html

- **New York:** Ulster County Deed Books 1, 2 & 3 Index

  archives.co.ulster.ny.us/deedsearchscreen.htm

- **North Carolina:** Alamance County Land Grant Recipients

  www.rootsweb.com/~ncacgs/ala_nc_land_grants.html

- **Oregon:** Oregon Historical Records Index

  genealogy.state.or.us/

- **Texas:** Land Grant Database

  wwwdb.glo.state.tx.us/central/LandGrants/LandGrants
  Search.cfm

- **Virginia:** Land Office Grants

  ajax.lva.lib.va.us/F/?func=file&file_name=find-b-clas30&
  local_base=CLAS30

- **Wisconsin:** Land Records

  searches.rootsweb.com/cgi-bin/wisconsin/wisconsin.pl

One exciting site relating to land records in the United States is the Bureau of Land Management, Eastern States, General Land Office Official Land Patents Records Site (www.glorecords.blm.gov). This site enables you to search the more than 3 million federal land title records for the Eastern States office issued between 1820 and 1908. Recently the database was expanded to include serial patent records issued after 1908, but this is still an ongoing project.

Follow these steps to search the records on this site:

1. **Go to the Land Patents Records Site (www.glorecords.blm.gov).**

2. **In the left green bar at the top of the page, click Search Land Patents and, on the following page, enter your ZIP code in the appropriate space and click Continue.**
   This brings you to a page displaying a form that you can fill out to search the patents. Matthew's interest, for example, is in finding land that one of his ancestors, Jacob Helm, owned in Illinois.

3. **Select the state that you're interested in from the State drop-down list.**
   We select Illinois.

4. **Type a first name and last name in the text boxes in the section where you enter the name of the patentee or warrantee, and then click Search.**
   We type **Helm** in the Last Name text box, **Jacob** in the First Name text box, and then click Search. This brings us to a page listing one result for Jacob Helm. The table tells us the name of the patentee, state, county, issue date, land office, document number, and accession number, and provides a button link that we can click for details on the entry or a button to view the image (looks like a piece of paper).

5. **Click the Patentee Name or Warrantee Name link.**

   The Land Patent Details page loads with the Patent Description showing. From this information, we can obtain the document number of the purchase, how many acres, how and when the land was purchased, and which land office recorded the transaction. Most databases stop here, but this site offers more, as you can see from the four tabs — Patent Description (what you're currently viewing), Legal Land Description, Document Image, and Certified Copy.

6. **Click the Document Image tab to view a digitized copy of the patent.**

   We can choose one of four ways to view the document: a small GIF image, a large GIF image, a TIFF image, or a PDF document. We can then save the copy of the document on our computer. Figure 5-12 shows the patent for Jacob Helm.

At the BLM site, you can also see digitized surveys for the states of Alabama, Arkansas, District of Columbia, Florida, Georgia, Idaho, Louisiana, Maryland, Michigan, Minnesota, Mississippi, North Carolina, New Mexico, New York, Oklahoma, Pennsylvania, Tennessee, Texas, Virginia, and West Virginia. For surveys in Illinois, see the Federal Township Plats of Illinois site at land plats.ilsos.net/Flash/FTP_Illinois.html.

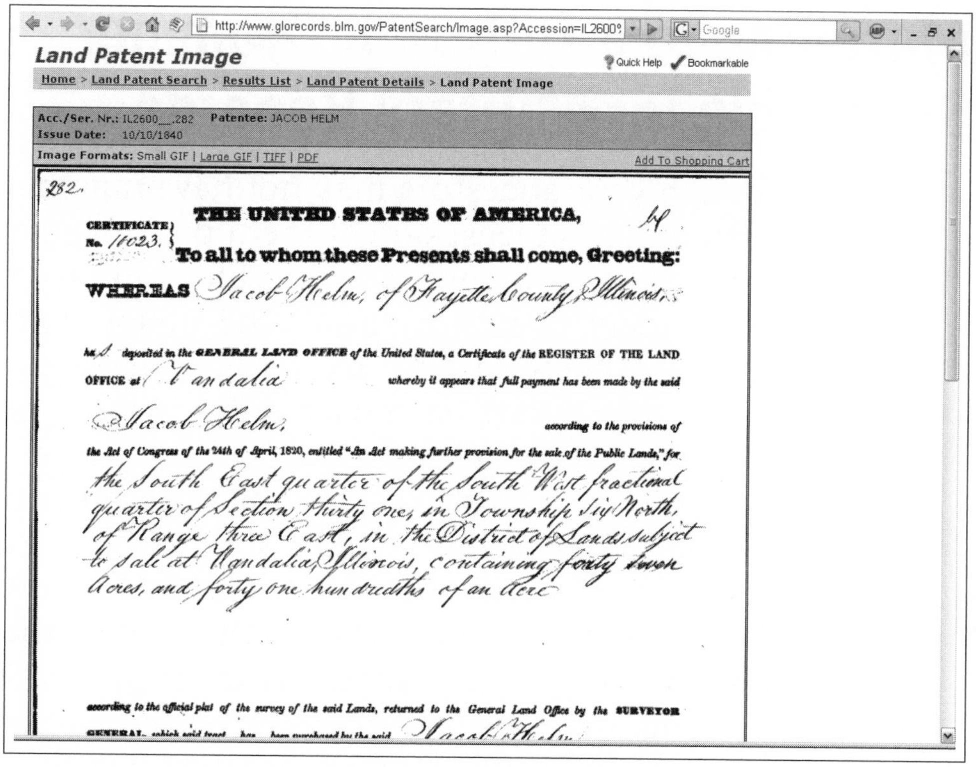

Figure 5-12: The land patent for Jacob Helm at the General Land Office site.

In addition to the methods we mention so far in this section, you may want to check out geography-related resources, such as the USGenWeb project (www.usgenweb .org) or the WorldGenWeb project (www.worldgen web.org). These sites organize their resources by location (country, state, and/or county, depending on which you use). For more information about USGenWeb, see Chapter 4. Of course, if your attempts to find land records and information through comprehensive sites and geography-related sites don't prove as fruitful as you'd like, you can always turn to a search engine such as AltaVista (www.altavista.com) or Google (www.google.com).

Marching to a Different Drummer: Searching for Military Records

Although your ancestors may not have marched to a different drummer, at least one of them probably kept pace with a military beat at some point in life. Military records contain a variety of information. The major types of records that you're likely to find are service, pension, and bounty land records. Draft or conscription records may also surface in your exploration.

Service records chronicle the military career of an individual. They often contain details about where your ancestors lived, when they enlisted or were *drafted* (or *conscripted,* enrolled for compulsory service), their ages, their discharge dates, and, in some instances, their birthplaces and occupations. You may also find pay records (including muster records that state when your ancestors had to report to military units) and notes on any injuries that they sustained while serving in the military. You can use these records to determine the unit in which your ancestor served and the time periods of their service. This information can lead you to pension records that can contain significant genealogical information because of the level of detail required to prove service in order to receive a pension. Also, service records can give you an appreciation of your ancestor's place within history — especially the dates and places where your ancestor fought or served as a member of the armed forces.

Pensions were often granted to veterans who were disabled or who demonstrated financial need after service in a particular war or campaign; widows or orphans of veterans also may have received benefits. These records are valuable because, in order to receive pensions, your ancestors had to prove that they served in the military. Proof entailed a discharge certificate or the sworn testimony of the veteran and

214

witnesses. Pieces of information that you can find in pension records include your ancestor's rank, period of service, unit, residence at the time of the pension application, age, marriage date, spouse's name, names of children, and the nature of the veteran's financial need or disability. If a widow submitted a pension application, you may also find records verifying her marriage to the veteran and death records (depending on when the veteran ancestor died).

Bounty lands are those lands granted by the government in exchange for military service that occurred between 1775 and 1855. Wars covered during this period include the American Revolution, War of 1812, Old Indian Wars, and the Mexican Wars. In order to receive bounty lands, soldiers were required to file an application. These applications often contain information useful to genealogical researchers.

If you are new to researching United States military records, take a look at the Research in Military Records page at the National Archives site (www.archives.gov/genealogy/military/). It contains information on the types of military records held by the archives, how you can use them in your research, and information on records for specific wars. Also, for the historical context of the time period that your ancestor served, see the U.S. Army Center of Military History Research Material page at www.army.mil/cmh-pg/html/bookshelves/resmat/resmat.html. This site contains links to chapters from *American Military History,* which covers military actions from the colonial period through the war on terrorism.

The largest collections for military records currently are housed within subscription sites. So, here is a quick rundown on what each site has within its collections.

Footnote.com (www.footnote.com) has partnered with the National Archives to place digitized images of microfilm held by the archives. As a result, most of the military records on Footnote are federal. Here are some examples of available record sets:

- ✔ Compiled Service Records of Soldiers Who Served in the American Army During the Revolutionary War

- ✔ Revolutionary War Pension and Bounty-Land Warrant Application Files

- ✔ Revolutionary War Rolls, 1775-1783 (includes muster rolls, payrolls, and personnel records of American Army Units)

- ✔ Organization Index to Pension Files of Veterans Who Served Between 1861 and 1900

- ✔ Compiled Service Records of Confederate Soldiers

- ✔ Mathew B Brady Collection of Civil War Photographs

- ✔ Case Files of Approved Pension Applications of Widows and Other Dependents of Civil War and Later Navy Veterans (Navy Widows' Certificates), 1861-1910

- ✔ Records of the American Section of the Supreme War Council, 1917-19

Ancestry.com (www.ancestry.com) has a number of indexes for American Revolution records, including

- ✔ American Revolutionary War Rejected Pensions

- ✔ Loyalists in the American Revolution: Miscellaneous Records

- ✔ U.S. Revolutionary War Miscellaneous Records (Manuscript File), 1775-1790s

- ✔ U.S. Civil War Soldiers, 1861-1865

- ✔ Confederate Service Records, 1861-1865

- Civil War POW Records

- U.S. Colored Troops Military Service Records, 1861-1865

- U.S. Marine Corps Muster Rolls

- World War I Draft Registration Cards

- U.S. World War II Army Enlistment Records

HistoryKat (www.historykat.com) features digital images from the following:

- Historical Register of Officers of the Continental Army during the War of the Revolution, April, 1775 to December, 1783

- Historical Register and Dictionary of the United States Army

- War of 1812 Military Bounty Land Warrants

- Returns of Killed and Wounded in Battles or Engagements with Indians and British and Mexican Troops, 1790-1848

- Military entries from A Register of Officers and Agents, Civil, Military, and Naval, in the Service of the United States 1829 and 1831

At WorldVitalRecords.com you can find textual records, including

- List of Officials, Civil, Military, and Ecclesiastical of Connecticut Colony, 1636-1677

- Spanish American War Volunteers — Colorado

- Korean War Casualties

✔ Army Casualties 1956-2003

✔ Muster Rolls of the Soldiers of the War of 1812: Detached from the Militia of North Carolina in 1812 and 1814

Here is a sampling of the different types of records that are available on free sites:

✔ Muster Rolls and Other Records of Service of Maryland Troops in the American Revolution

www.msa.md.gov/megafile/msa/speccol/sc2900/sc2908/000001/000018/html/index.html

✔ Ohio Historical Society War of 1812 Roster of Ohio Soldiers

www.ohiohistory.org/resource/database/rosters.html

✔ Illinois Black Hawk War Veterans Database

www.cyberdriveillinois.com/departments/archives/blkhawk.html

✔ South Carolina Confederate Pension Applications 1919-1926

www.archivesindex.sc.gov/Archives/default.asp

✔ Annual Report of the Adjutant General of Missouri, December 31, 1863

digital.library.umsystem.edu/cgi/t/text/text-idx?sid=d580ce6aa5df1d2b7af19a7357bb672d;c=umlib;idno=umlk000033

✔ Colorado Volunteers in the Spanish American War (1898)

> www.colorado.gov/dpa/doit/archives/military/span_am _war/

↙ Service Personnel Not Recovered Following World War II

> www.dtic.mil/dpmo/WWII_MIA/INDEX.HTM

Another set of valuable resources for researching an ancestor that participated in a war is information provided by a lineage society. Some examples include the Daughters of the American Revolution (www.dar.org), Sons of the American Revolution (www.sar.org), Society of the Cincinnati (www.thecincinnati.org), United Empire Loyalists' Association of Canada (www.uelac.org), National Society United States Daughters of 1812 (www.usdaughters1812.org), Daughters of Union Veterans of the Civil War (www.duvcw.org), and Sons of Confederate Veterans (www.scv.org).

One of the largest collections of military records at a free site is the Civil War Soldiers and Sailors System (CWSS). The CWSS site is a joint project of the National Park Service, Genealogical Society of Utah, and the Federation of Genealogical Societies. The site contains an index of over 6.3 million soldier records of both Union and Confederate soldiers. Also available at the site are regimental histories and descriptions of 384 battles.

Follow these steps to search the records on this site:

1. **Set your browser to the Civil War Soldier and Sailors System (www.itd.nps.gov/cwss/).**
   On the right side of the screen are links to information on the site, including links to soldiers, sailors, regiments, cemeteries, battles, prisoners, Medal of Honor, and National Parks.

2. Click on the appropriate link for the person you are looking for.

We are looking for a soldier who served, so we click the Soldier link.

3. Type in the name of the soldier/sailor in the appropriate field and click Submit Query.

If you know additional details, you can pick which side your ancestor fought on, the state they were from, unit, and function that they performed. We type **Helm** in the last name, **Uriah** for the first name, **Union** for the Union or Confederate field, and **Illinois** for State. One search result appears with that information.

4. Click on the name of the Soldier/Sailor to see the Detailed Soldier Record.

The soldier record shows that Uriah served in Company G, 7th Illinois Cavalry (see Figure 5-13). He entered and left the service as a private. His information is located on National Archives series M539 microfilm, roll 39.

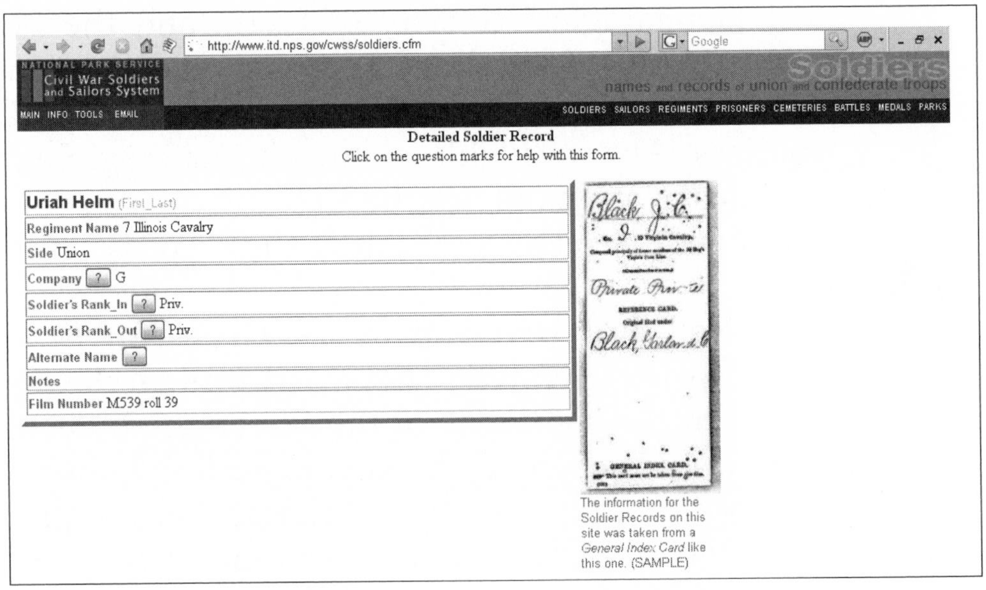

Figure 5-13: Detailed soldier record from the Civil War Soldiers and Sailors System.

Taxation with Notation

Some of the oldest records available for research are tax records — including property and inheritance records. Although several local governments have placed tax records online, they are usually very recent documents rather than historical tax records. Most early tax records you encounter were likely collected locally (that is, at the county level). However, many local tax records have since been turned over to state or county archives — some of which now make tax records available on microfilm, as do Family History Centers. (If you have a Family History Center in your area, you may be able to save yourself a trip, call, or letter to the state archives — check with the Family History Center to see whether it keeps copies of tax records for the area in which you're interested.) And a few maintainers of tax records — including archives and Family History Centers — are starting to make information about their holdings available online. Generally, either indexes or transcriptions of these microfilm records are what you find online and a lot of these are located on subscription sites.

Here are just a few examples of the types of online resources that you can find pertaining to tax records:

✔ **General Information:** Chapter 8, "Research in Land and Tax Records," by Sandra Hargreaves Luebking, in *The Source: A Guidebook of American Genealogy,* edited by Luebking and Loretto Dennis Szucs (Ancestry, Inc.).

✔ **Tax List:** 1790–1800 County Tax Lists of Virginia at homepages.rootsweb.com/~ysbinns/vataxlists/

✔ **Land and Poll Tax:** Benton County, Tennessee 1836 Land and Poll Tax List (www.rootsweb.com/~tnbenton/databas2.htm)

If you're locating records in the United States, try the USGenWeb site for the state or county. Here's what to do:

1. **Go to the USGenWeb site (www.usgenweb.org).**
   You see a page with two columns on it.

2. **Click a state in the left column of the page.**
   In our case, we select the <u>Pennsylvania</u> link because we're looking for tax records in Lancaster County.

   As a shortcut, you can always get to any USGenWeb state page by typing www.usgenweb.org and the two letter postal code for the state. For example, for Pennsylvania, we can type **www.usgenweb.org/pa**.

3. **From the USGenWeb state page (for the state that you choose), find a link to the county in which you're interested.**
   On the Pennsylvania Counties page, we click the <u>Lancaster</u> link to get to the Lancaster County GenWeb site.

4. **Click the link for Courthouse Records.**
   We click the <u>Courthouse Records</u> link because tax records were often kept in county courthouses. This leads us to another link called <u>Tax Lists</u>.

5. **Click the link for Tax Lists.**
   Clicking this link takes us to another page that offers tax lists for the county.

The state and county Web sites in the USGenWeb Project vary immensely. Some have more information available than the Pennsylvania and Lancaster County pages, while others have less. The amount of information that's available at a particular USGenWeb site affects the number of links you have to click through to find what you're looking for.

Don't be afraid to take a little time to explore and become familiar with the sites for states and counties in which your ancestors lived.

One other strategy for finding tax assessment information is to search local newspapers for the time period that your ancestor lived. A tax list was published in newspapers on a yearly basis in some localities. To find out more about searching newspapers online, see Chapter 9.

Was Your Ancestor a Criminal? Using Court Records

There's good news — your ancestor may not have to have been a criminal for court records to be useful in your genealogical research. Court records may also contain information about your model-citizen ancestors — those fine, upstanding citizens who made good witnesses.

Court cases and trials aren't just a phenomenon of today's world. Your ancestor may have participated in the judicial system as a plaintiff, defendant, or witness. Some court records can provide a glimpse into the character of your ancestors — whether they were frequently on trial for misbehavior or called as character witnesses. You can also find a lot of information on your ancestors if they were involved in land disputes — a common problem in some areas where land transferred hands often. Again, your ancestor may not have been directly involved in a dispute but may have been called as a witness. Another type of court record that may involve your ancestor is a probate case. Often, members of families contested wills or were called upon as executors or witnesses, and the resulting file of testimonies and rulings can be found in a probate record. Court records may also reflect appointments of ancestors to positions of public trust such as sheriff, inspector of tobacco, and justice of the peace.

Finding court records online can be tricky. They can be found using genealogically focused search engines such as TreEZy (www.treezy.com) or We Relate (www.werelate .org), a general search engine such as Lycos (www.lycos.com), or a subscription database service. Note, however, that good data can also be tucked away inside free databases that are not indexed by search engines. In this case, you will have to search on a general term such as "Berks County wills" or "Berks County court records." Here is an example:

1. **Go to the Lycos search engine site** (www.lycos.com).
    Near the top of the page is the search box (in the yellow area).

2. **Type your search terms into the search box and click Go Get It.**
    The results page is displayed. In our case, we type **Berks County wills** and receive 19,500 results.

3. **Click a link that looks relevant to your search.**
    We select the link to the Berks County Register of Wills at www.berksregofwills.com.

    This site contains a database where you can search more than 1 million records covering a variety of areas including birth, death, marriage, and estate.

Chapter 6

Going Beyond Borders: International Records

· ·

In This Chapter

▶ Strategies for finding international resources
▶ Canadian genealogical sites
▶ European sources
▶ Records from South and Central America
▶ Australian sites

· ·

In most cases, not all of your ancestors were born in the United States. So, at some point, you will want to "jump across the pond" in your research. Fortunately, in the last few years, the number of sites with international information has skyrocketed. In this chapter, we look at strategies for finding these sites and examine some of the key sites in each major geographical area.

Locating International Sources

Beginning research outside of the United States can be a daunting task, especially if you are not familiar with the record sets that are native to the country you need to research. One way to become familiar to a new area is to see if there is a research guide available for that geographic area. The Research Helps section of the FamilySearch.org site (www.familysearch.org/Eng/Search/Rg/frameset_rhelps .asp) contains maps, reference documents, research outlines, and research guides for some international locations. For example, if you are beginning to research your Finnish ancestors, you can find a research outline (see Figure 6-1) that contains information on the following items:

- ✔ Finnish language

- ✔ Maps of counties in 1939 and 1960

- ✔ Libraries and archives

- ✔ Censuses

- ✔ Church records

- ✔ Civil registrations

- ✔ Court records

- ✔ Emigration and Immigration

- ✔ Gazetteers

- ✔ History

- ✔ Military records

- ✔ Probate records

- ✔ Taxation

Figure 6-1: *A research outline for Finland at the Family Search site.*

Another place to look for help in getting started is the International Internet Genealogical Society site at www.iigs.org/index.htm.en. Although the site is currently limited in the areas that it covers, you can find Global Village Representatives that can help you with specific countries. There is also a list of current projects by group members and some online courses that provide an introduction to genealogy in Australia, New Zealand, Canada, Germany, and South Africa.

Speaking of projects, the WorldGenWeb Project (www.worldgenweb.org) contains links to Web sites for 254 countries and areas in the world. To find a specific country, follow these steps:

1. **Go to the WorldGenWeb Project site (www.worldgenweb.org).**
    You see a page with a map and a list of resources along the left side of the page (below the map).

2. **Choose the link to the Country Index under the Resources column.**
    For our example, we're looking for information on civil registrations in Jamaica.

3. **Click on the link in the WorldGenWeb Region column for your target country.**
    We click on the CaribbeanGenWeb link next to the entry for Jamaica. This link takes us to the region project page. In our case, the Caribbean GenWeb page has three versions — in English, French, and Spanish. We choose the English version.

4. **From the region page, find a link to the countries represented within the project.**
    On the CaribbeanGenWeb page, we select the Island Links link located near the top of the page in the second column. If you didn't choose the same region, you'll have to find the appropriate link on your particular region page.

5. **Select the link to your country.**
    We click on the Jamaica link that takes us to the Genealogy of Jamaica page.

6. **Choose a link to a resource that interests you.**
    On the front page of the Genealogy of Jamaica page, there is a list of resources available on the site. We select the Civil Registration link that takes us to the Civil Registrations of Jamaicans page (see Figure 6-2).

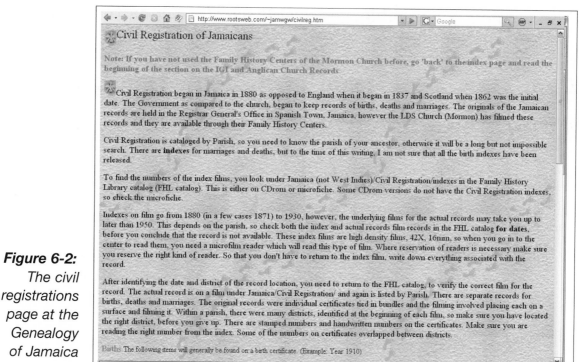

Figure 6-2:

The civil registrations page at the Genealogy of Jamaica site.

Because international genealogical sites are being added to the Web at a brisk pace, it is a good idea to use general search engines to keep abreast of the current sites. You can use a search term such as "Finnish genealogy" to get an idea of how much information is out on the Web about the geographic area that interests you. However, keep in mind that such general searches are likely to yield thousands of search results (at the time this book was written, "Finnish genealogy" yielded 703,000 hits). As we discuss elsewhere in this book (for example, in Chapter 4), you can get more focused results using a genealogically focused search engine such as TreEZy (www.treezy.com) or WeRelate (www.werelate.org).

Of course, you can also find links to international Web sites at comprehensive link sites or help sites. For instance, the genealogy site at About.com has a section that contains genealogy links by country. To find it, go to genealogy.

about.com/od/localities and select a region from the list at the top of the page.

Crossing Just Beyond the Border: North American Resources

The key to researching genealogy in North America is to know what types of records were being kept during the time period that interests you. At different points in history, you might encounter Spanish, French, Dutch, or English records. As each of these countries had distinct types of records, you may need to learn a few different methods to complete your research in a particular geographic area.

Heading north for Canadian records

So you want to research your ancestors from Canada, eh? Well, the first place to start is the Canadian Genealogy Centre (www.collectionscanada.ca/genealogy/index-e.html) maintained by Library and Archives Canada. The site contains information for beginners including what to do first, and search strategies for a variety of record types. Within the Guides section, see the online version of the Tracing Your Ancestors in Canada brochure (www .collectionscanada.ca/genealogy/022-607.001-e.html) if you are new to Canadian resources. Also, at the top of the Canadian Genealogy Centre Web page, you can find a search engine that provides results for the databases maintained by Library and Archives Canada.

To get an idea of what online resources are available for Canadian research, there are some genealogical link sites that specialize in Canada. These include Canadian Genealogy and History (www.islandnet.com/~jveinot/cghl/cghl .html), CanGenealogy (www.cangenealogy.com), and

Canadian Genealogy Resources (www.canadiangenealogy
.net).

For resources on a more local basis, go to the Canada
GenWeb Project site at www.rootsweb.com/~canwgw. The
project site includes links to genealogical sites, research
queries, look-ups, and a timeline. There is also a branch of
the site that is oriented to kids at www.rootsweb.com/
~cangwkid. The following provinces also have a GenWeb
Project page:

- **Alberta**: users.rootsweb.com/~canab/index.html

- **British Columbia**: www.rootsweb.com/~canbc/

- **Manitoba**: www.rootsweb.com/~canmb/index.htm

- **New Brunswick**: www.rootsweb.com/~cannb/

- **Newfoundland/Labrador**:
  www.rootsweb.com/~cannf/index.html

- **Nova Scotia**: www.rootsweb.com/~canns/index.html

- **Northwest Territories & Nunavut**:
  www.rootsweb.com/~cannt

- **Ontario**: www.geneofun.on.ca/ongenweb/

- **Prince Edward Island**:
  www.islandregister.com/pegenweb.html

- **Québec**: www.rootsweb.com/~canqc/index.htm

- **Saskatchewan**:
  www.rootsweb.com/~cansk/Saskatchewan/

- **Yukon**: www.rootsweb.com/~canyk/

Although Acadia is not a province, there is also an Acadian GenWeb site at www.geocities.com/Heartland/Acres/
2162/.

When it comes time to do some on-site research, you will want to look at the directory of archives at the Canadian Council of Archives. The Web site search interface (www.cdncouncilarchives.ca/directory_adv.html) allows you to search by an archive name or by province. The information on the site includes an overview of the collections of each archive, along with its hours of operation.

There are a number of sites that contain abstracts of Canadian records. Olive Tree Genealogy (www.olive treegenealogy.com) has free databases of ship and passenger lists, civil registrations, and cemetery records. inGeneas (www.ingeneas.com) is a pay site that offers access to passenger, immigration, census, vital statistic, land, and military records. Automated Genealogy (automatedgenealogy .com) has indexes to the 1851, 1901, 1906 (a special census that only included the provinces of Alberta, Saskatchewan, and Manitoba), and 1911 censuses. If your family immigrated to Canada between 1928 and 1971, take a look at the Pier 21 Immigration Museum site (www.pier21.ca). The site gives a brief overview of the function of Pier 21 and information on the research services available on site.

If you are looking for local genealogical experts, there are a number of genealogical societies in Canada. An example of a society Web site is Alberta Family Histories Society (www.afhs.ab.ca). The site includes the monthly schedule of meetings of the society, publications for sale, document transcriptions, research aids, queries, and information about the society library.

As Canada has a history of immigration of a number of different ethnicities, you might also check to see if there is a site dedicated to the ethnic group that you are researching. For example, the Chinese-Canadian Genealogy site (www.vpl.ca/ccg) maintained by the Vancouver Public Library contains information on the early Chinese immigrations, Chinese name characteristics, biographic resources, and a survey of the types of record sets associated with the Canadian Chinese population.

A number of digitized documents are available online for Canadian sources. Library and Archives Canada maintains images of the 1851, 1901, 1906, and 1911 censuses online through its ArchiviaNet research tool (www.collections canada.ca/archivianet/index-e.html). The images are not indexed by name, so you have to browse the images to find your ancestors (see Figure 6-3). You can also find images for the following record sets:

- Chinese Immigration Registers (1887-1908)

- Canadians in the South African War (1899-1902)

- Attestation Papers of Soldiers of the First World War (1914-1918)

- Upper Canada and Canada West Naturalization Records (1828-1850)

- Ward Chipman, Muster Master's Office (1777-1785) [Loyalist registers]

- Immigrants from the Russian Empire

- Canadian Patents, 1869-1894

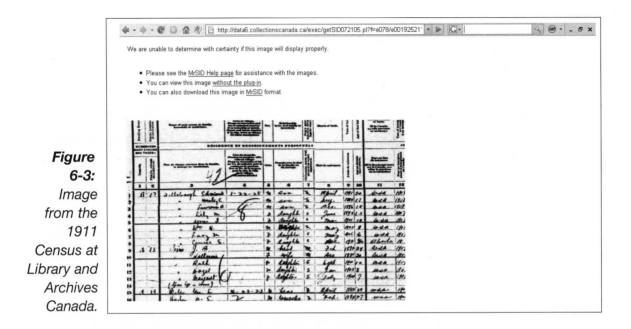

Figure 6-3: *Image from the 1911 Census at Library and Archives Canada.*

A subscription site containing a number of records is the Ancestry.ca site maintained by The Generations Network (www.ancestry.ca). The database contains name indexes for the 1851, 1901, 1906, and 1911 censuses; immigration records (1780-1908); border crossings (1895-1956); birth, marriage, and death records; military records; civil service lists, and land/gazetteer records.

Exploring south of the border: Mexican sources

To get your feet wet with resources from Mexico, take a look at the Mexico Research Outline at the FamilySearch site (www.familysearch.org/eng/Search/RG/frameset_rg .asp?Dest=G1&Aid=&Gid=&Lid=&Sid=&Did=&Juris1= &Event=&Year=&Gloss=&Sub=&Tab=&Entry=&Guide= Mexico.ASP). The outline covers archives and libraries, cemeteries, church records, emigration and immigration, gazetteers, land and property, military records, probate records, and societies. You can find a primer on tracing your ancestors on the Mexico Genealogy 101 page at the About.com genealogy site (genealogy.about.com/od/mexico/a/records.htm).

The MexicoGenWeb site (www.rootsweb.com/~mexwgw/) contains links to a few Mexican genealogical resources. Only a few of the state pages have been "adopted" by volunteers. These include

- **Baja California Sur**: www.californiagenealogy.org/labaja/

- **Chiapas**: www.geocities.com/Heartland/Acres/6769/Chiapas.html

- **Chihuahua**: www.rootsweb.com/~mexchi/

- **Coahuila**: www.rootsweb.com/~mexcoahu/index.html

- **Distrito Federal**: www.rootsweb.com/~mexwgw/DF.html

- **Durango**: www.rootsweb.com/~mexdur/Durango.html

- **Morelos**: www.rootsweb.com/~mexmorel/Morelos.html

- **Nuevo León**: www.geocities.com/Heartland/Prairie/6728/

- **San Luis Potosí**: www.rootsweb.com/~mexsanlu/

- **Sonora**: homepages.rootsweb.com/~windmill/sonora/

- **Tabasco**: www.rootsweb.com/~mextab/

- **Tamaulipas**: www.rootsweb.com/~mextam/

- **Zacatecas**: www.geocities.com/Athens/Acropolis/

The Genealogy of Mexico site (members.tripod
.com/~GaryFelix/index1.htm) features several sets of transcribed records including lists of individuals who accompanied Cortez, early entrants into New Spain, surnames contained in literature on Mexico, and a DNA project. If your
ancestors came from northeast Mexico, the Lower Rio
Grande Valley/Northeast Mexico Genealogical Research
page (129.113.50.6/info/speccoll/lrgvgen.html) contains a
bibliography of resources available at the University of
Texas — Pan American Library.

An index to vital records from Mexico is available on the
FamilySearch.org site (www.familysearch.org/Eng/Search/
frameset_search.asp?PAGE=vr/search_VR.asp&clear_form
=true). After putting in the name that you are researching,
make sure that you set the country to Mexico before exe-
cuting the search. The search results include information
on the vital record including the date of the event, individuals involved, age of the individual, the film or fiche number containing the record, and the collection housing the
record. For example, Figure 6-4 shows an entry for a marriage between Jose Lopez and Adelaida Ortiz in 1876. Jose
was 20 years old when the marriage took place in Mineral
del Chico, Hidalgo, Mexico. The record is contained within
the La Purisima Concepcion; Catolica collection and is located on LDS Film Number 638889.

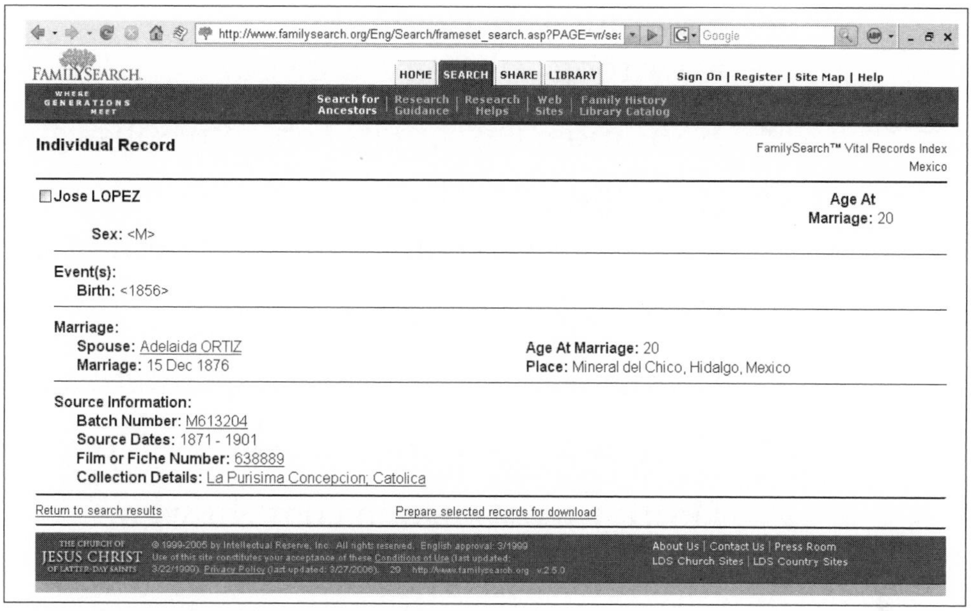

Figure 6-4: Family Search.org Vital Records entry for Jose Lopez.

Swimming through Caribbean genealogy

To be successful in researching Caribbean genealogy, you have to be aware of the history of the particular island that you are researching. Some islands will have a variety of record sets that may differ significantly depending upon what country was in control of the island.

A place to start your research is the CaribbeanGenWeb Project page at www.rootsweb.com/~caribgw/. The project is an umbrella site for each of the individual islands that have their own project pages. The site contains a list of the transcribed data sets held within the CaribbeanGenWeb Archives portion of the project, along with a global search engine for searching those data sets; descriptions of the mailing lists available for each island; links to surname resources; and some research tips. The individual island pages include

✔ **Anguilla**: www.britishislesgenweb.org/~anguilla/

- **Antigua and Barbuda**: www.rootsweb.com/~atgwgw/

- **Bahamas**: www.rootsweb.com/~bhswgw/

- **Bermuda**: www.rootsweb.com/~bmuwgw/bermuda.htm

- **Cuba**: www.cubagenweb.org

- **Dominica**: www.britishislesgenweb.org/~dominica/

- **Grenada**: www.britishislesgenweb.org/~grenada/

- **Haiti**: www.rootsweb.com/~htiwgw/

- **Jamaica**: www.rootsweb.com/~jamwgw/index.htm

- **St. Kitts and Nevis**: www.tc.umn.edu/~terre011/genhome.html

- **St. Vincent & the Grenadines**: www.rootsweb.com/~vctwgw/

- **Trinidad and Tobago**: www.rootsweb.com/~ttowgw/

- **U.S. Virgin Islands**: www.rootsweb.com/~usvi/

You can also find information on some islands on the GenWeb Project page of the mother country. For example, Guadeloupe and Martinique genealogical data can be found on the FranceGenWeb Project page at www.france genweb.org/~sitesdgw/outremer/. Another resource for the French islands is the Genealogie et Histoire de la Caraibe (www.ghcaraibe.org). The site contains some transcribed records and articles on the history of the area.

If you have a question about a specific individual, you can post a query on the Caribbean Surname Index (CARSUR-DEX) at www.candoo.com/surnames/index.php. The site has message boards based upon the first letter of the surname and has research specialty boards for the French West Indies, Dutch West Indies, and Spanish West Indies.

Reviewing Central American sites

The countries within Central America are tucked within the North American GenWeb Project site at www.rootsweb.com/~nrthamgw/. Sites are available for the following countries:

- ✔ **Belize**: www.rootsweb.com/~blzwgw/
- ✔ **Costa Rica**: www.rootsweb.com/~criwgw/
- ✔ **El Salvador**: www.rootsweb.com/~slvwgw/
- ✔ **Guatemala**: www.rootsweb.com/~gtmwgw/indexen.html
- ✔ **Honduras**: www.rootsweb.com/~hndwgw/
- ✔ **Nicaragua**: www.rootsweb.com/~nicwgw/
- ✔ **Panama**: www.rootsweb.com/~panwgw/

You can see a list of archives and libraries in Central American and Caribbean countries at the Repositories of Primary Sources page (www.uidaho.edu/special-collections/latam.html).

For more on Hispanic genealogical resources, see the Hispanic Roots section in Chapter 8.

Flying Across the Pond: European Sites

There are many different traditions within European countries when it comes to recordkeeping. Some countries have had a stable existence and more records are generally available, whereas other countries have been under several different governments and have suffered through the destruction of records. This section highlights some of the major sites for European genealogy.

Also keep in mind that we discuss European genealogy from an ethnic perspective in Chapter 8.

GenWeb sites

Due to the number of European countries, there is no single European GenWeb Project site. Instead, there are four European region sites, including

- **BritishIslesGenWeb** (www.britishislesgenweb.org) includes projects for Caribbean Islands, Channel Islands, England, Falkland Islands, Gibraltar, Ireland, Isle of Man, Northern Ireland, Scotland, St. Helena, and Wales.

- **CenEuroGenWeb** (www.rootsweb.com/~ceneurgw/) lists pages for Belgium, Denmark, Greenland, Germany, Iceland, Latvia, Liechtenstein, Lithuania, Luxembourg, Netherlands, Norway, Poland, Sweden, and Switzerland.

- **EastEuropeGenWeb** (www.rootsweb.com/~easeurgw/) contains sites for Albania, Austria, Croatia, Czech Republic, Estonia, Finland, Montenegro, Serbia, Slovak Republic, Slovenia, and Yugoslavia.

- **MediterraneanGenWeb** (www.mediterraneangenweb.com/indexe.html) has projects pages for Azores, France, Italy, Madeira, Portugal, and Spain.

Gathering information from England, Northern Ireland, Scotland, and Wales

Your first stop in getting acquainted with the British Isles is the Family Records.gov.uk site (familyrecords.gov.uk). The site is a partnership between the following groups:

- ✔ **Access to Archives** (www.a2a.org.uk) is a consortium of archives in England and Wales. The Access to Archives site features a database with descriptions of the holdings of 414 record offices and repositories.

- ✔ **British Library — India Office Records** (india family.bl.uk/UI/) holds records of the government of pre-1947 India. The site features a bibliographical index containing more than 300,000 entries.

- ✔ **Commonwealth War Graves Commission** (www.cwgc.org) is responsible for maintaining the 1.7 million graves of those who died in the two world wars. The CWGC Web site includes the Debt of Honour Register that provides basic information on those covered by the Commission.

- ✔ **Family Records Centre** (familyrecords.gov.uk/frc/) is run jointly by the General Register Office and the National Archives. The FRC site provides online access to leaflets that can help you begin your search into British records.

- ✔ **General Register Office** (www.gro.gov.uk/gro/content/) holds birth, marriage, and death records in England and Wales from 1 July 1837 up to one year ago. The GRO Web site details how to get copies of certificates and has some basic guides on researching genealogy.

- **General Register Office for Scotland** (www.gro-scotland.gov.uk) holds birth, marriage, divorce, adoption, and death records in Scotland from 1855. The GROS is also responsible for the periodic censuses for Scotland.

- **Imperial War Museum** (www.iwm.org.uk) chronicles the wars of the twentieth century from 1914. Its Web site contains fact sheets on tracing ancestors who served in the armed forces and an inventory of war memorials.

- **National Library of Wales/Llyfrgell Genedlaethol Cymru** (www.llgc.org.uk) holds documents such as electoral lists, marriage bonds, probate and estate records, and tithe maps. The Library's Web site contains a list of independent researchers and you can search databases including an index to the gaol files, applicants for marriage licenses, and descriptions of the Library's archival holdings.

- **National Archives** (www.nationalarchives.gov.uk) has a variety of records for genealogists including military service records, wills, records of non-conformists, and census records. The Archives' Web site has online documents including wills, World War I Campaign Medal lists, World War II Seamen's Medals, and Victorian prisoner lists.

- **National Archives of Scotland** (www.nas.gov.uk) contains records of when Scotland was its own kingdom, as well as modern Scotland. Records housed there include land transfers, records of the Church of Scotland parishes, estate papers, court papers, and taxation lists.

- **Public Record Office of Northern Ireland** (www.proni.gov.uk) holds items such as estate, church, business, valuation and tithe, school, and wills records.

- **Scottish Archives Network** (www.scan.org.uk) is a joint project between the National Archives of Scotland, Heritage Lottery Fund, and the Genealogical Society of Utah. The project has placed the holdings of 50 Scottish archives into an online catalog and has digitized more than two million records.

There are a number of online sources for transcribed and digitized documents. BMD Registers (www.bmdregisters .co.uk) features images of birth, baptism, marriage, and death records taken from non-parish sources from 1534 to 1865. You can conduct a search of their database; however, you must purchase credits before being able to view an image of the digitized document. The subscription site, The Genealogist (www.thegenealogist.co.uk), has a complete index of birth, marriage, and death records for England and Wales; census transcripts from 1841 to 1891; census indexes from 1841 to 1901; parish records; directories; and landowner records. The site also features a tool that allows users to create a surname distribution map from 1851 to 2002. Surname distribution maps can help you determine the geographical areas where particular surnames were concentrated. If you are looking for free birth, marriage, and death records, see the FreeBMD project at www.freebmd.org.uk. This volunteer effort has transcribed more than 114 million records — although the collection is still not complete.

There are two principal sources for images of census records. The 1841, 1851, 1861, 1871, 1881, 1891, and

1901 censuses are available from Ancestry.uk (www .ancestry.co.uk/) and are indexed by name for every person in the household. 1901CensusOnline.com (www .1901censusonline.com) also has the 1841, 1851, 1861, 1871, 1881, 1891, and 1901 censuses, as well as birth, marriage, and death records. The FreeCEN project (www.freecen.org.uk) is transcribing the censuses and offering the results at no cost. At the time this book was written, the project had transcribed records on more than 11 million individuals.

The ScotlandsPeople site (www.scotlandspeople.gov.uk) is the official government site for Scottish records. The subscription site contains statutory registers of births (1855-1906), marriages (1855-1931), and deaths (1855-1956); old parish registers of births and baptisms (1553-1854) and banns and marriages (1553-1854); census records (1841-1901); and wills and testaments (1513-1901). Scots Origins (www.scotsorigins.com) allows users to order record transcriptions of birth, baptism, marriage, or death records (1700-1900) or census transcriptions (1861 and 1871).

British Origins (www.britishorigins.com) includes a variety of records, including censuses for England and Wales (1841, 1861, and 1871), Boyd's Marriage Index, marriage license allegation index, wills indexes, probate indexes, apprenticeship records, court records, burial records, militia records, and passenger lists.

Another subscription site is findmypast.com (www.findmypast.com). You can find birth, marriage, and death records, census records (1841-1891), migration records, and military records.

To contact other genealogists interested in British genealogical research, see the Society of Genealogists (www.sog.org.uk). The site includes information on membership, publications, and the Society's online library catalog. For Scottish ancestors, see the Scottish Genealogy Society page at www.scotsgenealogy.com. Also, take a look at the North of Ireland Family History Society (www.nifhs.org) site, if you have ancestors from the north of Ireland. For societies at a local level, consult the list of members of the Federation of Family History Societies (www.ffhs.org.uk). The Federation's site includes information on its current projects and on upcoming events, as well as a set of subscription databases.

If you are not finding what you are looking for in one of the above sites, your next stop should be the GENUKI: United Kingdom and Ireland Genealogy site at www.genuki.org.uk. The GENUKI site is similar to the GenWeb sites in that it contains sub-sites for the various counties. You can find a variety of guides, transcribed records, and other useful data on the GENUKI sites.

Traversing the Emerald Isle

As we mentioned in the previous section, the GENUKI site (www.genuki.org.uk) contains information on a variety of geographic areas in the United Kingdom and Ireland. There are pages for all 32 counties of Ireland and you can find brief articles on a variety of topics including cemeteries, censuses, church records, civil registrations, court records, emigration and immigration, land and property, newspapers, probate records, and taxation. You can also find county pages at the Ireland Genealogy Projects site (irelandgenealogyprojects.rootsweb.com).

To get an overview on Irish genealogy, take a look at the Directory of Irish Genealogy at homepage.eircom.net/ ~seanjmurphy/dir/. In particular, look at the Beginner's Guide section that is available as a link at the top of the site's home page. You can also find information on genealogy courses and articles on Irish genealogy on this site. On the parent page to this site, the Centre for Irish Genealogical and Historical Studies (homepage.tinet.ie/~seanjmurphy/), are guides to the National Archives to Ireland and the General Register Office of Ireland. Another resource for those new to Irish research is the Irish Ancestors pages hosted by the Irish Times at www.ireland.com/ancestor/.

There are a few sites that contain databases and transcriptions of Irish records of interest to genealogists. Irish Family Research (www.irishfamilyresearch.co.uk) contains both free and subscription content including a directory of headstones, electoral registers, city directories, Griffiths Valuation, hearth rolls, school records, and a variety of other sources. My Irish Ancestry (myirishancestry.com) allows users to search Griffith's Valuation at no cost.

If you are looking for maps, Past Homes (www.pasthomes.com) has a subscription site with Irish townland maps. The maps on the site were surveyed between 1829 and 1843.

At some point, you may need to do some research on-site or need to find a particular work that is located within a public library. Familia (www.familia.org.uk) is an online directory of family history resources located in public libraries in the United Kingdom and Ireland. For information on Irish historical records, see the databases at the National Archives of Ireland Web site at www.nationalarchives.ie.

Getting to German sites

As German-speaking peoples have migrated to several places within Europe, as well as to the United States, you could very well encounter an ancestor of German descent. GermanRoots (home.att.net/~wee-monster) contains a variety of information to help you get started in researching

246

your German roots. It contains a directory of Web sites, a basic research guide, and links to articles on record sets useful in completing your research.

To get a bird's-eye view of available German genealogical sites, a good place to start is Genealogy.net (www .genealogienetz.de/index_en.html). The site includes home-pages for German genealogical societies, general information on research, gazetteer, a ships database, a passenger database, and a list of links to Web sites. Ahnenforschung.net (ahnenforschung.net) is a German-language genealogically focused search engine and index to genealogy Web sites.

The German Emigrants Database (www.deutsche-auswanderer-datenbank.de) maintained by the Historisches Museum Bremerhaven contains information on emigrants who left Europe for the United States from German ports between 1820 and 1939. At the time this book was written, the database contained more than 4.4 million emigrants. The site allows users to search an index of individuals and order records for a fee based upon the results. For more information on emigrants from the port of Hamburg, see Ballinstadt Hamburg (www.ballinstadt.de/en/index.php), a site that describes the emigrant experience at the Hamburg port.

The Generations Network recently launched a new subscription site for German genealogy at www.ancestry.de. Ancestry.de provides access to the Hamburg Passenger lists (1850-1934), Mecklenburg-Schwerin censuses (1819, 1867, 1890, and 1900), Bremen sailor registers (1837-1873), and Bremen ship lists (1821-1873).

Remembering French resources

For an overview of genealogy in French-speaking regions, drop by the Franco Gene site at www.francogene.com. The site features resources for Quebec, Acadia, the United

States, France, Belgium, Switzerland, and Italy. If you are not familiar with French surnames, you might want to see how common a surname is in France. At Geopatronyme .com (www.geopatronyme.com), you can view the surname distribution of more than 1.3 million names.

GeneaBank (www.geneabank.org) contains transcribed records created by French genealogical societies. To access the information in the site's databases, you must be a member of a society participating in the project. GeneaNet (www.geneanet.org) is a fee-based site that has transcriptions of some civil registers. The Lecture et Informatisation des Sources Archivistiques site (www.lisa90.org) contains a database with more than 165,000 transcribed parish records covering the eighteenth and nineteenth centuries, and Migranet (migranet.geneactes.org) houses a database of more than 45,000 French marriages where one of the participants was listed as a migrant.

Ancestry.fr (www.ancestry.fr) has a small collection of records in its subscription databases. These records include census tables from the French Colony of Louisiana (1699-1732), some French-language local and family histories, and a few marriage and church records.

Scanning Scandinavian countries

It is a good idea to get an overview of genealogical record sets in Scandinavian countries. The Beginner's Guide to Finnish Family History Research (members.aol.com/ dssaari/guide.htm) covers how to use parish, birth, marriage, death records, and communion books. MyDanish-Roots.com (mydanishroots.com) contains articles on vital records, census lists, place names, emigration, and Danish History. The Federation of Swedish Genealogical Societies/Sveriges Släktforskarförbund hosts the site Finding Your Swedish Roots (www.genealogi.se/roots/) that includes helpful articles on church, legal, and tax records, information on the collection in the Swedish Archives, and a brief history of Sweden. For help with your Norwegian ancestors, see the article Basics of Norwegian Research at www.rootsweb.com/~wgnorway/list-basics.htm.

A key database to consult when beginning your research is the Vital Records Index at FamilySearch.org (www.familysearch.org/Eng/Search/frameset_search.asp? PAGE=vr/search_VR.asp). The Index includes records for Denmark, Norway, Sweden, and Finland. The Dansk Demografisk Database (ddd.dda.dk/DDD_EN.HTM) includes censuses and lists of emigrants and immigrants for Denmark.

You can find transcriptions of passport lists for the Åland Islands in Finland at the Transcription of the Borough Administrator's Passport List 1882-1903 (www.genealogia.fi/ emi/magistrat/indexe.htm) and Sheriff's Passport List 1863-1916 (www.genealogia.fi/emi/krono/indexe.htm) sites. The database at DISBYT Finland contains more than 160,000 individuals who lived in Finland (www.dis.se/ search_fi_index_e.htm) prior to 1913. The Genealogy Society of Finland maintains a list of christenings, marriages, burials and moves as part of its HisKi Project at hiski.genealogia.fi/historia/indexe.htm.

The Swedish DISBYT database (www.dis.se) contains 15.4 million Swedes living before 1905. The Institute of Migration/Siirtolaisuusinstituutti (www.migrationinstitute .fi/index_e.php) maintains a database of more than 550,000 emigrants from Finland. Genline.com (www.genline.com) has over 16 million Swedish church records from 1860. Ancestry.se (www.ancestry.se) is a subscription site that contains emigration lists from 1783-1751; passenger and immigration lists from the 1500s to 1900s; and some local histories and published genealogies.

Accessing Australian Sources

When researching Australian ancestors, there are two distinct paths — aboriginal records and the sources for later settlers. For an introduction to aboriginal records, see Australian Aboriginal Genealogy Resources at mc2.vicnet.net .au/home/pmackett/web/index.html. The Australian Family History Compendium (www.cohsoft.com.au/afhc/) offers information on a wider range of record types, as well as information on archives, maps, glossary, and societies.

A transcription of the convicts on Australia's first three fleets and the Irish convicts that came to New South Wales from 1791 to 1834 are located at members.pcug.org .au/~pdownes/.

The Heraldry and Genealogy Society of Canberra maintains a database of Australian memorials of Australians in the Boer War (1899-1902) at www.hagsoc.org.au/sagraves/ abwmdb/abwm-search.php. The Metropolitan Cemeteries Board of Western Australia has a database of internments in five cemeteries at www.mcb.wa.gov.au/NameSearch/ GenResearch.html.

An index to the 1841 Census is maintained by the New South Wales Government at www.records.nsw.gov.au/ archives/1841_census_1068.asp. The index only contains the name of the head of household and contains just over 9,000 entries. The Donegal Relief Fund site (free pages.genealogy.rootsweb.com/~donegal/relief.htm) includes a description of the background of the Relief Fund, passenger lists, and subscription lists for those who donated to the Fund. A searchable index of birth, marriage, and death records for New South Wales is available at www.bdm.nsw.gov.au/familyHistory/search.htm.

Ancestry.com.au (www.ancestry.com.au) is a subscription site that contains a variety of record sets, including

- Electoral Rolls
- First Fleet, Second Fleet, and Third Fleet Lists
- Convict Musters, Pardons, and Lists
- Census of New South Wales, 1828
- Sands Directories (Sydney and New South Wales)

Part III
Adding Color to Your Research

The 5th Wave — By Rich Tennant

"The good news is that I've located Pinnochio's natural mother. The bad news is she's part of the parquet flooring at a bowling alley in upstate New York."

In this part . . .

These chapters help you add some pizzazz to your research by examining how to find geographically related and ethnic-based resources. These types of resources often offer perspectives into your ancestors' lives. We also explore some interesting genealogical byways, such as adoption records, molecular genealogy, and records associated with religious groups and fraternal orders.

Chapter 7

Your Ancestors: Here, There, and Everywhere

Say that while researching census records, you find that your great-great-great-grandfather lived in Winchester, Virginia. But where is Winchester? What was the town like? Where exactly did he live in the town? What was life like when he lived there? To answer these questions, you need to dig a little deeper than just retrieving documents — you need to look at the life of your ancestor within the context of where he lived.

Geography played a major role in the lives of our ancestors. It often determined where they lived, worked, and migrated (as early settlers often migrated to lands that were similar to their home state or country). It can also play a major role in how you research your ancestor. Concentrat-

255

ing on where your ancestor lived can often point you to area-specific record sets or provide clues about where to research next. In this chapter, we look at several ways to use geographical resources to provide a boost to your family history research.

Are We There Yet?: Researching Where "There" Was to Your Ancestors

What did "there" mean for your ancestors? You have to answer this question to know where to look for genealogical information. These days, a family that lives in the same general area for more than two or three generations is rare. If you're a member of such a family, you may be in luck when it comes to genealogical research. However, if you come from a family that moved around at least every couple of generations (or not all members of the family remained in the same location), you may be in for a challenge.

So how do you find out where your ancestors lived? In this section, we look at several resources you can use to establish their location, including using known records, interviewing relatives, consulting gazetteers, looking at maps, using GPS devices, and charting locations using geographical software. As we go through these resources, we use a "real-life" example to show how the resources can be used together to solve a research problem — finding the location of the final resting place of Matthew's great-great-grandfather.

Using documentation you already have in your possession

When you attempt to geographically locate your ancestors, start by using any copies of records or online data that you or someone else has already collected. Sifting through all of those photocopies and original documents from the attic and printouts from online sites provides a good starting point for locating your ancestors geographically. Pay particular attention to any material that provides a definite location during a specific time period. You can use these details as a springboard for your geographical search.

For example, Matthew's great-great-grandfather, Uriah Helm, is listed in the family trees at the WorldConnect Web site (for more on the WorldConnect project — wc.rootsweb.com — see Chapter 4). In the record, the submitter states that Uriah was buried in the German Reformed Cemetery in Fayette, Illinois, around 22 February 1911. The mention of Fayette, Illinois, gives us a place to begin our search.

If you have information about places where your ancestors lived, but not necessarily the time frame, you can still be reasonably successful in tracking your ancestors based on the limited information you do have. Aids are available to help you approximate time frames, such as the Period Approximation Chart (www.myroots.net/extras/tidbits3 .htm). For example, say you know the birth dates of your great-great-grandmother's children, but you don't know when great-great-grandma and great-great-grandpa were married. You can use the Period Approximation Chart to calculate a date range in which you can look for the marriage record. The Period Approximation Chart uses average ages for events in history and typical lifespans during certain periods of time to make the calculations.

For additional information about using documents you already have, take a look at Chapter 2.

Grilling your relatives about what they know

Your notes from interviews with family members, or from other resources you've found on your ancestors, most likely contain some information about locations where the family lived and hopefully the approximate time frames.

Chances are you have at least some notes with statements, such as "Aunt Lola recalled stories about the old homestead in LaRue County, Kentucky." Of course, whether Aunt Lola recalled stories firsthand (those that she lived through or participated in) or her recollections were stories she heard from those before her has an effect on the time frames within which you look for records in LaRue County. Either way, these stories give you a starting point.

For details on interviewing your family members, see Chapter 2.

Where is Llandrindod, anyway?

At some point during your research, you're bound to run across something that says an ancestor lived in a particular town or county, or was associated with a specific place, but contains no details of where that place was — no state or province or other identifiers. How do you find out where that place was located?

A *gazetteer,* or geographical dictionary, provides information about places. By looking up the name of the town, county, or some other kind of place, you can narrow your search for your ancestor. The gazetteer identifies every place by a particular name and provides varying information (depending on the gazetteer itself) about each. Typically, gazetteers provide at least the names of the principal region where the place is located. Many contemporary gazetteers also provide the latitude and longitude of the place.

By adding the information you get from the online gazetteer to the other pieces of your puzzle, you can reduce the list of common place names to just those you think are plausible for your ancestors. By pinpointing where a place is, you can look for more records to prove whether your ancestors really lived there.

For research in the United States, one of your first stops should be the U.S. Geological Survey's Geographic Names Information System (GNIS) Web site. The GNIS site contains information on more than 2 million places within the United States and its territories (including those in Antarctica).

To find the precise location of the cemetery where Uriah Helm is buried, we can use the Geographic Names Information System (GNIS) site.

1. **Start your Web browser and head to the U.S. Geological Survey's Geographic Names Information System (GNIS) at** geonames.usgs.gov/pls/gnispublic.
   This page contains the search form for the United States and its territories (see Figure 7-1).

2. **Enter any information that you have, tabbing or clicking between fields; click Send Query when you're finished.**
   If you're not sure what a particular field asks for but you think you may want to enter something in it, click the title of the field for an explanation.
   We enter **German Reformed Cemetery** in the Feature Name field and select **Illinois** from the state drop-down box.

Figure 7-2 shows the result of the search. The only result was the German Reformed Cemetery in Fayette County, located at 38 degrees, 55 minutes, 58 seconds North latitude and 88 degrees, 54 minutes, 18 seconds West longitude. With this information, we can now plot the location on a map. (See the following section, "Mapping your ancestor's way," for more details on using maps.)

 In addition to the GNIS database, some online gazetteers identify places in other countries as well as places in the United States. Here are some for you to check out:

- **Alexandria Digital Library Gazetteer Server** (which has a worldwide focus): middleware.alexandria.ucsb.edu/client/gaz/adl/index.jsp

- **Autoriserede stednavne i Danmark (in Danish):** levende.kms.dk/su/sunavn.htm

- **Belgian Place Names:** belgium.rootsweb.com/bel/_places/index.html

- **Geoscience Australia Place Name Search:** www.ga.gov.au/map/names

- **Canada's Geographical Names:** geonames.nrcan.gc.ca/search/search_e.php

- **Gazetteer for Scotland:** www.geo.ed.ac.uk/scotgaz/

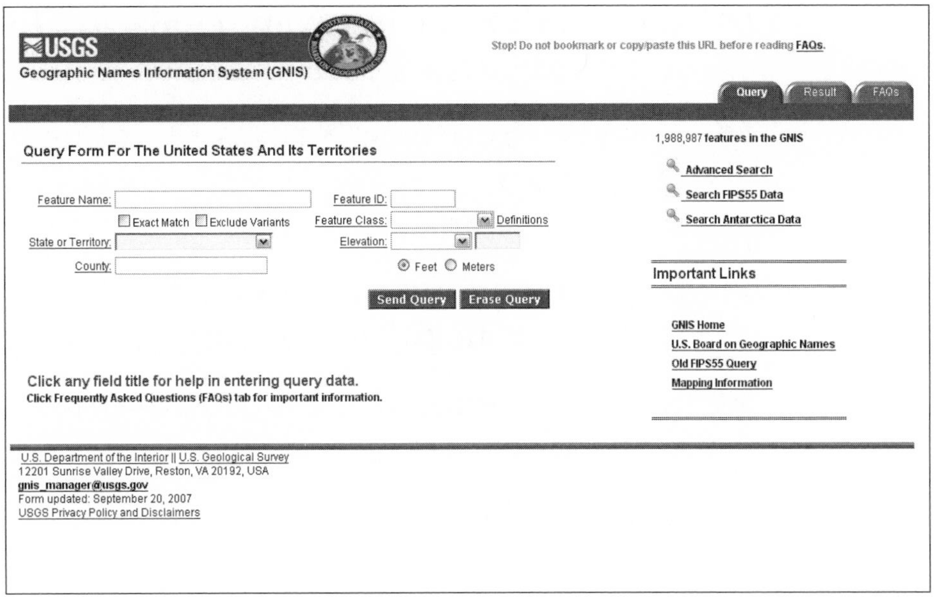

Figure 7-1:
Use the query form on the U.S. Geological Survey's Geographic Name Information System (GNIS) site to search the system for places in the United States.

Gazetteer of British Place Names:
www.gazetteer.co.uk

GEOnet Names Server (GNS):
gnswww.nga.mil/geonames/GNS/index.jsp

German Genealogy Gazetteer (in German):
gov.genealogy.net

Institut Géographique National (France):
www.ign.fr/rubrique.asp?rbr_id=1652&lng_id=EN

IreAtlas Townland Data Base (Ireland):
www.seanruad.com

Map.es (Spain):
www.map.es/documentacion/entes_locales/registro_entidades_locales.html

Metatopos.org (Netherlands):
www.metatopos.org/

National Gazetteer of Wales:
homepage.ntlworld.com/geogdata/ngw/home.htm

- ✔ **Land Information New Zealand (LINZ):**
  www.linz.govt.nz/core/placenames/index.html

- ✔ **KNAB, the Place Names Database of EKI (Estonia):**
  www.eki.ee/knab/knab.htm

- ✔ **Registro de Nombres Geograficos (Mexico):**
  mapserver.inegi.gob.mx/rnng/?c=730

- ✔ **South African Geographic Names System:**
  sagns.dac.gov.za

- ✔ **Statens Kartverk (Norway):**
  ngis2.statkart.no/norgesglasset/default.html

- ✔ **Swedish Gazetteer:**
  www.sna.se/gazetteer.html

- ✔ **World Gazetteer:**
  world-gazetteer.com

Most online gazetteers are organized on a national level and provide information about all the places (towns, cities, counties, landmarks, and so on) within that country. However, there are exceptions. Some unique gazetteers list information about places within one state or province. One such example is the Kentucky Atlas and Gazetteer (www.uky.edu/KentuckyAtlas), which has information only about places within — you guessed it — Kentucky. For each place, it provides the name of the place, the type of place (civil division, school, cemetery, airport, and so on), source of information, topoquad (topographic-map quadrangle that contains the feature), latitude, longitude, area (if applicable), population (if applicable), date of establishment, elevation, and a link to a map showing you where the place is.

In addition to online gazetteers, there are also a number

of software gazetteers. One such gazetteer geared toward genealogists is the World Place Finder by Progeny Software (www.progenygenealogy.com/placefinder.html).

If you can't find a place in current gazetteers, you may need to consult a historical gazetteer. Some examples of these include the place information section of A Vision of Britain through Time (British) available at www.gbhgis.org, and the 1853 Wisconsin Gazetteer at quod.lib.umich.edu/cgi/t/text/text-idx?c=moa;idno=AFK4346.0001.001.

Figure 7-2:
The results of a GNIS search for German Reformed Cemetery in Illinois.

≊USGS
Geographic Names Information System (GNIS)

Stop! Do not bookmark or copy/paste this URL before reading **FAQs**.

Query   Result   FAQs

Geographic Names Information System Feature Query Results

Click the feature name for details and to access map services
Click any column name to sort the list ascending ▲ or descending ▼

Feature Name	ID	Class	County	Latitude	Longitude	State	Map	Elev(ft)	BGN	Entry Date
German Reformed Cemetery	1802263	Cemetery	Fayette	385558N	0885418W	IL	Brownstown	581	-	21-JUL-1998

1 - 1

View & Print all   Save as pipe "|" delimited file

Note: If data are returned and the column headings display but no data appear, click any column heading

U.S. Department of the Interior || U.S. Geological Survey
12201 Sunrise Valley Drive, Reston, VA 20192, USA
gnis_manager@usgs.gov
Form updated: September 20, 2007
USGS Privacy Policy and Disclaimers

Mapping your ancestor's way

After you find out where the place is located, it's time to dig out the maps. Maps can be an invaluable resource in your genealogical research. Not only do maps help you track your ancestors, but they also enhance your published genealogy by illustrating some of your findings.

Different types of online sites have maps that may be useful in your genealogical research:

✔ **Historical maps:** Several Web sites contain scanned or digitized images of historic maps. In a lot of cases, you can download or print copies of these maps.

263

Such sites include these:

- **David Rumsey Map Collection:**
  www.davidrumsey.com

- **Perry-Castañeda Library Map Collection, University of Texas at Austin:**
  www.lib.utexas.edu/maps/index.html

- **American Memory Map Collections of the Library of Congress:**
  memory.loc.gov/ammem/gmdhtml/gmdhome.html

You can also find local collections of maps at several university and historical-society sites.

✔ **Digitized historical atlases:** In addition to map sites, individuals have scanned portions or the entire contents of atlases, particularly those from the nineteenth century. Examples include

- **Countrywide atlases.** An example is the 1895 U.S. Atlas:
  www.livgenmi.com/1895

- **County atlases.** An example is the 1904 Maps from the New Century Atlas of Cayuga County, New York:
  www.rootsweb.com/~nycayuga/maps/1904/

- **Specialty atlases.** An occupational example is the 1948 U.S. Railroad Atlas:
  trains.rockycrater.org/pfmsig/atlas.php

✔ **Interactive map sites:** A few sites have interactive maps that you can use to find and zoom in on areas. After you have the view you want of the location, you can print a copy of the map to keep with your genealogical records. Some such sites are

- **Google Maps** (maps.google.com) includes road and satellite maps for countries around the world. You can also get directions for places within the United States and Canada.
- **MapQuest** (www.mapquest.com) has interactive maps for over 200 countries, although some of these look down from too high a level to get much detail. Street level maps are available for the United States and Canada. Driving directions are available for the United States, Canada, and a few European countries.
- **Microsoft Live Search** (maps.live.com) features road and aerial maps of North and South America. In some areas, a bird's-eye view is available, which is a close-up satellite view of the area.
- **National Geographic MapMachine** (plasma.nationalgeographic.com/mapmachine/index.html) includes a world atlas with road, satellite, and physical maps. For some areas thematic maps are available, such as those related to weather, farming, and population density.
- **The U.K. Street Map Page** (www.streetmap.co.uk) identifies streets in London or places in the United Kingdom.

Interactive maps are especially helpful when you're trying to pinpoint the location of a cemetery or town you plan to visit for your genealogical research, but they're limited in their historical helpfulness because they typically offer only current information about places.

✔ **Specialized maps:** You can view specialized maps on Web sites such as these:

- **Topozone** has interactive topographic maps for the entire United States: www.topozone.com

- **OffRoute.com** lets you order custom-made waterproof topographical maps, perfect for those cemetery trips: www.offroute.com

Zeroing in

We've looked at a few different types of maps, but the real promise of mapping technology is the ability to use different maps together to see the whole picture of where your ancestors lived. One of the ways of doing this is by using mapping layers.

A good example of this is the Google Earth technology. Google Earth (earth.google.com) is a downloadable program that combines Google searches with geographic information. When you launch the program, you see the Earth represented as a globe. Enter a place name or a longitude and latitude coordinate and the system maps it for you. Then you can add additional map layers to see other information about that particular place.

Here's an example of how the layering works: In the cemetery example used in the previous sections, we know two pieces of information about where that cemetery is located. The WorldConnect entry states that the cemetery is in Fayette, Illinois; the GNIS tells us that the cemetery is in Fayette County, Illinois, at a specific latitude and longitude. As Matthew wants to see the gravestone for himself, we can use Google Earth to give us an idea of how to get to the cemetery and what that area looked like at the time his ancestors lived there.

Here is how to generate a Google Earth map by latitude and longitude (you will need to download the Google Earth program from www.earth.google.com to your machine before following these steps):

1. **Open the Google Earth program.**
   When Google Earth launches, you will see the Earth as viewed from space. In the upper-left corner of the screen is the Search area, where you can enter a coordinate (see Figure 7-3 for a view of the Google Earth interface).

2. **In the Search area, click on the tab marked Fly To.**
   Enter the latitude and longitude in the field and click on the magnifying glass to the right of the field. For our example, we enter the latitude and longitude from the GNIS entry for the cemetery — 38 55.58 N, 088 54.18' W.

3. **The Google Earth application "flies" to the location on the map.**
   The location is marked with a crosshair and the latitude and longitude label appears to the right. If the map zooms in too far, you can use the scale in the upper right corner of the map to zoom out. Just move your cursor to the area where the circle with the "N" is. A scale with a plus and minus appears to the right of the compass. Click on the scale and move it down (towards the minus) and the map will zoom out.

4. **Add a placemark to label the location.**
   Move your cursor to the top of the screen and click on the placemark icon. (It looks like a yellow pushpin.) When you click on the icon, a dialog box

appears where you can title the placemark, add a description, and change attributes of the placemark. We enter "Uriah Helm's Grave" into the Name field and a brief description on the description tab (see Figure 7-3).

5. **Overlay the roads layer.**
   The bottom box on the left contains a list of the available layers. We click the layer marked Roads. From this layer we can see that Illinois Route 185 runs past the cemetery.

6. **Add the featured content layer.**
   Visiting the Layers area again, we click on the Featured Content item and then click Rumsey Historical Maps. Under that category we select the United States 1833 layer. A map of the area as of 1833 appears. Although Uriah Helm lived several decades after the map was made, his grandfather moved into the area just seven years after the map was made — so, we can see what the area looked like when the family arrived (see Figure 7-4).

While interactive maps are good for getting a general idea of where a place is, more specific maps are sometimes necessary for feature types such as cemeteries. Topographic maps are especially good set to use for these purposes; they contain not only place names, but also information on features of the terrain (such as watercourses, elevation, vegetation density, and, yes, cemeteries). At the TopoZone site (www.topozone.com), you can view interactive topographic maps produced by the United States Geological Survey.

To generate a topographic map from GNIS coordinates, follow these steps. (Or, you can click on the TopoZone.com link directly from the GNIS results page that we generated in the earlier section titled, "Where is Llandrindod, any-way?".)

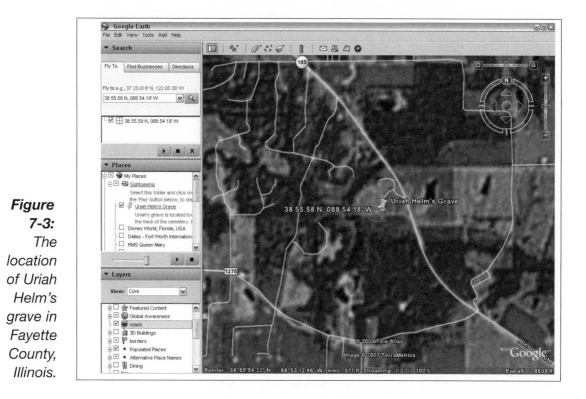

Figure 7-3: *The location of Uriah Helm's grave in Fayette County, Illinois.*

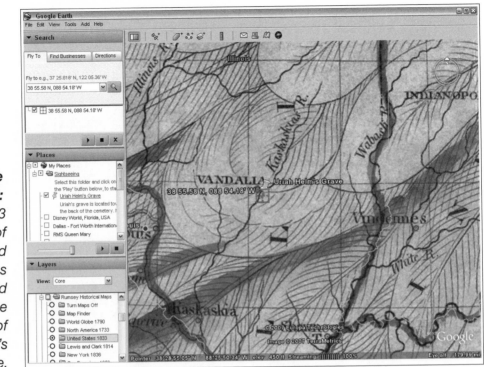

Figure 7-4:

The 1833 Map of the United States overlaid on the map of Uriah's grave.

1. **Direct your browser to www.topozone.com.**

2. **Click on the link marked <u>View Maps</u>, which takes you to a page where you can browse maps.**

3. **Click the <u>Deg/min/sec</u> link in the left column, and you pop down to that section of the form.**

4. **Type the latitude and longitude and click Map.** You will need to use the negative sign in the degrees field to denote western longitude.

The topographic map produced by TopoZone appears in Figure 7-5. A small red cross marks the location of the coordinates. On the topographic map, the letters *CEM* indicate the location of a cemetery. You can also get an idea of the area surrounding the cemetery — which appears to be quite rural.

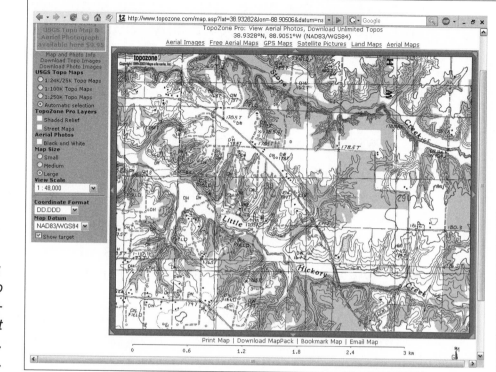

Figure 7-5:
A map generated at TopoZone.com.

Crossing the line

Just as maps help you track your ancestors' movements and where they lived, they can also help you track when your ancestors *didn't* really move. Boundaries for towns, districts, and even states have changed over time. Additionally, for towns and counties to change names wasn't unheard of. Knowing whether your ancestors really moved or just appeared to move because a boundary or town name changed is important when you try to locate records for them.

To determine whether a town or county changed names at some point, check a gazetteer or historical text on the area. (Gazetteers are discussed earlier in this chapter, in the section, "Where is Llandrindod, anyway?".) Finding boundary changes can be a little more challenging, but resources are available to help you. For example, historical atlases illustrate land and boundary changes. You can also use online sites that have maps for the same areas over time, and a few sites deal specifically with boundary changes in particular locations. A couple of examples are

- ✔ The Boundaries of the United States and the Several States site:
  www.ac.wwu.edu/~stephan/48states.html

- ✔ Atlas of Historical County Boundaries:
  www.newberry.org/ahcbp/

- ✔ The Counties of England, Scotland, and Wales Prior to the 1974 Boundary Changes site:
  www.genuki.org.uk/big/Britain.html

You can also use software designed specifically to show boundary changes over time. Programs like these can help you find places that have disappeared altogether:

- ✔ The Centennia Historical Atlas tracks boundary changes in Europe. Its Web site is
  www.clockwk.com

- ✔ AniMap Plus tracks boundary changes in the United States. Its Web site is
  goldbug.com/store/page1.html

Here's a quick walk-through using the AniMap Plus demonstration to see how some counties have changed over time:

AniMap opens to a 1683 map that shows the 12 original counties of New York. All counties are named in the upper-left corner of the map. Abbreviations of each are explained in the County Codes box; you can see the county boundaries on the map.

2. **Double-click Start Demo in the upper-left corner of the screen.**

3. **Click Next to advance to the next map of New York to see changes that took place between 1683 and 1686.**

    The box in the upper-left corner briefly explains the changes that took place and which counties still existed in New York in 1686.

4. **You can advance through the maps in sequential order by clicking the Next button or you can skip to other years by double-clicking the years identified in the Go To box.**

Positioning your family: Using global positioning systems

After learning the location of the final resting place of great-great-great-grandpa Nimrod (yes, that is the name of one of April's ancestors), you just might get the notion to travel to the cemetery. Now, finding the cemetery on the map is one thing, but often finding the cemetery "on the ground" is a completely different thing. That is where global positioning systems come into play.

A *global positioning system* (GPS) is a device that uses satellites to determine the exact location of the user. The technology is pretty sophisticated, but in simple terms, satellites send out radio signals that are collected by the GPS receiver — the device that you use to determine your location. The receiver then calculates the distances between the satellites and the receiver to determine your location. These receivers can come in many forms, ranging from ve-hicle-mounted receivers to those that fit in your hand. (We frequently use a GPS receiver mounted inside Matthew's cell phone for quick readings.)

While on research trips, we not only use GPS receivers to locate a particular place, but we also use them to document the location of a specific object within that place. For example, when we visit a cemetery, we take GPS readings of the gravesites of ancestors and then enter those readings into our genealogical databases. That way, if the marker is ever destroyed, we still have a way to locate the grave. As a final step, we take that information and plot the specific location of the sites on a map, using geographical information systems software. (See the following section for more details on geographical information systems.)

We should also mention that a project is under way that combines genealogy with the use of GPS devices. The U.S. GeoGen project (geogen.org) was established to create county-level pages with coordinates of some places of interest to genealogists (such as cemeteries, mines, homesteads, and historical post offices). At present, these resources are being developed for 23 states.

Plotting against the family

While finding the location where your ancestors lived on a map is interesting, it is even more exciting to create your own maps that are specific to your family history. One way genealogists produce their own maps is by plotting land records: They take the legal description of the land from a record and place it into land-plotting software, which then creates a map showing the land boundaries. A couple of programs for plotting boundaries are DeedMapper by Direct Line Software (www.directlinesoftware.com/factsht.htm) and Metes and Bounds by Sandy Knoll Software (www.tabberer.com/sandyknoll/more/metesandbounds/metes.html). You can also find a number of commercial plotting programs by using a search engine such as

Google (www.google.com).

Another way to create custom maps is through geographical information systems (GIS) software. GIS software allows you to create maps based upon layers of information. For example, you may start with a map that is just an outline of a county. Then you might add a second layer that shows the township sections of the county as they were originally platted. A third layer might show the location of your ancestor's homestead based upon the legal description of a land record. A fourth layer might show watercourses, or other terrain features within the area. The resulting map can give you a great appreciation of the environment in which your ancestor lived.

To begin using GIS resources, you first have to acquire a GIS data viewer. This software comes in many forms, including free software and commercial packages. One popular piece of free software is ArcReader, which is available on the ESRI site at www.esri.com/software/arcgis/arcreader/about/features.html. Then you download (or create) geographical data to use with the viewer. There are a number of sites that contain data, both free and commercial. Starting points for finding data include Geography Network (www.geographynetwork.com) and GIS Data Depot (data.geocomm.com). For more information on GIS software, see GIS.com at www.gis.com.

You can also use maps from other sources and integrate them into a GIS map. For example, when visiting cemeteries, we like to use GIS resources to generate an aerial photograph of the cemetery and plot the location of the grave markers on it. When we get back home, we use the aerial photograph as the base template and then overlay the grave locations on it electronically to show their exact positions.

Using our example of grave-hunting in the German Reformed Cemetery (discussed earlier in the chapter), we generate an aerial view by going to Microsoft Virtual Earth (maps.live.com, or you can get to the site through a link under Mapping Services on the GNIS results page that you generated if you followed the step lists in the section titled, "Where is Llandrindod, anyway?").

Figure 7-6 shows the photograph at its maximum zoom. The cemetery is the slightly lighter, triangular gray area near the center of the photograph (it's bordered on the west by the highway and on the east by a grove of trees). This view of the cemetery helps a lot when we try to find it "on the ground."

From the photograph, we know it's right off of the highway, in between two farms, and across from a triangular lake (although we have to keep in mind that the aerial photograph may have been taken long ago — some things might have changed since then).

After plotting the gravestone locations based on GPS readings at the cemetery, we generate the picture in Figure 7-7. We store that picture in our genealogical database so it's easy to find gravestones at that cemetery should we (or anyone else) wish to visit it in the future.

Figure 7-6: *An aerial map generated at the Microsoft Virtual Earth site.*

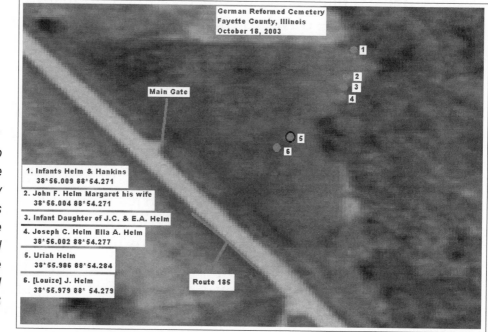

Figure 7-7: *An aerial map on which we plotted family gravestones that we visited and for which we gathered GPS readings.*

There's No Place Like Home: Using Local Resources

A time will come (possibly early in your research) when you need information that's maintained on a local level — say, a copy of a record stored in a local courthouse, confirmation that an ancestor is buried in a particular cemetery, or just a photo of the old homestead. So how can you find and get what you need?

Finding this information is easy if you live in or near the county where the information is maintained — you decide what it is you need and where it's stored, and then go get a copy. Getting locally held information isn't quite as easy if you live in another county, state, or country. Although you can determine what information you need and where it may be stored, finding out whether the information is truly kept where you think it is and then getting a copy is another thing. Of course, if this situation weren't such a common occurrence for genealogists, you could just make a vacation out of it — travel to the location to finish researching there and get the copy you need while sightseeing along the way. But unfortunately, needing records from distant places is a common occurrence, and most of us can't afford to pack the bags and hit the road every time we need a record or item from a faraway place, which is why it's nice to know that resources are available to help.

From geographic-specific Web sites to local genealogical and historical societies to libraries with research services to individuals who are willing to do lookups in public records, a lot of resources are available to help you locate local documents and obtain copies. Some resources are totally free, others may charge you a fee for their time, and still others will bill you only for copying or other direct costs.

Geographic-specific Web sites

Geographic-specific Web sites are those pages that contain information only about a particular town, county, state, country, or other locality. They typically provide information about local resources, such as genealogical and historical societies, government agencies and courthouses, cemeteries, and civic organizations. Some sites have local histories and biographies of prominent residents online. Often, they list and have links to other Web pages that have resources for the area. Sometimes they even have a place where you can post *queries* (or questions) about the area or families from there, in the hope that someone who reads your query will have some answers for you.

How can you find geographic-specific Web sites, you ask? Doing so is easy:

1. **Using your Web browser, go to the Genealogy Toolbox** at www.genealogytoolbox.com.

2. **Scroll down to the Places section.**
   The Places section contains a list of states and countries.

3. **Click the country or geographic link that interests you.**
   Doing so brings up a list of links to general sites or to counties or subdivisions.

4. **Click the subdivision of your choice.**
   This takes you to a page that lists all Internet sites pertaining to the subdivision you selected that are indexed in the Genealogy Toolbox. Each entry includes a brief abstract of the site and a link to that site; you can select sites that sound promising.

You can find several good examples of general geographic-specific Web sites:

- ✔ **The USGenWeb Project** (www.usgenweb.org) conveys information about the United States. The USGenWeb Project is an all-volunteer online effort to provide a central genealogical resource for information (records and reference materials) pertaining to counties within each state. (See the sidebar "The USGenWeb project" in this chapter for more information.)

- ✔ **GENUKI: UK + Ireland Genealogy** (www.genuki.org.uk) is an online reference site containing primary historical and genealogical information in the United Kingdom and Ireland. It links to sites containing indexes, transcriptions, or digitized images of actual records. All of the information is categorized by locality — by country, then county, then parish.

- ✔ **The American Local History Network** (www.alhn.org) organizes its resources by state and by topic.

- ✔ **The WorldGenWeb project** (www.worldgenweb.org) attempts the same type of undertaking as USGenWeb, only on a global scale.

Genealogical and historical societies

Most genealogical and historical societies exist on a local level and attempt to preserve documents and history for the area in which they are located. Genealogical societies also have another purpose — to help their members research their ancestors whether they lived in the local area or elsewhere. (Granted, some surname-based genealogical societies, and even a couple of virtual societies, are exceptions because they aren't specific to one particular place.) Although historical societies usually don't have a stated purpose of aiding their members in genealogical research, they are helpful to genealogists anyway. Often, if you don't live in the area from which you need a record or information, you can contact a local genealogical or historical society to get help. Help varies from look-up services in books and documents the society maintains in its library to volunteers who actually locate records for you and get copies to send you. Before you contact a local genealogical or historical society for help, be sure you know what services it offers.

Many local genealogical and historical societies have Web pages and identify exactly which services they offer to members and nonmembers online. To find a society in an area you're researching, try this:

1. **Using your Web browser, go to Genealogy Resources on the Internet: World Wide Web at** www-personal.umich.edu/~cgaunt/gen_int1.html.

2. **Select the link for World Wide Web sites and scroll down (if necessary) and click a link for *[Insert Place Name Here]* Resources, using the location where you're looking for an association or society as the place name.**

   For example, if you're looking for a genealogical or historical society in Belgium, scroll down and click the <u>Belgium Resources</u> link. This action takes you to a page that identifies and links to all sorts of genealogical sites pertaining to Belgium.

3. **Look through the list of links to see if any associations or societies exist for the area you are interested in. If so, click the link to visit the site.**

   Visit the group or society home page to see what

The USGenWeb project

The USGenWeb Project provides a central resource for genealogical information (records and reference materials) pertaining to counties within each state. USGenWeb offers state-level pages for each state within the United States that have links to pages for each county, as well as links to other online resources about the state. At the county level, the pages have links to resources about the county.

In addition to links to other Web sites with genealogical resources that are geographic-specific, most of the county-level pages have query sections in which you can post or read queries (or questions) about researching in that county. Some of the county-level pages offer other services in addition to the query section, such as a surname registry for anyone researching in the county and a look-up section that identifies people who are willing to look up information for others.

Although some states have uniform-looking county pages with the same standard resources for each county, other states don't. The content and look of USGenWeb state and county pages vary tremendously from state to state.

In addition to state- and county-level pages, the USGenWeb Project includes special projects that cross state and county lines. Some of these projects include the following:

- A project to collect and transcribe tombstone inscriptions so genealogists can access the information online.

- An undertaking to transcribe all federal census data for the United States and make it available online.

- The Pension project — an attempt to transcribe pensions for all wars prior to the year 1900.

- A lineage project to provide resources for individuals researching all descendants of a particular ancestor.

✏ The Digital Map Library project is designed to provide free, high-quality digital maps to researchers.

✏ The Kidz Project, a resource page for kids interested in genealogy.

The various pages and projects that make up the USGenWeb Project are designed and maintained by volunteers. If you're interested in becoming involved, visit the USGenWeb home page (www.usgenweb.org).

services that group or society offers to members and nonmembers. If the group or society offers a service you need (lookup, obtaining copies of records, and so on), use whatever contact information the site provides to get in touch and request help.

You can also use a search engine to effectively locate genealogical and historical societies. Typically, typing in the name of the location you're looking for, followed by either "genealogical society" or "historical society," is all you need to be successful. Keep in mind, however, that you may need to search on the county name rather than the town name — some societies are formed at the county level rather than the town level.

Libraries and archives

Often, the holdings in local libraries and archives can be of great value to you — even if you can't physically visit the library or archive to do your research. If the library or archive has an Internet site, go online to determine whether that repository has the book or document you need. (Most libraries and archives that have Web pages or other Internet sites make their card catalogs or another listing of their holdings available online — and some are even adding indexes or images of actual documents online.) After seeing whether the repository has what you need, you can contact it to borrow the book or document (if they participate in an interlibrary loan program) or to get a copy of what you need. (Most libraries and archives have services to copy information for people at a minimal cost.)

To find online catalogs for libraries in particular places, follow these steps:

1. **Using your Web browser, go to LibDex: The Library Index at** www.libdex.com.

2. **Click the <u>Country</u> link.**
    This brings up a Geographic Index of links sorted by country.

    For example, you can look for the National Library of Australia to see whether its collection has books that would help your Australian research.

3. **Scroll down and click the link for Australia.**
    Clicking the link for Australia takes you to a page that lists regions in Australia.

4. **Click a region and browse through the list to find a library of interest.**
    Depending on the link you select, you are taken to a page for that particular location. For example, selecting the <u>Tasmania</u> link takes us to the Geographic: Countries: Australia: Tasmania page, where we can scroll through a list of catalogs.

5. **Click the <u>State Library of Tasmania</u> link in the Government section.**
    Selecting the <u>State Library of Tasmania</u> link under Government takes you to a description page with a

link to the State Library's catalog. The main Web page for the library contains a list of resources available on the site, including a link to Family History.

From this point on, follow the site's instructions to search for books of interest and applicability to your particular research.

Professional researchers

Professional researchers are people who research your genealogy — or particular family lines — for a fee. If you're looking for someone to do all the research necessary to put together a complete family history, some do so. If you're just looking for records in a particular area to substantiate claims in your genealogy, professional researchers can usually locate the records for you and get you copies. Their services, rates, experience, and reputations vary, so be careful when selecting a professional researcher to help you. Look for someone who has quite a bit of experience in the area in which you need help. Asking for references or a list of satisfied customers isn't out of the question. (That way you know who you're dealing with before you send the researcher money.) Chapter 11 provides a list of questions we recommend you ask when looking for a professional researcher to hire, as well as provides some steps to follow in finding a professional researcher online.

Looking at directories and newspapers

If you have a general idea of where your family lived at a particular time, but no conclusive proof, city and county directories and newspapers from the area may help. (Census records, which we discuss in Chapters 2 and 5, are quite helpful for this purpose, too.) Directories and newspapers can help you confirm whether your ancestors indeed lived in a particular area and, in some cases, they can provide even more information than you expect. A friend of ours has a great story — morbid as it is — that illustrates just this point. He was looking through newspapers for an obituary about one of his great-uncles. He knew when his great-uncle died but could not find mention of it in the obituary section of the newspaper. As he set the newspaper down (probably in despair), he glanced at the front page — only to find a very graphic description of how a local man had been killed in a freak elevator accident. And guess who that local man was? That's right, he was our friend's great-uncle! The newspaper not only confirmed for him that his great-uncle lived there, but also gave our friend a lot more information than he ever expected.

Directories

Like today's telephone books, the directories of yesteryear contained basic information about the persons who lived in particular areas, whether the areas were towns, cities, districts, or counties. Typically, the directory identified at least the head of the household and the location of the house. Some directories also included the names and ages of everyone in the household and occupations of any members of the household who were employed.

Unfortunately, no centralized resource on the Web contains transcriptions of directories or even an index to all directories that may exist on the Internet. But don't be discouraged. Some sites can direct you to directories for particular geographic areas, but they are by no means universal. You can find a list of city directories available on microfilm at the Library of Congress for nearly 700 American towns and states through the U.S. City Directories on Microfilm in the Microform Reading Room Web page (www.loc.gov/rr/microform/uscity). Another list of city directories can be found at the City Directories of the United States of America site (www.uscitydirectories.com). This site contains the years of the city directories and which repositories house them. Right now, the site only contains information on the collections in twenty repositories; however, the site is still growing. If you are looking for city directories for England and Wales, look at the Historical Directories site (www.historicaldirectories.org). The site contains digitized directories from 1750 to 1919. You can also often find lists of city directories on the Web sites of local and state libraries.

Some individuals have also posted city directories in their areas. An example of this is the Fredericksburg, Virginia City Directory 1938 page at

departments.umw.edu/hipr/www/fredericksburg/1938directory.htm

And a commercial effort from Ancestry.com is attempting to recreate the 1890 Census through city directories. For more information on this subscription-based project, see its Web site at

www.ancestry.com/search/rectype/census/1890sub/main.htm

For tips on using city directories, see the article "City Directories," by Brian Andersson, at

www.ancestry.com/learn/library/article.aspx?article=2634

 Some societies and associations have made a commitment to post the contents of directories for their areas or at least an index of what their libraries hold online so that you know before you contact them whether they have something useful to you. To help you find out whether such a project exists for an area you're researching, use the location-specific search engine at TreEZy (www.treezy.com). This tool enables you to search the full text of several genealogical Web sites at once.

Newspapers

Unlike directories that list almost everyone in a community, newspapers are helpful only if your ancestors did something newsworthy — but you'd be surprised at what was considered newsworthy in the past. Your ancestor didn't necessarily have to be a politician or a criminal to get his picture and story in the paper. Just like today, obituaries, birth and marriage announcements, public records of land transactions, advertisements, and gossip sections were all relatively common in newspapers of the past.

Finding copies online of those newspapers from the past is a challenge. Most of the newspaper sites currently on the Web are for contemporary publications. Although you can read about wedding anniversaries and birthdays in England and Sweden today, you can't necessarily access online information about your ancestor's death in the 1800s in one of those countries. Many researchers are beginning to recognize the potential that the Web holds for making historical information from newspapers available worldwide. However, the lack of committed resources (time and money, primarily) prevents them from doing so as quickly as we'd like.

Here's what you're likely to find online pertaining to newspapers:

- ✔ **Indexes:** A variety of sites serve as indexes of newspapers that are available at particular libraries, archives, and universities. Most of these list the names and dates of the periodicals that are held in the newspaper or special collections. Examples of index sites include the following:

- **The Newspapers at Library and Archives Canada page:** www.collectionscanada.ca/8/16/index-e.html

- **The Newspaper Collection at the State Library of Victoria, Australia:** www.slv.vic.gov.au/collections/newspapers/index.html

- **New England Old Newspaper Index Project of Maine:** www.rootsweb.com/~megenweb/newspaper/project

- **The Online Newspaper Indexes Available in the Newspaper and Current Periodical Reading Room of the Library of Congress:** lcweb.loc.gov/rr/news/npindex2.html

✔ **Transcriptions:** A few sites contain actual transcriptions of newspaper articles, entire issues, and/or excerpts. Typically, the contents at these sites are limited to the topic and geographic interests of the person who transcribed the information and posted it for public access on the Web. Here are a couple of examples:

- **Old Newspaper Articles of Henderson County Texas:** www.rootsweb.com/~txhender/Newspapers.htm

- **The Knoxville Gazette:** www.rootsweb.com/~tnnews/kgmain.htm

- **Ireland Old News:** www.irelandoldnews.com

✔ **Collectors' issues for sale:** Although they don't provide information directly from the newspaper online for you to use in your genealogical pursuits, these sites can help you find out about collectors' editions of newspapers and possibly even buy them online. The sites that sell old newspapers generally market their papers as good gift ideas for birthdays and anniversaries. For the services to be really useful to you as a genealogist, you have to know the date and place of the event you want to document (and a newspaper name helps, too), as well as be willing to pay for a copy of that paper. Here are a couple of newspaper collector sites to check out:

- **History Buff's Home Page by the Newspaper Collectors Society of America:** www.historybuff.com

- **Historic Newspaper Archives:** www.historicnewspaper.com

✔ **Online newspaper projects:** Many people are beginning to recognize the important role newspapers play in recording history and the value of putting newspaper information on the Web. We've seen an increasing number of online projects to catalog or transcribe newspapers — some of the projects are organized on a state level, and others are for cities or particular newspapers. The Web sites for these projects explain the purpose of the project, its current status, and how to find the newspapers if they've been transcribed or digitized and placed online. Here are a few examples:

- **Chronicling America: Historic American Newspapers (see Figure 7-8):** www.loc.gov/chroniclingamerica/

- **GenealogyBank.com:**

www.genealogybank.com

- **NewspaperArchive.com:**
  www.newspaperarchive.com

- **Ancestry.com:**
  www.ancestry.com

Now you know what newspaper resources you may find online, but how do you find these sites? One option is to use a geographic category in a comprehensive genealogical site (though most may not list newspaper transcriptions if the transcriptions are buried under a larger site). A better option may be to use a genealogically focused search engine, or even a general Internet search engine — especially if you know the location and time frame for the newspaper.

Figure 7-8:
The Chronicling America Web site.

291

Localizing your search

To find a lot of detail about a specific area and what it was like during a particular time frame, local histories are the answer. Local histories often contain information about when and how a particular place was settled and may have biographical information on earlier settlers or principal people within the community who sponsored the creation of the history.

Online local histories can be tucked away in geographically specific Web sites, historical society pages, library sites, and Web-based bookstores. There are also a few sites that feature local histories:

- Ancestry.com (www.ancestry.com) features several thousand works in its family and local history collection.

- A collection of Canadian local histories is available at Our Roots/Nos Racines (www.ourroots.ca).

- A growing collection of local histories can be found on Google Books (books.google.com).

For an example of a local history site, take a gander at Figure 7-9. It shows an example page of the History of Sangamon County, Illinois, on Google Books.

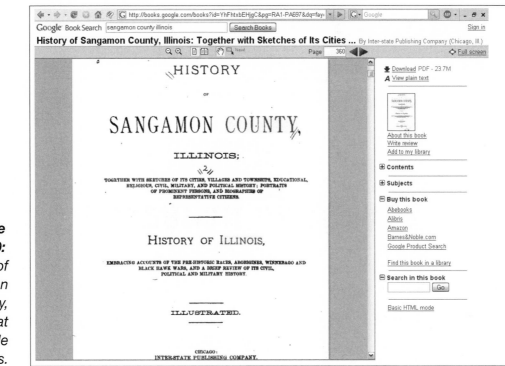

Figure 7-9: *History of Sangamon County, Illinois, at Google Books.*

Chapter 8

Ethnic Research

. . . .

In This Chapter

▶ Discovering African ancestry
▶ Finding American Indian sites
▶ Identifying Hispanic roots
▶ Researching European ethnic groups

. . . .

Researching ethnic groups can often be frustrating. Even though every ethnic group has records that are unique to it, some ethnic groups have historically been very mobile or have passed down their most important information through oral tradition — making written records for it hard to find. And in some cases, records were destroyed during periods of war. Despite the difficulties in finding some of these records, ethnicity-based research can be very rewarding. By looking for records specific to ethnic groups, you get a clearer picture of your ancestor's part in history and find unique sources of information that can add color to your family's story. This chapter examines some of the online resources available to assist you in finding ethnic-specific records.

If you're looking for a good reference resource that covers ethnic research, we recommend *The Source: A Guidebook of American Genealogy,* edited by Loretto Dennis Szucs and Sandra Hargreaves Luebking (Ancestry, Inc.).

Researching African Ancestry

It's a common misconception that tracing African ancestry is impossible. In the past decade or so, much has been done to dispel that perception. If your ancestors lived in the United States, you can use many of the same research techniques and records (census schedules, vital records, and other primary resources) that genealogists of other ethnic groups consult back to 1870. Prior to 1870, your research resources become more limited, depending on whether your ancestor was a freedman or a slave. To make that determination, you may want to interview some of your relatives. They often possess oral traditions that can point you in the right direction.

If your ancestor was a slave, try consulting the slave owners' probate records (which you can usually find in local courthouses), deed books (slave transactions were often recorded in deed books — which you also find in local courthouses), tax records, plantation records, Freedman's Bureau records, and runaway-slave records. These types of records can be helpful because they identify persons by name.

Although your first inclination may be to turn to a slave schedule in the U.S. Census (slave schedules show the owner's name and the age, sex, and color of slaves), such schedules are not as useful as other sources in your research because the *enumerators* who collected the census information didn't record the names of slaves, nor did the government require them to do so. This fact doesn't mean that looking at slave schedules is a total waste of time; the schedules simply don't identify your ancestor by name. You need to find other resources that name your ancestor specifically.

If your ancestors served in the American Civil War, they may have service and pension records. You can begin a search for service records in an index to Civil War records of the United States Colored Troops or, if your ancestor joined a state regiment, in an Adjutant General's report. (An *Adjutant General's report* is a published account of the actions of military units from a particular state during a war; these reports are usually available at libraries or archives.) A good place to begin your search for Civil War records is the Civil War Soldiers and Sailors System at www.itd.nps.gov/cwss/.

Two other sources of records to keep in mind are the Freedmen's Bureau and the Freedmen's Savings and Trust:

- ✔ **The Freedmen's Bureau** (its full name was the Bureau of Refugees, Freedmen and Abandoned Lands) was established in 1865 to assist ex-slaves after the American Civil War. For more on the Bureau, see the article by Elaine Everly at www.archives.gov/publications/prologue/1997/summer/freedmens-bureau-records.html

- ✔ **The Freedmen's Bureau Online** offers examples of Freedmen's Bureau records at www.freedmensbureau.com

- ✔ **The Freedman's Savings and Trust Company** was also established in 1865 as a bank for ex-slaves. For more information, see the article by Reginald Washington at www.archives.gov/publications/prologue/1997/summer/freedmans-savings-and-trust.html

Several of the bank's contributors were members of the United States Colored Troops during the American Civil War. Although the company failed in 1874, its records are now kept at the National Archives and Records Administration, along with the records for the Freedmen's Bureau. You can also find information on the Freedman's Bank Records CD-ROM available from the FamilySearch.org store:

www.ldscatalog.com/webapp/wcs/stores/servlet/Category Display?catalogId=10151&storeId=10151&categoryId=13706 &langId=-1&cg1=13701&cg2=&cg3=&cg4=&cg5=

✔ **The National Archives and Records Administration** provides information about Freedman's Savings records (and their availability on microfilm) at www.archives.gov/research/guide-fed-records/groups/105.html

 For more information on using records to research your African ancestry, try the following resources:

✔ *The Source: A Guidebook of American Genealogy,* edited by Loretto Dennis Szucs and Sandra Hargreaves Luebking (Ancestry, Inc.). In particular, see Chapter 15, "Tracking African American Family History," written by David Thackery.

✔ *Black Roots: A Beginners Guide to Tracing the African American Family Tree,* written by Tony Burroughs (Fireside).

✔ *Black Family Research: Records of Post-Civil War Federal Agencies at the National Archives* available online at www.archives.gov/publications/ref-info-papers/108/.

- ✔ *Slave Genealogy: A Research Guide with Case Studies,* written by David H. Streets (Heritage Books).

Mailing lists focusing on African research

When you look for key records that are specific to African ancestral research, it's a good idea for you to interact with other researchers who may already be knowledgeable about such resources. One place to start is the *AfriGeneas* mailing list. This mailing list focuses primarily on African genealogical research methods. On the Web page for the mailing list (www.afrigeneas.com), you find the following resources (see Figure 8-1):

- ✔ A beginner's guide to researching genealogy

- ✔ Links to census schedules and slave data on the Internet

- ✔ A digital library of transcribed resources

- ✔ A link to a database of African American surnames and their corresponding researchers

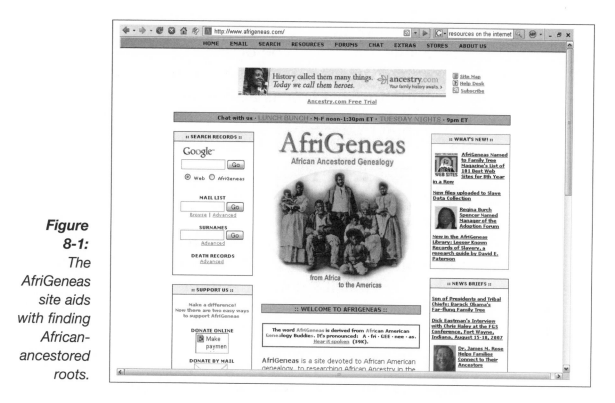

Figure 8-1:
The AfriGeneas site aids with finding African-ancestored roots.

Here's how to subscribe to the AfriGeneas mailing list:

1. **Start your favorite e-mail program.**
   How you start your e-mail program depends on which one you use. Generally, you can begin the program by double-clicking the program's icon (or, in Windows, by opening the program from the Start button). If you're not sure how to start your e-mail program, see the documentation that came with the program.

2. **Create a new e-mail message.**
   Normally you create a new e-mail message by clicking an icon in your e-mail program's toolbar or by using a menu. If you don't know how to create a new e-mail message, consult the documentation that came with the program.

3. **Type** majordomo@lists.msstate.edu **in the To line.**
   Make sure that you type *only* majordomo@lists.msstate.edu in the To line. You subscribe to AfriGeneas at this listserv e-mail account. If you type anything more, your e-mail message won't be delivered, and your attempt to subscribe fails.

4. **Make sure that your e-mail address is in the From line.**
   Most e-mail programs automatically fill in your e-mail address in the From line. In that case, just make sure that it's correct. Otherwise, type the e-mail address where you want to receive postings to the AfriGeneas mailing list.

5. **In the body of the message, type** subscribe afrigeneas **or** subscribe afrigeneas-digest**.**
   Use **subscribe afrigeneas-digest** if you want to receive fewer e-mail messages a day from the list. In the digest form, the listserver compiles all the messages that people post throughout the day into one e-mail. For example, if April subscribes to the mailing list in its regular format, where each posting arrives separately, she'd type **subscribe afrigeneas** in the body of her message. Again, don't type anything more than this line in the message body, or you confuse the automatic program that adds you to the mailing list — and it rejects your attempt to subscribe.

6. **Send the e-mail message.**
   Your e-mail program probably features a Send button that sends the message after you click it. If you don't see a Send button or a Send command in one of the drop-down menus, consult your e-mail

program documentation for details on sending a message.

Another resource is the Ethnic-African Mailing Lists page at lists.rootsweb.com/index/other/Ethnic-African.

This page identifies more than 80 mailing lists of interest to those conducting African-ancestored research. For mailing lists with a little broader focus, see the list at Genealogy Resources on the Internet at www.rootsweb.com/~jfuller/gen_mail_african.html.

Genealogical resource pages on the Web

In addition to the AfriGeneas Web site, a number of online resources are available to assist you in finding your African ancestry.

You can find a high-level overview of the subject at African American Lives (www.pbs.org/wnet/aalives). The site is the companion to the PBS show that originally aired in early 2006 (see Figure 8-2). Items on the site include

- Profiles of individuals featured on the show

- Tips on how to effectively use documentation in researching African ancestral roots

- A brief primer on DNA testing

- An introduction to some of the issues and pitfalls surrounding research

- A list of stories from other researchers

For a brief list of resources that you can use, see the University of Pennsylvania African Studies Center bibliography page at www.africa.upenn.edu/Bibliography/menu_Biblio .html.

Other sites with helpful content include

- Sankofa's Slave Genealogy Wiki (www.sankofagen.com)

- Slave Archival Collection Database (www.rootsweb.com/%7Eilissdsa/text_files/database_intro2.htm)

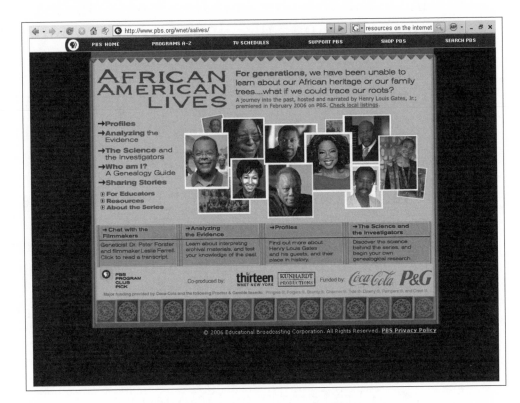

Figure 8-2:
African American Lives Web site.

Transcribed records pertaining to ancestors with African roots

Many genealogists recognize the benefits of making transcribed and digitized records available for other researchers. More and more of these Web sites are popping up every day. A few Web sites have transcribed records that are unique to the study of African ancestry online. Following are some examples:

302

- **Cemetery records:** For a transcribed list of cemeteries, see African American Cemeteries Online at

  `www.prairiebluff.com/aacemetery/`

- **Freedman's Bureau records:** You can find transcribed Freedman's Bureau records at the Freedman's Bureau Online at

  `www.freedmensbureau.com/index.html`

- **Manumission papers:** For examples of manumission papers (documents that reflect a slave was granted freedom), see Bourbon County Deeds of Manumission Abstracts site at

  `www.rootsweb.com/~kyafamer/Bourbon/manumissions.htm`

- **Registers:** At the Valley of the Shadow site, you can view transcribed Registers of Free Blacks in Augusta County, Virginia, at

  `valley.vcdh.virginia.edu/govdoc/free.html`

- **Slave schedules:** You can find transcriptions of slave schedules (lists of slave owners and the number of slaves owned by them) at the African American Census Schedules Online site at

  `www.afrigeneas.com/aacensus/`

  Although some of these schedules don't identify ancestors by name, they're useful if you know the name of the slave owner.

- **Wills and probate records:** Slaves were often mentioned in the disposition of wills. A list of slaves mentioned in probate records of Noxubee County, Mississippi, can be found at

earphoto.tripod.com/SlaveNames.html

The preceding sites are a few examples of transcribed records that you can find on the Internet. To see whether online records exist that pertain specifically to your research, visit a comprehensive genealogical site and look under the appropriate category.

Special ethnic pages about African ancestry

Many Web sites include information on a particular subset of individuals of African ancestry. Here are some you may want to visit:

- ✔ The African-Native Genealogy home page provides details on the Estelusti, a tribe of Black Indians in Oklahoma (www.african-nativeamerican.com).

- ✔ You can find information on French Creoles on the French Creoles Free People of Color Web site (www.frenchcreoles.com/CreoleCulture/freepeople ofcolor/freepeopleofcolor.htm).

To find additional sites containing unique information about researching your African ancestry, visit a comprehensive genealogical site and look under the appropriate category to review a list of links to such sites or use a genealogical search engine.

Original records

You can find digitized original records online at some subscription sites. For example, Ancestry.com (www.ancestry .com) has images of the 1850 and 1860 Slave Schedules. This collection includes both the images and an index of names. Footnote (www.footnote.com) has the federal and Supreme Court case files for the case involving the seizure of the Amistad, a ship carrying slaves seized by the U.S. Navy in 1839 (see Figure 8-3).

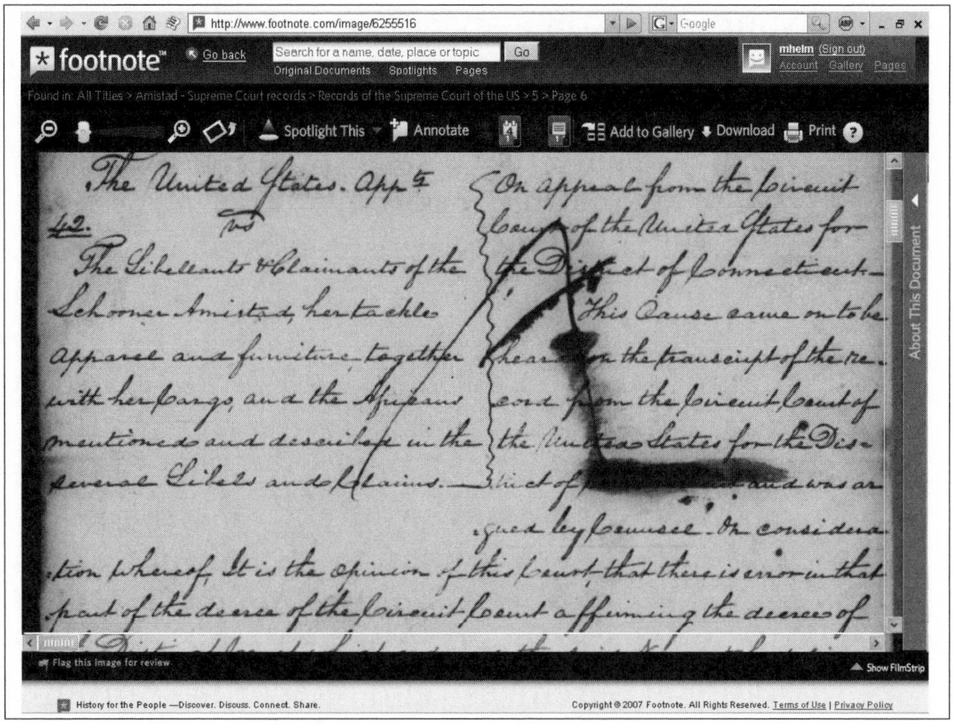

Figure 8-3:
The decree freeing the slaves of the Amistad from Footnote.

American Indian Resources

Tracing your American Indian heritage can be challenging. Your ancestor may have moved frequently and, most likely, few written records were kept. However, your task isn't impossible. With a good research strategy, you may be able to narrow down your search area and find primary resources to unlock some of the mysteries of your ancestors.

One key to your research is old family stories that have been passed down from generation to generation. Interviewing your family members is a good way to find out what tribe your ancestor belonged to and the geographic area in which that ancestor lived. After you have this information, a trip to your local library is well worth the effort to find a history of the tribe and where it migrated throughout time. From this research, you can then concentrate your search on a specific geographic area and gain a much better chance of success in finding records of genealogical value.

Fortunately, the government of the United States did compile some records on American Indians. For example, you can find annual census lists of American Indians, dating from 1885 to 1940, in the National Archives — as well as digitized copies of the censuses on Ancestry.com (see Figure 8-4). You can also find probate and land records at the federal level, especially for transactions occurring on reservations. You can also find in federal repositories school records for those who attended schools on reservations. Additionally, the Bureau of Indian Affairs has a vast collection of records on American Indians. For more information about American Indian resources available from the National Archives and Records Administration, visit www.archives.gov/research/alic/reference/native-ameri cans.html.

You may also be able to find records on your ancestor in one of the many tribal associations in existence. To find out how to contact tribes recognized in the United States, go to the American Indian Tribal Directory at www.indians.org/Resource/FedTribes99/fedtribes99.html.

 For more information about researching American Indian records, see the following resources:

- *The Source: A Guidebook of American Genealogy,* edited by Loretto Dennis Szucs and Sandra Hargreaves Luebking (Ancestry, Inc.). In particular, see Chapter 14, "Tracking Native American Family History," written by Curt B. Witcher and George J. Nixon.

- *Native American Genealogical Sourcebook,* edited by Paula K. Byers and published by Gale Research.

- *Guide to Records in the National Archives of the United States Relating to American Indians,* written by Edward E. Hill and published by the National Archives and Records Services Administration.

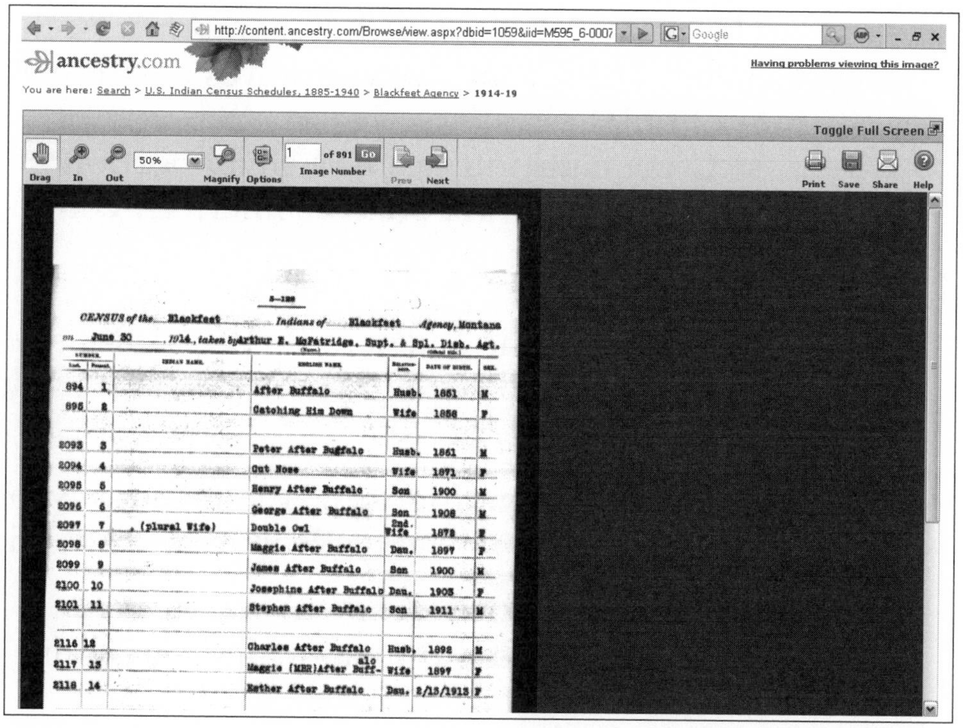

Figure 8-4: Blackfeet Indian Census of 1914 on Ancestry.com.

Where to begin looking for information about American Indians

For a general look at what Internet resources are available on American Indians, see the NativeWeb site (www.nativeweb.org). NativeWeb includes a resource center with hundreds of links to other Internet sites on native peoples around the world.

When you're ready to dive into research, you may want to join the INDIAN-ROOTS-L mailing list, which is devoted to discussing American Indian research methods. To subscribe to the list, type **SUB INDIAN-ROOTS-L *your first name your last name*** in the body of an e-mail message and send it to listserv@listserv.indiana.edu.

Another resource worth exploring is the National Archives and Records Administration's Archival Research Catalog (ARC) at www.archives.gov/research_room/arc/index.html.

ARC contains indexes to a small portion of the archive's holdings. Among the Native American collections in ARC are the following:

- Images of the Index to the Final Rolls of the Citizens and Freedmen of the Five Civilized Tribes in Indian Territory

- Images of the Index to Applications Submitted for the Eastern Cherokee Roll of 1909 (Guion Miller Roll)

- Records of the Bureau of Indian Affairs Truxton Canon Agency

- Record of Applications under the Act of 1896 (1896 Citizenship Applications) received by the Dawes Commission

- Descriptions for records of the Cherokee Indian Agency and the Seminole Indian Agency

- Descriptions for records of the Navajo Area Office, Navajo Agency, and the Window Rock Area Office of the Bureau of Indian Affairs

- Some images of Cherokee, Chicasaw, Creek, and Seminole Applications for Enrollment to the Five Civilized Tribes (Dawes Commission)

- Images of the Kern-Clifton Roll of Cherokee Freedmen

- Images of the Wallace Roll of Cherokee Freedmen in Indian Territory

- Surveys of Indian Industry, 1922

- Classified Files of the Extension and Credit Office, 1931–1946

- Selected Documents from the Records of the Bureau of Indian Affairs, 1793–1989

- American Indians, 1881–1885

To search ARC, try this:

1. **Go to**
   www.archives.gov/research_room/arc/index.html.

2. **Click the Search button located near the ARC logo.**
   This link takes you to the ARC Basic Search interface.

3. **Type the name or keyword you're looking for and click Go.**
   For example, if April is looking for a person with the

name Annie Abbott, she simply types **Annie Abbott** in the blank text box and then clicks Go. After you submit the search, you are taken to the ARC Search Results page. Each result contains the title of the document, creator, type of material, description level, and physical location.

4. **Click the link to see the full record description.** This takes you to a screen displaying the available information on the document, including a description of its content.

At this point, ARC contains descriptions of only 55 percent of the Archives' total holdings. So, if you don't find something in it, that does not mean it does not exist.

For general information on how to begin researching American Indian resources, see the article "How-To Guide for Native Americans" at members.aol.com/bbbenge/page12.html.

A brief outline of tracing American Indian ancestry is found on the U.S. Department of the Interior site (www.doi.gov/ancestry.html). Another page that you may want to visit is Tawodi's American Indian Genealogy site (members.aol.com/tawodi/). It contains a how-to guide, a list of American Indian texts online, and links to several tribal and American Indian pages.

American Indian resource pages on the Web

Researching American Indian roots would be much easier if some sites were dedicated to the genealogical research of specific tribes. If your ancestor's tribe passed through the state of Oklahoma, you may be in luck. Volunteers with the Oklahoma USGenWeb project developed the Twin Territories site at www.rootsweb.com/~itgenweb/index.htm.

(For more information about USGenWeb, see Chapter 7.) Here are some links to various tribes available on the World Wide Web:

- Cherokee Nation Indian Territory at

  www.rootsweb.com/~itcherok/

- Cherokee Archival Project at

  www.rootsweb.com/~cherokee/

- NC Cherokee Reservation Genealogy at

  www.rootsweb.com/~ncqualla/index.htm

- Cheyenne-Arapaho Lands Indian Territory at

  www.rootsweb.com/~itcheyen/

- Chickasaw Nation, Indian Territory 1837–1907 at

  www.rootsweb.com/~itchicka/

- Choctaw Nation, Indian Territory at

  www.rootsweb.com/~itchocta/

- Kiowa, Comanche, Apache Lands Indian Territory at

  www.rootsweb.com/~itkiowa/

- Muscogee (Creek) Nation of Oklahoma at

  www.rootsweb.com/~itcreek/index.htm

- Native Genealogy People of the Three Fires (Chippewa, Ottawa, and Potawatomi) at

  www.rootsweb.com/~minatam/

- ✔ Osage Nation Genealogical Web site at www.rootsweb.com/~itosage/

- ✔ Quapaw Agency Lands Indian Territory at www.rootsweb.com/~itquapaw/index.htm

- ✔ Seminole Nation in Indian Territory at www.seminolenation-indianterritory.org/

- ✔ Sovereign Nation of the Kaw at www.rootsweb.com/~itkaw/KanzaNation.html

Transcribed American Indian records

Some Web sites have transcribed records that are unique to researching American Indian roots. Here are some examples:

- ✔ **The Chickasaw Historical Research Page:** This page contains transcriptions of marriage records, a partial census roll of 1818, land sale records, court records, treaty letters, and guardianship records, all at www.chickasawhistory.com/.

- ✔ **1851 Census of Cherokees East of the Mississippi:** This site provides a transcription of the census, including names, family numbers, ages, and relationships to head of household, all at members.aol.com/lredtail/siler.html.

- ✔ **South Dakota Native American Genealogy page:** You can find several transcribed records at www.geocities.com/Heartland/Plains/8430/. These records include marriage lists, agency rolls,

Many families have legends that they are descended from famous American Indians. These claims should always be researched carefully and backed up with appropriate proof. One of the most prolific legends is descent from Pocahontas. If that legend runs through your family, you may want to visit the Pocahontas Descendants page for resources that can help you prove your heritage. You can find it at pocahontas.morenus.org/poca_gen.html.

Hispanic Roots

A growing number of genealogists are researching their Hispanic roots. If you have Hispanic ancestors, you can use several different types of records to pursue your genealogy, depending on when your ancestor immigrated.

If your ancestor immigrated in the nineteenth or twentieth century, look for vital records, military records, photographs, passports, church records, passenger lists, naturalization papers, diaries, or other items that can give you an idea of the birthplace of your ancestor. For those ancestors who immigrated before the nineteenth century, you may want to consult Spanish colonial records after you exhaust any local records in the region where your ancestor lived.

 For more information on researching Hispanic records, see the following:

- *The Source: A Guidebook of American Genealogy,* edited by Loretto Dennis Szucs and Sandra Hargreaves Lueb King (Ancestry, Inc.). In particular, see Chapter 16, "Tracking Hispanic Family History," written by George Ryskamp.

- *Hispanic Family History Research in a L.D.S. Family History Center,* written by George R. Ryskamp

(Hispanic Family History Research).

Where to begin searching for genealogical information on Hispanic ancestors

If you aren't sure where to begin your research, check out the messages that people post to the GEN-HISPANIC-L mailing list at lists.rootsweb.com/index/intl/ESP/GEN-HISPANIC.html.

If your genealogical interests lie in a specific country or ethnic subgroup, you may want to join one of the following mailing lists:

- **Basque-L:** This list discusses Basque culture and periodically includes genealogical postings. To subscribe to the mailing list, type **SUBSCRIBE BASQUE-L *your first name your last name*** in the body of an e-mail message and send it to listserv@cunyvm.cuny.edu.

- **Columbia:** COLEXT is a general mailing list on Columbia. To subscribe to the mailing list, type **SUBSCRIBE COLEXT *your first name your last name*** in the body of an e-mail message and send it to listserv@ cuvmb.columbia.edu.

- **Costa Rica:** This mailing list is devoted to people who have a genealogical interest in Costa Rica. To subscribe to the mailing list, send a message to costa-rica-l-request@rootsweb.com with only the word *subscribe* in the body of the message.

- **Cuba:** This mailing list is devoted to people who have a genealogical interest in Cuba. To subscribe to the mailing list, send a message to cuba-l-request @rootsweb.com with only the word *subscribe* in the body of the message.

- ✔ **Dominican Republic:** This mailing list is for people with a genealogical interest in the Dominican Republic. To subscribe to the mailing list, send a message to republica-dominicana-l-request@ rootsweb.com with only the word *subscribe* in the body of the message.

- ✔ **Ecuador:** This mailing list is devoted to people who have a genealogical interest in Ecuador. To subscribe to the mailing list, send a message to ecuador-l -request@rootsweb.com with only the word *subscribe* in the body of the message.

- ✔ **El Salvador:** This mailing list is devoted to people who have a genealogical interest in El Salvador. To subscribe to the mailing list, send a message to elsalvador-l-request@rootsweb.com with only the word *subscribe* in the body of the message.

- ✔ **Guatemala:** This mailing list is devoted to people who have a genealogical interest in Guatemala. To subscribe to the mailing list, send a message to guatemala-l-request@rootsweb.com with only the word *subscribe* in the body of the message.

- ✔ **Honduras:** This mailing list is devoted to people who have a genealogical interest in Honduras. To subscribe to the mailing list, send a message to honduras-l-request@rootsweb.com with only the word *subscribe* in the body of the message.

- ✔ **Mexico:** This mailing list is for anyone with an interest in genealogy in Mexico. To subscribe to the mailing list, send a message to mexico-l-request @rootsweb.com with only the word *subscribe* in the body of the message.

- ✓ **Nicaragua:** This mailing list is devoted to people who have a genealogical interest in Nicaragua. To subscribe to the mailing list, send a message to nicaragua-l-request@rootsweb.com with only the word *subscribe* in the body of the message.

- ✓ **Paraguay:** This mailing list is for anyone with an interest in genealogy in Paraguay. To subscribe to the mailing list, send a message to paraguay-l-request @rootsweb.com with only the word *subscribe* in the body of the message.

- ✓ **Spain:** This list is devoted to people who have a genealogical interest in Spain. Send a message to spain-l-request@ rootsweb.com with only the word *subscribe* in the body of the message to subscribe to the list.

- ✓ **Venezuela:** This mailing list is for anyone with an interest in genealogy in Venezuela. Send a message to venezuela-l-request@rootsweb.com with only the word *subscribe* in the body of the message to subscribe to the mailing list.

Hispanic resource pages on the Web

The Hispanic Genealogy Center (www.hispanic genealogy.com) is a Web page that the Hispanic Genealogical Society of New York maintains to promote genealogy among Hispanic Americans. For a list of Hispanic resources by location, the Puerto Rican/Hispanic Genealogical Society maintains a page of links to genealogical resources at www.rootsweb.com/~prhgs/ (see Figure 8-5).

The Colorado Society of Hispanic Genealogy (www.hispanicgen.org) also maintains a Web site dedicated to people researching ancestors in the Southwest area of the United States (formerly known as New Spain). For resources specific to a country or area, see the following sites:

- ✔ Argentina WorldGenWeb at www.rootsweb.com/~argwgw/

- ✔ Genealogie d'Haiti et de Saint-Domingue at www.rootsweb.com/~htiwgw/

- ✔ GuatemalaGenWeb at www.rootsweb.com/~gtmwgw/

- ✔ Honduras GenWeb at www.rootsweb.com/~hndwgw/

- ✔ Genealogia de El Salvador at www.rootsweb.com/~slvwgw/

- ✔ La Genealogia de Puerto Rico at www.rootsweb.com/~prwgw/index.html

- ✔ Mexican GenWeb Project at www.rootsweb.com/~mexwgw/

- ✔ Panama GenWeb at www.rootsweb.com/~panwgw/

- ✔ Peru — The WorldGenWeb Project at www.rootsweb.com/~perwgw/

Transcribed records for Hispanic ancestors

Transcribed records are also available on sites that focus on Hispanic ancestors. For example, you can view transcribed records from the 1757, 1780, 1791, 1823, and 1860 censuses of the village of Guerrero in Mexico (along with baptismal records) at members.aol.com/gallegjj/viejo.html.

Other transcribed records are available online; visit a comprehensive genealogical site if you're interested in discovering whether other sites pertain more specifically to your research.

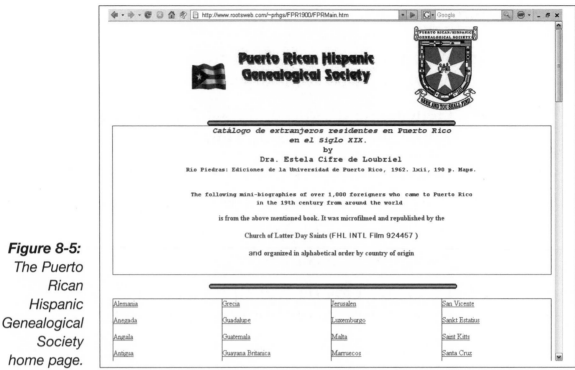

Figure 8-5:
The Puerto
Rican
Hispanic
Genealogical
Society
home page.

European Resources

If your ancestors came from Europe, you may want to consult information on one of the continent's many ethnic groups. Your level of genealogical success with European ethnic records depends greatly on the history of the group and the areas in which your ancestors lived. There may be fewer surviving records for ancestors from places that weathered several wars and border changes than for those who lived in a more stable environment. Here is a sampling of European ethnic-research sites:

✔ **Austrian:** AustriaGenWeb
(www.rootsweb.com/~autwgw/)

✔ **Belarusian:** Belarusian Genealogy
(www.belarusguide.com/genealogy1/index.html)

318

- ✔ **Bosnia-Herzegovina:** Bosnia-Herzegovina Web Genealogy Project (www.rootsweb.com/~bihwgw/)

- ✔ **Bulgarian:** Bulgarian GenWeb (www.rootsweb.com/~bgrwgw/)

- ✔ **Croatian:** CroatiaGenWeb (www.rootsweb.com/~hrvwgw/)

- ✔ **Czech:** Czech Republic Genealogy (www.rootsweb.com/~czewgw/)

- ✔ **Danish:** DIS Danmark (www.dis-danmark.dk/dis-english.asp)

- ✔ **Dutch:** DutchGenealogy.com (www.dutchgenealogy.com/)

- ✔ **Estonian:** Estonian GenWeb (www.fortunecity.com/meltingpot/estonia/200/genweb.html)

- ✔ **Federation of East European Family History Societies (FEEFHS):** If you're looking for research guides for Eastern Europe, start here. The federation's pages (feefhs.org) have information on the Albanian, Armenian, Austrian, Belarusian, Bohemian, Bulgarian, Carpatho-Rusyn, Croatian, Czech, Danish, Finnish, Galician, German, Hutterite, Hungarian, Latvian, Lithuanian, Polish, Moravian, Pomeranian, Romanian, Russian, Silesian, Slavic, Slavonian, Slovak, Slovenian, Transylvanian, Ukrainian, and Volhynian ethnic groups.

- ✔ **Finnish:** Family History Finland (www.open.org/~rumcd/genweb/finn.html)

- ✔ **French:** Francogene (www.francogene.com/) focuses on genealogy of French-speaking groups,

319

including French Canadians, Acadians, Cajuns, Belgians, and Swiss.

- ✔ **German:** The German Genealogy Pages (www .genealogy.net/gene/genealogy.html) focus on research of German, Austrian, Swiss, Alsatian, Luxemburger, and Eastern European genealogy. Also, Ahnenforschung.net (www.ahnenforschung .net) is a search engine dedicated to German genealogy.

- ✔ **Greek:** GreeceGenWeb (www.rootsweb.com/~grcwgw/)

- ✔ **Hungarian:** HungaryGenWeb (www.rootsweb.com/~wghungar/)

- ✔ **Icelandic:** Iceland Genealogy (www.rootsweb.com/~islwgw/)

- ✔ **Irish:** Irish Ancestors (www.ireland.com/ancestor/) provides guides on sources of genealogical information in Ireland, a list of county heritage centers, record sources, and useful addresses.

- ✔ **Italian:** The Italian Genealogy Homepage (www.italgen.com) covers many topics including medieval genealogy, tips for researching in Italy, records repositories, common surnames, and history.

- ✔ **Latvian:** LatvianGenWeb (www.rootsweb.com/~lvawgw/)

- ✔ **Liechtenstein:** LiechGen (www.rootsweb.com/~liewgw/)

- ✔ **Luxembourg:** Luxembourg Home Page (www.rootsweb.com/~luxwgw/)

- ✔ **Maltese:** MaltaGenWeb

(www.rootsweb.com/~mltwgw/)

- ✔ **Moldava:** MoldavaGenWeb
  (www.rootsweb.com/~mdawgw/)

- ✔ **Norwegian:** Norway Genealogy
  (www.rootsweb.com/~wgnorway/)

- ✔ **Polish:** PolandGenWeb
  (www.rootsweb.com/~polwgw/polandgen.html)

- ✔ **Romanian:** Romania World GenWeb
  (www.rootsweb.com/~romwgw/index.html)

- ✔ **Russian:** RussiaGenWeb
  (www.rootsweb.com/~ruswgw/)

- ✔ **Serbian:** SerbiaGenWeb
  (www.rootsweb.com/~serwgw/)

- ✔ **Slovak:** Slovak Republic Genealogy
  (www.rootsweb.com/~svkwgw/)

- ✔ **Slovenia:** Genealogy and Heraldry in Slovenia
  (genealogy.ijp.si/)

- ✔ **Spanish:** Espana GenWeb
  (www.genealogia-es.com/)

- ✔ **Swedish:** Sweden Genealogy
  (www.rootsweb.com/~wgsweden/)

- ✔ **Swiss:** Swiss Genealogy on the Internet
  (www.eye.ch/swissgen/gener-e.htm)

- ✔ **UK and Ireland Genealogical Information
  Service (GENUKI):** GENUKI
  (www.genuki.org.uk) includes details on English,
  Irish, Scottish, Welsh, Channel Islanders, and Manx
  ethnic groups.

✔ **Ukrainian:** Ukraine World GenWeb
(www.rootsweb.com/~ukrwgw/index.html)

To find information on European ethnic groups, your best bet is to consult a comprehensive genealogy site. The following steps provide an example of how to conduct such a search:

1. **Go to the Genealogy Resources on the Internet site:**
   www.rootsweb.com/~jfuller/internet.html
   In the first paragraph of the home page, you see a list of resources including mailing lists, Usenet newsgroups, anonymous File Transfer Protocol (FTP), Gopher, World Wide Web, Telnet, and e-mail.

2. **Click the <u>World Wide Web</u> link.**
   This link takes you to an alphabetical listing of categories of genealogical Web sites.

3. **Click a geographic location or name of an ethnic group.**
   We're interested in finding information on individuals of Dutch ancestry, so we choose the Dutch Resources link. This brings up a page with a list of Dutch-related links.

4. **Choose a link from the list that interests you.**

Asian Resources

If your ancestors came from Asia or the Pacific Rim, your success at finding records depends greatly on the history of the ancestor's ethnic group and its recordkeeping procedures. Currently, there isn't much online genealogical information that pertains to these areas and peoples. Here's a sampling of Asian and Pacific Rim resources:

- ✔ **Australia:** AustraliaGenWeb at www.australiagenweb.org/

- ✔ **Bangladesh:** Bangladesh Genealogy at www.rootsweb.com/~bgdwgw/

- ✔ **Bhutan:** Bhutan Genealogy at www.rootsweb.com/~btnwgw/

- ✔ **China:** ChinaGenWeb at www.rootsweb.com/~chnwgw/

- ✔ **Japan:** Japan GenWeb at www.rootsweb.com/~jpnwgw/

- ✔ **Lebanon:** Lebanon GenWeb at www.rootsweb.com/~lbnwgw/

- ✔ **Melanesia:** MelanesiaGenWeb Project at www.rootsweb.com/~melwgw/

- ✔ **Philippines:** Philippines Genealogy Web Project at www.geocities.com/Heartland/Ranch/9121/

- ✔ **Polynesia:** PolynesiaGenWeb at www.rootsweb.com/~pyfwgw/

- ✔ **Saudi Arabia:** Saudi Arabia GenWeb at www.angelfire.com/tn/BattlePride/Saudi.html

- ✔ **South Korea:** South Korea GenWeb at www.rootsweb.com/~korwgw-s/

- ✔ **Syria:** Syria GenWeb at www.rootsweb.com/~syrwgw/

- ✔ **Sri Lanka:** Sri Lanka GenWeb at www.rootsweb.com/~lkawgw/

- **Taiwan:** TaiwanGenWeb at www.rootsweb.com/~twnwgw/

- **Tibet:** TibetGenWeb at www.rootsweb.com/~tibetwgw/

- **Turkey** Turkish Genealogy at www.rootsweb.com/~turwgw/

- **Vietnam:** Vietnamese Genealogy at www.rootsweb.com/~vnmwgw/

- **Various:** Genealogical Gleanings (genealogies of the rulers of India, Burma, Cambodia, Thailand, Fiji, Tonga, Hawaii, and Malaysia) at www.uq.net.au/~zzhsoszy/index.html

Chapter 9

Records Off the Beaten Path

● ●

In This Chapter

▶ Seeking information in religious group records
▶ Using photographs as research aids
▶ Checking out adoption records
▶ Digging through newspapers

● ●

Many people who are familiar with genealogy know to use census records, vital records, tax lists, and wills to find information on their ancestors. These records offer historical "snapshots" of an individual's life at particular points in time. But as a family historian, you want to know more than just when your ancestors paid their taxes — you want to know something about them as people.

For example, April once came across a photograph of her great-great-grandfather while she was looking through some pictures. He was dressed in a uniform with a sash and sword and was holding a plumed hat. As far as April knew, her great-great-grandfather hadn't been in the military, so she decided to dig for some information about the uniform.

Although part of the picture was blurry, she could make out three crosses on the uniform. One was on his sleeve, the second was on the buckle of his belt, and the third was a different kind of cross that was attached to his sash. April suspected that the symbols were Masonic. She visited a few Masonic sites on the World Wide Web and found that the crosses indicated that her great-great-grandfather had been a member of the Order of the Temple within the Masonic organization. Of course, she would never have known that he was a member of that organization had she depended solely upon the usual group of records used by genealogists.

This chapter looks at some examples of unique or hard-to-find records that can be quite useful in family history research. These records include those kept by religious groups and fraternal orders, photographs, and adoption records.

Religious Group Records

In the past, several countries required attendance at church services or the payment of taxes to an ecclesiastical authority. Although your ancestors may not have appreciated those laws at the time, the records that were kept to ensure their compliance can benefit you as a genealogist. In fact, before governments started recording births, marriages, and deaths, churches kept the official records of these events. For those places where no such laws were in effect, you can use a variety of records kept by church authorities or congregations to develop a sketch of the everyday life of your ancestor.

Some common records that you may encounter include baptismal records, parish registers, marriage records, death or burial records, tithes, welfare rolls, meeting minutes, and congregation photographs. Each type of record may include several different bits of information. For example, a baptismal record may include the date of birth, date of baptism, parents' names, and where the parents lived.

Several sites provide general information and links to all sorts of resources that pertain to specific religions and sects. Here are a few examples:

- **Anabaptist:** www.gameo.org
  The Global Anabaptist Mennonite Encyclopedia Online (GAMEO) site contains over 8,000 articles related to Amish, Mennonite, Hutterite, and Brethren in Christ congregations. You can find genealogical databases of Anabaptists at the Swiss Anabaptist Genealogical Association site at www.omii.org.

- **Baptist:** www.baptisthistory.us
  The American Baptist Historical Society site contains an overview of its collections and the services that the Society provides.

- **Catholic:** home.att.net/~Local_Catholic/
  The Local Catholic Church History & Genealogy Research Guide includes links to information on diocese and genealogy, categorized by location. If you are looking for British resources, see www.catholic-genealogy.com.

- **Church of the Brethren:** www.cob-net.org/fobg/
  The Fellowship of Brethren Genealogists Web site contains information on the organization and the current projects sponsored by the Fellowship.

- **Church of Scotland:** www.scotlandspeople.gov.uk
  The General Register Office for Scotland site features searchable indexes of births/baptisms and banns/marriages from the Old Parish Registers dating from 1553 to 1854.

✔ **Huguenot:** huguenots-france.org/english.htm

The Huguenots of France and Elsewhere site contains genealogies of several Huguenot families. For information on Huguenots in America, see Experiences of the French Huguenots in America at pages.prodigy.net/royjnagy/ressegui.htm. Also, there is a surname index at the Australian Family Tree Connections site at www.aftc.com.au/Huguenot/Hug.html.

✔ **Hutterite:** feefhs.org/hut/frg-hut.html
The Hutterite Genealogy HomePage gives an introduction and links to resources for this denomination found in Austria, Bohemia, Moravia, Slovakia, Hungary, Romania, Canada, the United States, and the Ukraine. For links to a variety of Hutterite resources, see Hutterite Reference Links at home.westman.wave.ca/~hillmans/BU/hutterite.html.

✔ **Jewish:** www.jewishgen.org
JewishGen has information about the JewishGen organization and frequently asked questions about Jewish genealogy, as well as indices of other Internet resources, including searchable databases, special interest groups, and JewishGen family home pages.

✔ **Lutheran:**
www.lutheransonline.com/lutheransonline/genealogy/
The Lutheran Roots Genealogy Exchange has a registry of researchers looking for information about Lutheran ancestors and a message board to which you can post questions about your research.

✔ **Mennonite:**
www.ristenbatt.com/genealogy/mennonit.htm
The Mennonite Research Corner features general

information about Mennonites and a collection of online resources for researchers. For a Canadian perspective, visit the Mennonite Genealogy Data Index at www.mennonites.ca.

✔ **Methodist:**
www.geocities.com/Vienna/Choir/1824/methodistresearch.html
Researching Your Methodist Ancestors contains some general advice on getting started with your research and links to some online resources.

✔ **Moravian Church:** www.enter.net/~smschlack/
The Moravian Church Genealogy Links page features links to articles on the history of the church, as well as links to genealogical resources.

✔ **Quaker:** www.rootsweb.com/~quakers
The Quaker Corner contains a query board, a list of research resources, and links to other Quaker pages on the World Wide Web.

✔ **Seventh-day Adventist:**
www.andrews.edu/library/car/
The Center for Adventist Research at Andrews University site contains information on the University's archives and research center and databases including a periodical index, obituary index, bibliographies, and photographs.

A few church organizations have online descriptions of their archives' holdings:

✔ Archives of Brethren in Christ Church:
www.messiah.edu/archives/archives_bic.html

- ✔ Center for Mennonite Brethren Studies in Fresno, California: www.fresno.edu/library/cmbs/genealogical_resources.asp

- ✔ Concordia Historical Institute Department of Archives and History (Lutheran): chi.lcms.org

- ✔ Catholic Archives of Texas: www.onr.com/user/cat

- ✔ Friends University Library (Quaker): www.friends.edu/library/SpecialCollections/default.asp

- ✔ General Commission on Archives and History for the United Methodist Church: www.gcah.org/index.htm

- ✔ Greek Orthodox Archdiocese of America Department of Archives: www.goarch.org/goa/departments/archives/

- ✔ Moravian Archives: moravianchurcharchives.org

- ✔ United Church of Canada Archives: unitedchurcharchives.vicu.utoronto.ca

If you're curious about what types of information for religious groups are available on the Internet, here are a few examples:

- ✔ **Baptism Records:** You can find a list of those baptized in the Wesleyan Methodist Baptismal Register at

freepages.genealogy.rootsweb.com/~wjmartin/wm-index.htm

- ✔ **Cemetery Records:** The Quaker Burying Ground Cemetery, Galesville, Anne Arundel County, Maryland, site is

www.interment.net/data/us/md/anne_arundel/quaker.htm

It's part of the Cemetery Records Online site, provides transcribed burial information, including the person's name and dates of birth and death, as well as some other information. (See Figure 9-1.)

- ✔ **Marriage Records:** The Moravian Church, Lititz Marriages 1742–1800 page contains a list of marriage dates along with the names of the bride and groom performed in the church located in Lancaster County, Pennsylvania. Here's where you find it:

searches1.rootsweb.com/usgenweb/archives/pa/lancaster/church/moravianlititz.txt

- ✔ **Parish Directories:** The Holy Trinity Church, Boston, Massachusetts, site has a searchable 1895 parish directory, an ongoing project to identify and post information about church members who served in the Civil War, and a list of church members who served in World War I. Here's the URL:

homepages.rootsweb.com/~mvreid/bgrc/htc.html

Of course, in addition to some sites that focus specifically on one type of record, you may run across sites like the Genline Project (www.genline.com), which collects digitized copies of all sorts of records pertaining to a particular church. The goal of the Genline Project is to place all digital copies of Swedish church records online.

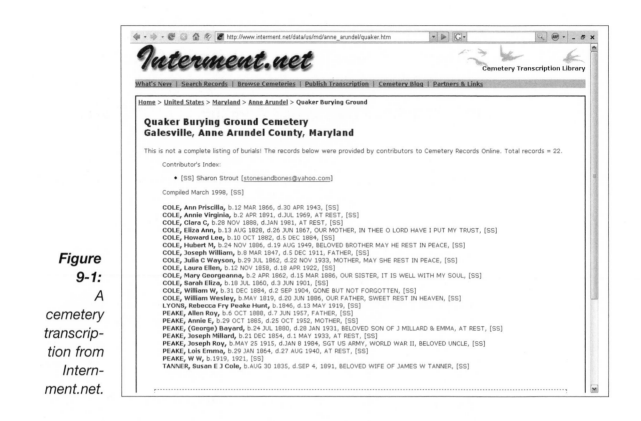

Figure 9-1: A cemetery transcription from Interment.net.

Fraternal Orders and Service Clubs

Were any of your ancestors members of fraternal orders or service clubs? Many such organizations are out there, and chances are, you have at least one ancestor who was a member of an order or club. Although most of the more commonly known organizations are for men, affiliated organizations for women exist, too. Here are a few general information sites on fraternal orders and service clubs:

✔ **American Legion:** www.legion.org

✔ **Ancient and Mystical Order Rosae Crucis:** www.amorc.org

✔ **Ancient Order of Hibernians in America:** www.aoh.com

- **Catholic Knights:**
  www.catholicknights.org/home/default.aspx

- **DeMolay International:**
  www.demolay.org/home/index.shtml

- **Eagles (Fraternal Order of Eagles):**
  www.foe.com

- **Elks (Benevolent Protective Order of the Elks):**
  www.elks.org

- **Freemasonry:** Freemasonry.org
  (www.freemasonry.org) and A Page About
  Freemasonry (web.mit.edu/dryfoo/www/Masons/
  index.html)

- **Improved Order of Red Men:** www.redmen.org

- **Job's Daughters (International Order of Job's
  Daughters):** www.iojd.org

- **Kiwanis International:** www.kiwanis.org

- **Knights of Columbus:** www.kofc.org/un/index.cfm

- **Lions Clubs:** LionNet (www.lionnet.com)

- **Military Order of the Loyal Legion of the
  United States:** www.suvcw.org/mollus/mollus.htm

- **Modern Woodmen of America:** www.modern-
  woodmen.org/Public

- **Moose International:**
  www.mooseintl.org/public/default.asp

- **Odd Fellows (Independent Order of Odd
  Fellows):** www.ioof.org

- **Optimist International:** www.optimist.org

- **Order of the Eastern Star (Grand Chapter Order of the Eastern Star):** www.easternstar.org

- **Orioles (Fraternal Order of Orioles):** www.fraternalorderorioles.homestead.com

- **Police (Fraternal Order of Police):** www.grandlodgefop.org

- **Rainbow for Girls (International Order of the Rainbow for Girls):** www.iorg.org

- **Rebekahs:** www.ioof.org/rebekahs.htm

- **Rotary International:** www.rotary.org

- **Shriners (The Shrine of North America):** www.shriners.com

- **Veterans of Foreign Wars of the United States:** www.vfw.org

Most of the online sites related to fraternal orders provide historical information about the clubs and current membership rules. Although the sites may not provide you with actual records (membership lists and meeting minutes), they do give you an overview of what the club is about and an idea of what your ancestor did as a member. The sites also provide you with the names and addresses of local chapters — you can contact them to see if they have original resources available for public use or if they can send you copies of anything pertaining to your ancestor.

An important thing to note is that having information about a fraternal order doesn't necessarily make a particular site the organization's *official* site. This is particularly true for international organizations. You may find Web pages for different chapters of a particular club in several different countries, and although each site may have some general club information in common, they are likely to have varying types of information specific to that chapter of the organization.

If you're looking for sites containing information on fraternal organizations, you may want to try some of the comprehensive genealogy sites. If you can't find sufficient information there, try one of the general Internet search engines. To find information on fraternal orders through a general Internet search engine, try this:

1. **Open your Web browser and go to the AltaVista search engine page (www.altavista.com) or substitute the address of your favorite search engine.**

2. **Type the name of a fraternal organization in the Search box and click Find.**
   We're interested in finding information about the Knights of Columbus, so we type that phrase in the Search box.

3. **Click a link that interests you from the search results page.**
   After you click Search, you see a page with the results of your search. Each result has the site's title and a brief abstract taken directly from the page. You can use these to determine whether the site contains information that you're interested in before visiting it.

A Photo Is Worth a Thousand Words

In Chapter 2, we discuss the value of photographs in your genealogical research. But a lot of us don't have photographs of our family beyond two or three generations, though it sure would be great to find at least an electronic copy of a picture of your great-great-grandfathers. Actually, a picture of your great-great-grandfather may exist. Another researcher may have posted it on a personal site or the photograph may be part of a collection belonging to a certain organization. You may also be interested in pictures of places where your ancestors lived. Being able to describe how a certain town, estate, or farm looked at the time your ancestor lived there adds color to your family history.

You can find various types of photographic sites on the Internet that can assist you with your research. Some of these sites explain the photographic process and the many types of photographs that have been used throughout history, some sites contain collections of photographs from a certain geographic area or time period in history, and some sites contain photographs of the ancestors of a particular family. Here are some examples:

- ✔ **General Information:** City Gallery has a brief explanation of the types of photography used during the nineteenth century, a photography query page, and a gallery of photographs from one studio of the period. (See Figure 9-2.) The Web site is www.city-gallery.com/learning.

- ✔ **Photograph Collections:**
  You can find images of the American West and Civil War at
  www.treasurenet.com/images/

  American Memory: Photographs, Prints, and Drawings:
  memory.loc.gov/cgi-bin/query/S?ammem/collections:@field(FLD003+@band(origf+Photograph)):heading=Original+Format%3a+Photos+&+Prints

Florida Photographic Collection:
www.floridamemory.com/PhotographicCollection

✔ **Photograph Identification:**
The DeadFred Genealogy Photo Archive contains over 30,000 photographs at www.deadfred.com

Each photograph includes descriptive information including where the photograph was taken, the names of the subjects, and an approximate time frame (see Figure 9-3).

✔ **Personal Photographs:**
The Harrison Genealogy Repository site is an example of a personal Web site with a photo gallery: freepages.genealogy.rootsweb.com/~harrisonrep/ Photos/ harrphot.htm

The gallery includes the likenesses of several famous Harrisons, including Benjamin Harrison V, President William Henry Harrison, and President Benjamin Harrison.

To find photographic sites, you may want to visit one of the comprehensive genealogy sites or general Internet search engines.

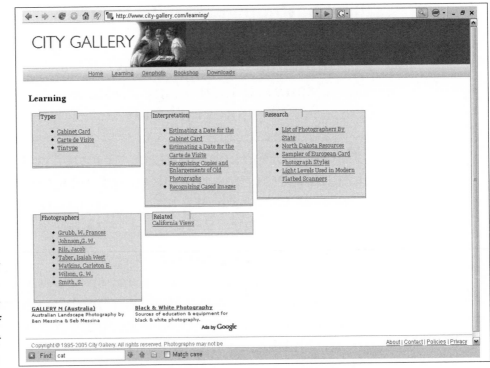

Figure 9-2:
Learn about photographic methods of the past at City Gallery.

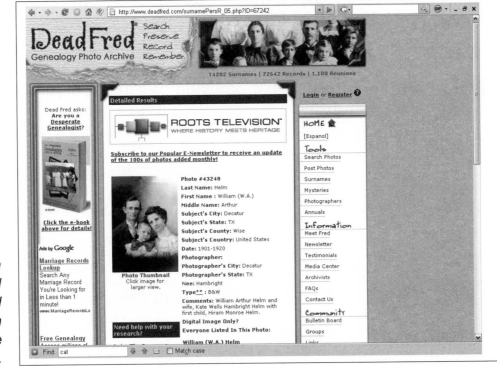

Figure 9-3:
An entry on the Dead Fred photograph archive site.

Adoption Records

Adoption records are of interest to a lot of genealogists, including those who were adopted themselves, those who gave up children for adoption, and those who have ancestors who were adopted.

If you fall into the first two groups (you were adopted or gave up a child for adoption), some online resources may help you find members of your birth family. The online resources include registries, reference materials, advice and discussion groups, and information on legislation pertaining to adoption. Registries enable you to post information about yourself and your adoption with the hope that a member of your birth family may see the posting and contact you. (Likewise, if you're the birth parent of an adoptee, you can post a message with the hope that the adoptee sees it and responds.)

Unfortunately, you won't find online sites that contain actual adoption records — for legal reasons, generally. Instead, you need to rely on registries and other resources that point you toward more substantial information about adoption. If you have a successful reunion with your birth parent(s) by registering with an online site, with any luck, you can obtain information about their parents, grandparents, and so on — so you know where to begin your genealogical pursuit of that family line.

Here are some online sites that have adoption registries, reference materials, advice and discussions, and/or legislative information:

- **Adoptees Internet Mailing List:** www.aiml.org

- **AdoptioNetwork:** www.adoption.org

- **About.com:** genealogy.about.com/od/adoption/index.htm

If you're interested in adoption records because you have ancestors who were adopted, you may have a more difficult time finding information. We have yet to discover any sites specifically designed to aid in research for adopted ancestors. In fact, you may have to rely on the regular genealogical resources — particularly query pages and discussion groups — and the kindness and knowledge of other researchers to find information about your adopted ancestors.

If you're searching for general types of adoption resources, using a general Internet directory like Yahoo! may be the best course of action. To find resources using Yahoo!, try this:

1. **Open your Web browser and go to Yahoo! at** dir.yahoo.com.

2. **Click the <u>Society And Culture</u> link, and click the <u>Families</u> link.**
   A second way to find items in Yahoo! (this may be a lot faster): You can type a search term in the box near the top of the screen and have Yahoo! search for the topic. For example, you can type **Adoption** in the box and click Search, which produces a results page that has links to take you directly to the appropriate page in Yahoo! containing adoption links.

3. **Under the Families category, click the <u>Adoption</u> link.**
   This takes you directly to the adoption page — even though it's a couple of levels down in the directory's hierarchy.

4. **Click a link to another subdirectory in Yahoo! or a link to an Internet site containing**

information that interests you.

Descriptions follow most of the links in Yahoo! to give you an idea of what kind of information is on the sites. Figure 9-4 shows an example of a Yahoo! page.

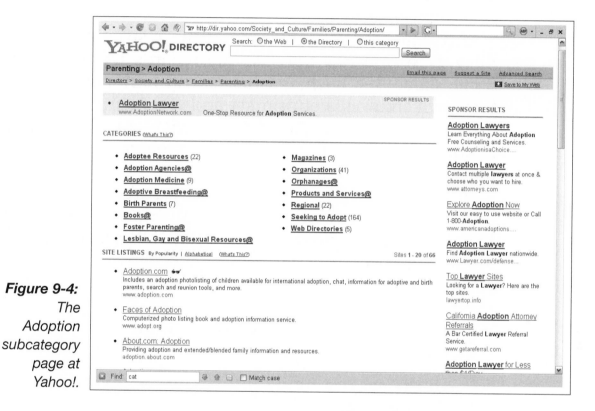

Figure 9-4:
The Adoption subcategory page at Yahoo!.

Preparing to Be Schooled

Beyond census records, relatively few records chronicle the early years of an individual. One type of resource that can help fill in the gaps are educational records. These records can take a number of forms including enrollment records, transcripts, yearbooks, directories, and fraternity and sorority records.

The first step is to find out what educational institution

your ancestor attended. If you are looking for an elementary or secondary school, you might try looking at the US-GenWeb (www.usgenweb.org) page for the county where your ancestor lived to see if there is information on the location of schools. If the USGenWeb page doesn't have information, try to find the Web site of the local historical or genealogical society.

After you discover the name of the institution, the next thing is to find out who has the records for that school. Some schools — such as colleges and universities — have their own archives. For primary and secondary schools, you may need to contact the school district — or if the school no longer exists, you need to find out where the records for that school were transferred.

To see if a college or university has an archive, look at the list of archives at the Repositories of Primary Sources site (www.uidaho.edu/special-collections/Other.Repositories .html). If you are not sure where the records are located, you can use WorldCat at www.worldcat.org.

1. **Use your Web browser to pull up www.worldcat.org.**

2. **In the search field, enter your criteria and then click Search.**
   In this example, we search for Harvard enrollment records.

3. **Choose a result that looks promising.**
   Figure 9-5 shows the results of our WorldCat search.

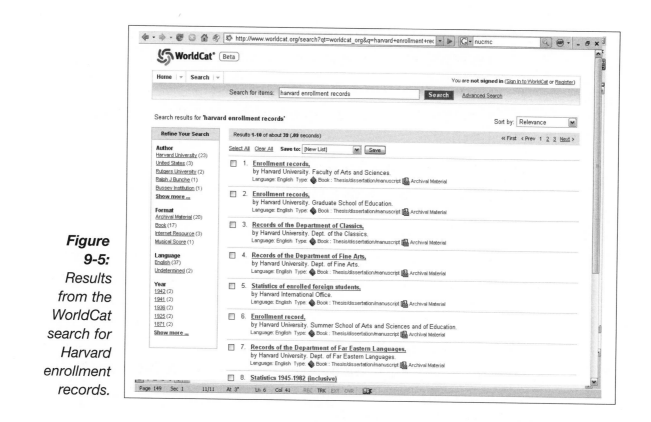

Figure 9-5:
Results from the WorldCat search for Harvard enrollment records.

Turning to Bible Records

Bible records are a great source of birth, death, and marriage information for time periods before vital records were required. As most of these are held by private individuals, it is sometimes very difficult to locate these records. Recognizing the importance of these records, groups have created Web sites to share the information contained within the Bibles. Here are a few sites worth visiting:

✔ **Ancestor Hunt Family Bible Records:**
www.ancestorhunt.com/family_bible_records.htm

✔ **Bible Records Online:** www.biblerecords.com

- **Family Bible Records in Onondaga County:**
  www.rootsweb.com/~nyononda/BIBLE.HTM

- **Maine Family Bible Archives:**
  www.rootsweb.com/~meandrhs/taylor/bible/maine.html

- **The Bible Archives:**
  www.geocities.com/Heartland/Fields/2403/

Similar to looking for educational records, you can also find Bible records in some archives. You can use WorldCat (www.worldcat.org) to see what is available in different institutions. For details on how to use WorldCat, see the previous section. Some subscription sites might also have Bible records. For example, Ancestry.com (www.ancestry.com) has Bible records from New York, Tennessee, Missouri, Virginia, as well as a collection called Old Southern Bible Records.

Nosing through Newspapers Records

A lot of the day-to-day details of your ancestor's life can be filled in by reading local newspapers. You can find obituaries, marriage announcements, social activities, and tax assessments information. Also, you can find background information on the locality that they lived in, so that you gain a better perspective of your ancestor's life.

There has been a lot of effort to digitize newspapers over the last couple of years. Ancestry.com (www.ancestry.com) has partnered with NewspaperArchive.com (www.newspaperarchive.com) to offer a collection of more than 1,000 newspaper databases online. The newspapers featured in the collection are digitized images that have been indexed by optical character recognition (OCR) — a software method where letters within an image are translated into characters (typically letters of the alphabet) that a computer can read. Each page of the newspaper is searchable. When a search result is found, the text is highlighted on the page. The optical character recognition system does not always know the context of the words on the page — so, the system sometimes generates false positive search results. Figure 9-6 shows the interface for the newspaper collection at Ancestry.com.

WorldVitalRecords.com (www.worldvitalrecords.com) also has select newspapers from the NewspaperArchive.com site. In addition, it also has newspapers from the SmallTownPapers.com site.

Figure 9-6: The Decatur Daily Review newspaper image at Ancestry.com.

Several large newspapers have also begun to place their back issues online — often with a subscription service. For example, you can find the Los Angeles Times back to 1881 online at pqasb.pqarchiver.com/latimes/advancedsearch.html, the Washington Post from 1877 at pqasb.pqarchiver.com/washingtonpost/search.html, and the Chicago Tribune from 1849 at pqasb.pqarchiver.com/chicagotribune/advancedsearch.html.

Chapter 10

Fitting into Your Genes: Molecular Genealogy

It sounds like something right out of a crime scene investigation: You swab your cheek, send the sample off to a lab, the results are analyzed, and presto! You find the identity of that long-lost ancestor. Although the science behind molecular genealogy traces its roots back to identifying individuals from crime scenes, it is not advanced to the point where you can simply take the test and watch your entire genealogy unfold.

Although it is just one of many tools to use in documenting your research, *deoxyribonucleic acid* (DNA) testing holds great potential for the future of genealogy. You may be familiar with the use of DNA testing in identifying the remains of Nicholas, the last Czar of Russia, and his fam-

347

ily; the debate about the last resting place of Christopher Columbus; or the true fate of Jesse James. The methods used in these investigations are the same methods that you can use to compliment your documentary research.

In this chapter, we provide an overview of how DNA testing works, where you can order tests, and what to do with the information that you discover during the testing process.

A Friendly Word of Caution

Before you embark into the world of molecular genealogy, we want you to consider two things. First of all, by taking a DNA test, you might find out something that you would rather not know. For example, some people have discovered that they are not biologically related to the family from which they've always claimed descent. Sometimes this occurs due to a "non-paternal event" where the biological father was not the person listed on the birth record (this may have occurred in the immediate family, or sometime in past generations). Others have discovered that they may not have the racial or ethnic composition that they have always identified themselves with. While both of these situations are rare, you need to be prepared just in case it happens to you or to someone you invite to participate in a study.

The second thing to remember is that molecular genealogy is a science — but not an absolute one. When looking at DNA test results, you are looking at the *probability* that something is true. (Probability is the likelihood that a specific fact or outcome will occur.) Nothing is ever 100 percent certain and, although it is rare, sometimes mistakes are made by the testing facility, or new research is discovered that changes the way that a test result is viewed. DNA testing for genealogy is still in its infancy and is going through some growing pains. As long as you can adapt to change and accept new technology, you'll be just fine in the world of DNA genealogy.

Delving into DNA

Some people might think that we are attempting the impossible — explaining how DNA testing works in one mere chapter of this book. But in this day and age, DNA testing for genealogical research is a very real resource that is becoming more and more widespread. Knowing this, we feel it is our duty to at least give you a basic introduction to genetic research so you can use all technological means available to you when digging for information on your ancestors. And first things first: You need an understanding of the terminology and how the testing process works to help you interpret your test results. If you find that our elementary explanations just whet your appetite, you can always get a healthy dose on the subject with *Genetics For Dummies* by Tara Rodden Robinson (Wiley Publishing).

What can molecular genealogy do for you?

Have you ever thought about the applications of genetic testing in genealogical research? It's a brave new world in which some of your family riddles may be answered and the brick walls in your research could be torn down. Molecular genealogy offers hope in many research realms, not the least of which are

- Determining if two people are related when one or both were adopted

- Identifying whether two people are descended from the same ancestor

- Discovering whether you are related to others with the same surname

- Proving or disproving your family tree research

- Providing clues about your ethnic origin

Getting down to bases

When we decided to conduct a molecular genealogy study on the surname Helm, we completed some basic research on genetics. While looking at the many resources available that describe *deoxyribonucleic acid,* or DNA, we found one in particular contained a model that helped us understand the basics better — it was a publication called "DNA Program Kit" published jointly by the National Genome Research Institute, United States Department of Energy, and the Science Museum of Minnesota. You can find this publication online at www.genome.gov/DNADay/DNA_Programming_Kit_Manual.pdf. We use a modified version of that model to help you understand the components of DNA that are used in molecular genealogy.

Being a family historian, you most likely have taken a research trip to a particular town to find the burial location for an ancestor. When you reached that town, your first stop was the local library. Entering the library, you quickly made your way to the reference room. You leafed through the reference room collection, looking for a cemetery index for that area. Finding an index, you located the chapter containing a list of gravestones for the cemetery where your ancestor is buried. Thumbing through the chapter, you find your ancestor's name, which is typed with some combination of 26 letters (assuming that there are no special characters and the book is in English).

You can think about the components of DNA like the library example mentioned above (see Figure 10-1 for a model of the components of DNA). The basic building blocks of humans are *cells* that function like little towns. Within each cell is a *nucleus,* the structure that contains all of the DNA. This nucleus acts as the library for the cell. Within the nucleus is the *genome.* The genome is the complete set of instructions for how the cell will operate — you can think of it as the reference book collection of the library.

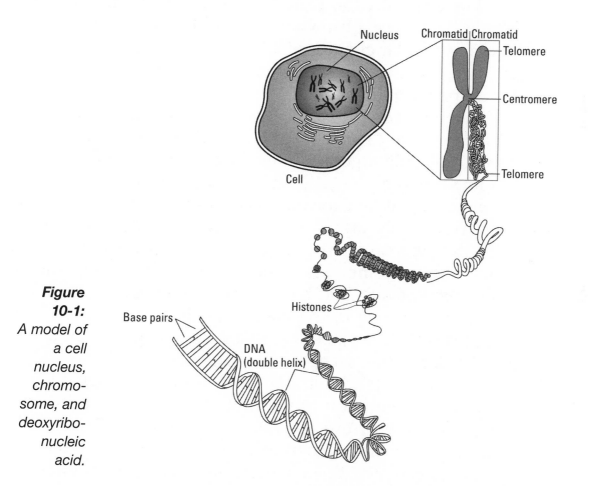

Figure 10-1:
A model of a cell nucleus, chromosome, and deoxyribonucleic acid.

Courtesy of the National Human Genome Research Institute

The human genome is composed of 23 pairs of *chromosomes.* A chromosome is the container that holds the strands of DNA. Each type of chromosome has a different set of instructions and serves a different purpose, much like a reference collection has several types of reference books. Particular sections of a chromosome are called *genes*. Genes contain specific sequences of information that determine a particular inheritable characteristic of a human. So, if chromosomes are the reference book, genes are the chapters within the book.

A particular gene can come in different forms called *alleles*. For example, the gene for eye color might come in a blue eye allele or a brown eye allele. To use our book analogy, a particular chapter of a book can be laid out in different ways. Alleles would be different layouts that a particular chapter could have.

Genes are composed of *bases*, also called *nucleotides*, which form the "rungs" of the DNA "ladder" that hold the DNA molecule together. There are four types of bases, including adenine (A), guanine (G), cytosine (C), and thymine (T). When forming the rungs of the DNA molecule, bases only attach in one way. Adenine always pairs with thymine on the opposite strand and guanine always pairs with cytosine. The attachment of bases together is called *base pairing*. The bases are the language of DNA. You read the sequence of the base pairs to determine the coding of the allele — just like reading the sequence of letters in a book forms a recognizable sentence.

Please understand that our DNA-library analogy is a very simplistic explanation of the molecular parts that are considered in genetic testing. DNA plays a much more complicated role in genetics than what we just covered. However, for the purpose of this chapter, our basic presentation on genetic structure should be sufficient for understanding the broader implications in DNA testing for molecular genealogy.

Selecting the Right Test for You

After you gain a basic understanding of molecular structure, you may find your curiosity piqued — are you ready to jump right in and gather DNA samples willy-nilly? Slow down a little! There's more to learn so that you don't lose time and momentum by submitting your swabs for the wrong types of tests.

There are three types of tests that have demonstrated usefulness in genealogical research:

- ✔ **Y chromosome DNA testing:** Humans have 23 pairs of chromosomes. Of these 23, males and females have 22 pairs that are in common and one pair that is not in common. In that one pair, males have one X and one Y chromosome, where females have two X chromosomes. The Y chromosome DNA test explores the Y chromosome in this uncommon pair of chromosomes. As you might suspect at this point, this particular test is only available for men because females do not carry the Y chromosome. However, just because you — the reader — might be female, don't fail to read the following section on Y chromosome DNA testing. You can always have a male relative (such as your father, brother, uncle, or cousin) take this test for you in order to discover the hidden secrets in your familial Y DNA.

- ✔ **Mitochondrial DNA testing:** The mitochondrion is considered by some to be the "power plant" of the cell. (Remember, the cell is the basic building block of the human body.) It sits outside the nucleus of the cell and it contains its own distinct genome — that means its genome is separate from the genome found within the nucleus of the cell. This distinct genome is known as mtDNA in genetic testing. The mtDNA is inherited only from the female parent, is passed to all offspring (male and female), and mutates (or changes) at a slow rate over generations. All of these aspects of the mtDNA make it good for identifying genetic relationships over hundreds of generations.

✔ **Autosomal DNA testing:** Also called admixture or bio-geographical tests, Autosomal DNA consists of 22 pairs of chromosomes that are non-sex specific found in the cell nucleus — this means that they don't contain the X or Y chromosomes. Autosomal DNA is found in males and females, and is the part of the DNA responsible for characteristics such as height and eye color. This DNA is inherited from both parents.

Given the complexity of molecular research, we expect the tests to be complicated as well. Hence, each test warrants its own attention. In the next sections, we explore them in a little more depth.

Y chromosome DNA testing

In the previous section, we introduced the concept that the Y chromosome DNA test examines the Y chromosome that men receive from their male ancestors. The Y chromosome is part of the one chromosomal pair that is not common between males and females; in males, the pair has an X and a Y chromosome, whereas in females, the pair has two X chromosomes. We also mentioned that this test is only available for men (although women can participate in Y chromosome projects by using a father, brother, or male cousin as a proxy). Now it's time to get into the details of the test.

"Junk" DNA is worth something

When scientists began studying chromosomes, they discovered that not all of the base pairs were used as instructions for the cell. These *non-coding regions,* sometimes referred to as "junk" DNA because they seem to just be hanging around without helping guide the cell to fulfill its larger purpose, contain alleles that differ from person to person. This means that the junk DNA has characteristics that distinguish individuals from each other. Scientists soon began to use these alleles to identify individuals, especially in criminal investigations.

As more research was done on the Y chromosome, scientists found that the non-coding regions could be used to define not only individual characteristics but characteristics of larger populations into which individuals with these characteristics fit. In essence, they discovered how to determine what population a particular human was a member of by using the non-coding regions of the DNA. They also discovered that the Y chromosome changes (or mutates) very little (or not at all) between fathers and sons. As the Y chromosome is only passed from father to son, it is only useful for tracing the direct paternal line of an individual's ancestry (as illustrated by Figure 10-2).

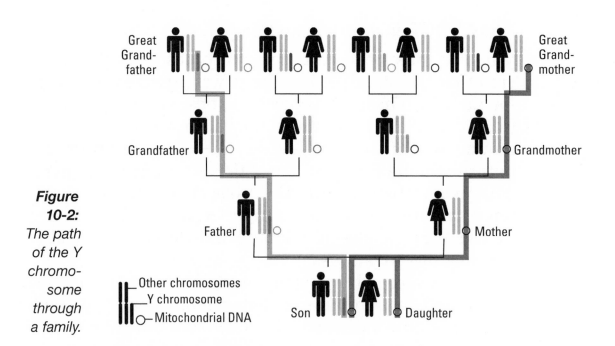

Figure 10-2:
The path of the Y chromosome through a family.

Grandfather   Grandmother

Father   Mother

Other chromosomes
Y chromosome
Mitochondrial DNA

Son   Daughter

The testing process

The process of testing the Y chromosome starts with a man swabbing the inside of his cheek with a sample collection device that usually looks something like a Q-Tip cotton swab. The swab collects cheek cells, which serve as the source for the DNA. After the laboratory receives the swab, the DNA is extracted using a process called polymerase chain reaction (PCR). This process makes thousands of copies of the DNA so that it can be analyzed.

After the copies are made, sequences of DNA at specific locations on the chromosome are analyzed. These sequences are called *markers* and the location of the markers on the chromosome is called the *locus* (or plural *loci*). The markers are read by the sequence of the bases. (Remember, as we mentioned in the "Getting down to bases" section earlier in this chapter, the bases are abbreviated A, G, C, and T). So, the sequence for the bases shown in Figure 10-3 would be the following:

Each marker is given a name that usually begins with *DYS* — short for DNA Y Chromosome Segment. When analyzing the markers, laboratory technicians look for the number of times that a segment of bases (usually three to five bases long) repeat. These segments of repeating bases are called *Short Tandem Repeat* polymorphisms (STRs).

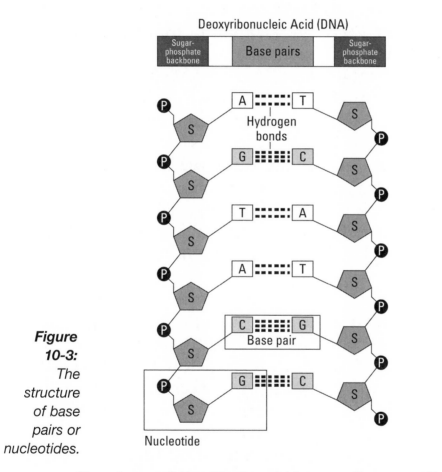

Figure 10-3: *The structure of base pairs or nucleotides.*

Courtesy of the National Human Genome Research Institute

Is your head spinning yet from all of the definitions that we just threw at you? Think about the book analogy to

357

recap what we just said in terms that are hopefully easier to follow. Think of this book as the Y Chromosome and this chapter as a gene on the chromosome. This page would be the locus where the segment is located — that is easily found by using the page number. The DNA Y Chromosome Segment is the following sentence:

I like this book VERY VERY VERY much.

The Short Tandem Repeat is the phrase "VERY VERY VERY" in the sentence — a set of letters that repeat.

Now see if you can make sense of a real sequence of bases for the marker DYS393, keeping in mind you can refer to our book example if needed:

gtggtcttctacttgtgtcaatac AGAT AGAT AGAT AGAT AGAT AGAT AGAT AGAT AGAT AGAT AGAT AGAT AGAT AGAT AGAT atgtatgtcttttctatgagacatacctcatttttt-gacttgagttc

To make it easier for you to see, we capitalized the letters and inserted spaces between the base segments composing the STR (which are AGAT). If you count the number of times the bases AGAT repeat, you'll find that the number of repeats for DYS393 for this individual is 15.

Comparing the results

After the number of repeats within a marker is calculated, we can compare the results of that marker plus a few other markers to see if two or more individuals are related. Most labs try to compare at least 12 markers. Table 10-1 shows a comparison between the markers of four individuals.

Table 10-1   A Comparison of 12 Markers for Four Individuals

ID	D	D	D	D	*D*	*D*	D	D	*D*	D	D	D
	Y	Y	Y	Y	Y	Y	Y	Y	Y	Y	Y	Y

	S	S	S	S	S	S	S	S	S	S	S	S
	3	3	1	3	3	3	4	3	4	3	3	3
	9	9	9	9	8	8	2	8	3	8	9	8
	3	0	/	1	5	5	6	8	9	9	2	9
				3	a	b					-	-
				9							1	2
				4								
A	13	25	14	11	11	11	12	12	13	13	13	29
B	13	25	14	11	11	11	12	12	12	13	13	29
C	13	25	14	11	11	11	12	12	12	13	13	29
D	13	25	14	11	11	11	12	12	12	13	13	29
Modal	13	25	14	11	11	11	12	12	12	13	13	29

If you compare the results between individuals A and B in Table 10-1, you will see that they have the same number of repeats in 11 of the 12 markers. Only at DYS439 is there a difference in the number of repeats, commonly called a *mutation.* Based on this information, we would say that there is a genetic distance of one between these two individuals. At 12 markers, a genetic distance of one would indicate that these two individuals are probably related — however, testing more markers would certainly give a better indication of how closely they may be related. There is a higher probability that individuals B, C, and D are related, as they match on all 12 markers.

The results of a set of markers for an individual are called a *haplotype.* So, in the preceding chart, the haplotype for individual A is DYS393 – 13, DYS390 – 25, DYS19/394 – 14, DYS391 – 11, DYS385a – 11, DYS395b – 11, DYS426 – 12, DYS388 – 12, DYS439 – 13, DYS389-1 – 13,

DYS392 – 13, DYS 389-2 – 29.

After you have haplotype results for an individual, it is important to get results from relatives of that individual — more specifically, it's important to get the haplotype results for relatives whose relationships can be documented by primary sources, including those in the extended family. These results help confirm the results of individual A and establish an overall specific haplotype for the family. For example, say that all of the individuals in Table 10-1 above are related and the fact is well documented with primary sources. After analyzing the results, a *modal haplotype* can be calculated by looking at the number of repeats that have the highest occurrence for each marker. As all of the results are the same for 11 out of 12 markers, the modal values for these are the same as the number of repeats for that marker. That only leaves one marker to calculate — DYS439. The results for DYS439 include one 13 and four 12s. That makes the modal value for that marker 12 — as it appears the most. So, the row marked "Modal" in Table 10-1 shows the haplotype for Individual A's family.

The modal haplotype for a family can be used to compare that family to other families with the same surname to determine the probability that the two families are related. A good way to see these relationships is to join a surname DNA project — we talk about how to find these in the section, "Helpful DNA Sites," later in this chapter.

Assessing the probability of a relationship

After the test is taken and the results compared, it's time to figure out what the probability is that two individuals are related. This probability is calculated by determining how often a change might occur to a marker over time. Fortunately, the testing companies calculate this for you and typically give you a tool (in the form of an online chart or written instructions) to compare two results.

Reviewing the data in Table 10-1, say that you want to determine how closely related Individual A may be to Individual B. To do this, you need to identify the *Time to Most Recent Common Ancestor* (TMRCA) for the two individuals. The Time to Most Recent Common Ancestor is pretty much what it sounds like — a calculation to determine when two individuals may have shared the same ancestor. As you'll see from this example, the calculation is not extremely precise, but it is enough to point you in the right direction as you begin looking for supporting documentation. By the way, if you want a more in-depth explanation of how TMRCA works, see the article by Bruce Walsh at nitro.biosci.arizona.edu/ftdna/TMRCA.html.

The easiest way to determine the TMRCA between two individuals is to use an online utility. If your testing company doesn't have one — or you are comparing results from more than one testing company — you can use the Y-Utility: Y-DNA Comparison Utility at www.mymcgee.com/tools/yutility. html. There are a lot of options with this utility, so we'll take it a step at a time.

1. **Point your Web browser to the Y-Utility Web site.**
   The page has a number of options and ways of displaying the data. We'll adjust some of these to make it easier to see the results.

2. **Ensure the Marker table includes those markers necessary for the calculation.**
   In the table at the top of the screen, there are 100 markers. In this example, you'll be working with the first thirteen markers from the left. Make sure that the following markers are checked "Exists" and "Enable" — DYS393, DYS390, DYS19/394, DYS391, DYS385a, DYS395b, DYS426, DYS388,

DYS439, DYS389-1, DYS392, and DYS 389-2. Be sure that DYS19b is not checked. The rest of the markers you can leave checked.

3. **Check the options that will provide the appropriate calculation.**
You are only looking for the TMRCA, so deselect the check boxes next to Ysearch, SMGF, Ybase, Yhrd, and Genetic Distance. Under the General Setup column, deselect the Create Modal Haplotype check box.

4. **Enter the marker values into the field marked Paste Haplotype Rows Here.**
Make sure that you separate the values with a space. For example, like this:

```
A 13 25 14 11 11 11 12 12 13 13 13 29
B 13 25 14 11 11 11 12 12 12 13 13 29
```

5. **Click Execute.**
A new browser window appears with the calculation. In this example, the Time to Most Recent Common Ancestor between individuals A and B is estimated at 1,110 years (the box with the TMRCA contains a blue background).

Figure 10-4 shows the estimated TMRCA for individuals A and B. Essentially, the results show that there is a 50 percent probability that individuals A and B shared a common ancestor within the past 1,110 years. So, as you can see, just testing on 12 markers really doesn't give you conclusive evidence of how closely two people are related. However, it can certainly indicate that two individuals are not related — especially if there are more than two markers out of twelve that do not match.

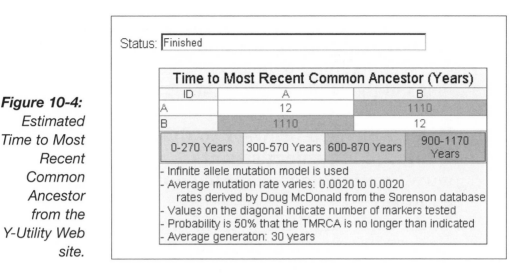

Status: Finished

Time to Most Recent Common Ancestor (Years)		
ID	A	B
A	12	1110
B	1110	12

0-270 Years	300-570 Years	600-870 Years	900-1170 Years

- Infinite allele mutation model is used
- Average mutation rate varies: 0.0020 to 0.0020
  rates derived by Doug McDonald from the Sorenson database
- Values on the diagonal indicate number of markers tested
- Probability is 50% that the TMRCA is no longer than indicated
- Average generaton: 30 years

Figure 10-4:
Estimated Time to Most Recent Common Ancestor from the Y-Utility Web site.

Haplogroups

We mentioned earlier in this chapter that haplotypes are a set of results of markers for a particular individual. When several similar haplotypes are categorized together, they compose a *haplogroup*. Haplogroups are useful for deep ancestry research (that is, research that is further back than the advent of surnames) and for placing a geographical context around the possible origin of the individuals within the haplogroup.

Y chromosome haplogroups are categorized by the letters A through R by the Y Chromosome Consortium (YCC). (The Y Chromosome Consortium is a group that studies and publishes findings about the Y chromosome. You can find out more about it at ycc.biosci.arizona.edu/.) These letter designations are based on mutations of certain locations of the Y chromosome. For instance, if an individual has a mutation at the M89 loci, they fall into a haplogroup between F and J. If the individual has a mutation at both the M89 and M170 loci, they are classified in the I haplogroup.

When you submit a sample to a DNA testing company,

the results you receive usually include your haplogroup. You can then take that haplogroup and go to the National Geographic Genographic Project page to learn more about the origins of the haplogroup — here's how:

1. **Point your Web browser to the National Geographic project site at www3.nationalgeographic.com/genographic/index.html.**
   At the top of the blue portion of the page are links to the different sections of the site including <u>Main Menu</u>, <u>Genetics Overview</u>, <u>Atlas of the Human Journey</u>, and <u>Your Genetic Journey</u>.

2. **Click on the <u>Atlas of the Human Journey</u> link.**
   This page contains a timeline followed by an introductory paragraph about the Atlas. Beneath the introduction in the black area are two buttons — <u>Genetic Markers</u> and <u>Journey Highlights</u>.

3. **Select <u>Genetic Markers</u>.**
   In the right column is a listing of haplogroups for both mitochondrial and Y chromosome. Scroll down to the Y chromosome area.

4. **Click on the Y chromosome haplogroup that interests you.**
   We are interested in Haplogroup I. So, we click on the link titled <u>Y chromosome Haplogroup I</u>.

Figure 10-5 shows a map of the migration path of Haplogroup I and some text describing attributes of the haplogroup. The haplogroup migrated from the Middle East into the Balkans and later into central Europe.

Haplogroups can also be used to show the genetic distribution of individuals in a particular geographic area. For example, Doug McDonald maintains a map of the distribu-

364

tion of haplogroups at www.scs.uiuc.edu/~mcdonald/WorldHaplogroupsMaps.pdf. So, if you are interested in finding out the distribution of Haplogroup I in Europe, you can match the color (pink) on the pie charts to determine how prevalent the haplogroup is in a particular area. From this chart, you can see that Haplogroup I has a strong concentration in Scandinavia and northwest Europe. Another Y chromosome haplogroup map is located on the DNA Heritage site at www.dnaheritage.com/ysnptree.asp. This map is interactive and allows you to filter the map to show only the haplogroup that interests you. Figure 10-6 shows the map. At the top of the map are letters representing the haplogroups. To filter the haplogroups, move your mouse pointer over one of the letters. The map will only show the distribution for that haplogroup.

As haplogroups are large collections of haplotypes, it is useful to break down haplogroups into subgroups that have common traits. These subgroups are referred to as *subclades*. Subclades can help genealogists get a clearer picture of the geographical setting of that portion of the haplogroup.

Although the typical Y chromosome test can suggest a haplogroup, it normally takes additional testing to confirm the haplogroup and a subclade to that haplogroup. In these additional tests, particular positions of the Y chromosome are examined for differences called *single nucleotide polymorphisms* (SNP) or "snips." Some SNPs are very common and apply to a large population of people within a haplogroup. Other SNPs can be unique to an individual or a family — referred to as private SNPs. New SNPs are constantly being discovered and that sometimes results in changes to the labels of subclades or the discovery of new subclades. To find the most up-to-date list of subclades, take a look at the International Society of Genetic Genealogy (ISOGG) Y-DNA Haplogroup Tree at www.isogg.org/tree/Main06.html.

Figure 10-5:
Explanation of Y chromosome Haplogroup I at the National Geographic Genographic Project site.

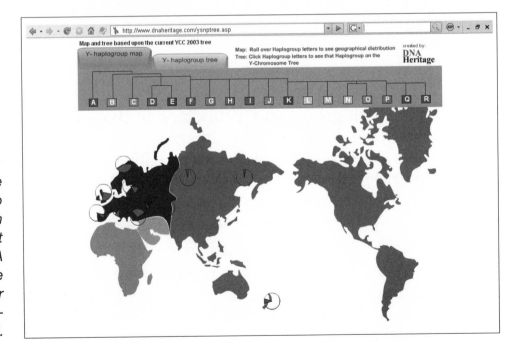

Figure 10-6:
Interactive haplogroup distribution map at DNA Heritage filtered for Haplogroup I.

To illustrate how subclades work, look at our Haplogroup I example. As you can see from the haplogroup distribution map in Figure 10-5, Haplogroup I has a concentration in Northern Europe and a concentration in the Balkans. If you are in that haplogroup, you might be curious about which region your direct male ancestor came from. To find this out, SNP tests would be conducted on several areas of the Y chromosome including those called M253, M307, P30, P40, S31, and P37.2. If a mutation is found at loci M253, M307, P30, P40, the subclade is I1a — a subclade found in southern Norway, southwestern Sweden, and Denmark. If mutations are found at S31 and P37.2, the subclade is I1b1* — found in the western Balkans. Figure 10-7 shows the subclades of Haplogroup I.

After you discover the haplogroup of your results, you can then join a Y chromosome project for particular haplogroup. Through a haplogroup project, you might be able to find out more about the origins of the haplogroup or the subclade within the haplogroup and communicate with others who are studying the same genetic group. To find a project for your haplogroup, see if your DNA testing company already has a project for it, or do a search using a general Internet search engine such as Google for something like "Y-DNA Haplogroup I project."

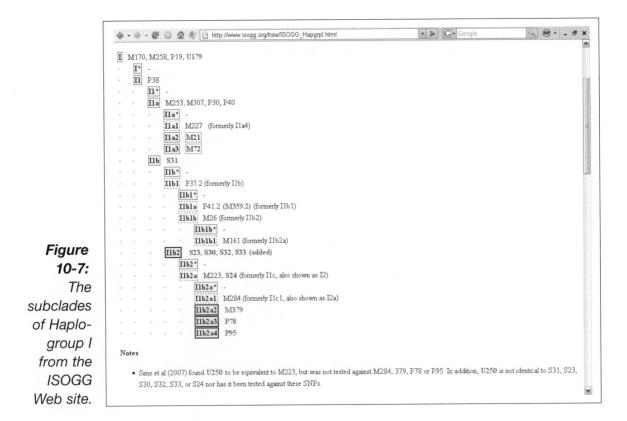

Figure 10-7:
The subclades of Haplogroup I from the ISOGG Web site.

Getting tested

Have you decided it's time to take the plunge and get a Y chromosome test? If you are female (or if you are a male but you are not a direct line descendant from the family for which you want to test), you need to find a male relative that is a direct line descendant of the family you are researching. Then it's just a matter of selecting a testing company and following their specific instructions.

There are a number of testing companies that offer Y chromosome testing. Some of these include

✔ **African Ancestry:** africanancestry.com

✔ **DNA Ancestry:**
dna.ancestry.com/learnMorePaternal.aspx

- ✔ **DNA Heritage:** www.dnaheritage.com/ystr.asp

- ✔ **FamilyTreeDNA:** www.ftdna.com

- ✔ **Genebase:** www.genebase.com

- ✔ **Oxford Ancestors:**
  www.oxfordancestors.com/service-yline-classic.html

- ✔ **Sorenson Molecular Genealogy Foundation:**
  www.smgf.org

- ✔ **Trace Genetics:**
  www.tracegenetics.com/dnaancestry.html

Locating others with the same results

Spending the money to have a Y chromosome test doesn't do you much good unless you have something to compare the results with. To find others who have tested and received results, you should first look for a surname project currently underway for your direct male line. Some of the testing companies have established mechanisms for people to set up the projects that are housed on the testing companies' servers. For example, you can find a list of projects at the FamilyTreeDNA site at www.familytreedna .com/surname.aspx.

Even if you are a member of a surname project, you may want to distribute your results to a wider audience in the hopes of locating others with matching results. Here are some sites that you can use to "broadcast" your Y chromosome results:

- ✔ **Ybase:** ybase.org

- ✔ **Ysearch:** www.ysearch.org

If you don't want your results to be publicly accessible, you can use these sites to search for others with your same haplotype and contact them directly. Say that you want to see if there are any matches for the surname Abell in Ysearch.

1. **Open your Web browser and go to www.ysearch.org.**

   At the top of the page are blue tabs with labels such as Create a New User, Edit an Existing User, Alphabetical List of Last Names, Search by Last Name, Search for Genetic Matches, Search by Haplogroup, Research Tools, and Statistics.

2. **Click the tab entitled Search by Last Name.**

   The resulting page contains two ways to search. You can search by entering a surname or by using a User ID. Also, the search can be limited to a specific geographic area.

3. **Type the surname you are researching into the field marked Type Last Names to Search For and click Search.**

   Note that you can search for multiple names at the same time using commas to separate them. It is a good idea to do this if the last name has some common derivations. For the purposes of this example, type in Abell, Abel, Able.

4. **Choose a match by clicking on a link within the results table.**

   In our example, the results page shows that there is one result for the surname Abel. There are no results for the surnames Abell or Able — although there are some pedigree charts with those names associated with them. When we click on the Abel result, the screen shows us that the origin of the individual is Hesse, Germany and that their haplogroup is R1b1*.

5. **Click on the User ID link to see the DNA**

results for this individual.
Figure 10-8 shows the test results for this individual.
There is also a link on the page where you can
e-mail the individual who submitted the result to
Ysearch.

Although you cannot add your own results to the database, you can search the Sorenson Molecular Genealogy Foundation Y-Chromosome Database at www.smgf.org/ychromosome/search.jspx. The database allows searches by surname or by haplotypes. The results contained within the database include pedigree charts submitted by the participants of the study. Unfortunately, one limitation of the database is that there is not a direct way of contacting the participant to share research findings. A few other searchable Y chromosome databases are also available. The Y Chromosome Haplotype Reference Database at www.yhrd.org allows you to see the distribution of a particular haplotype; however, it is a scientific database geared towards DNA researchers, so it doesn't contain a lot of information useful to genealogists. Oxford Ancestors also allows its database to be searched, if you login as a guest. The database is located at www.oxfordancestors.com/members/.

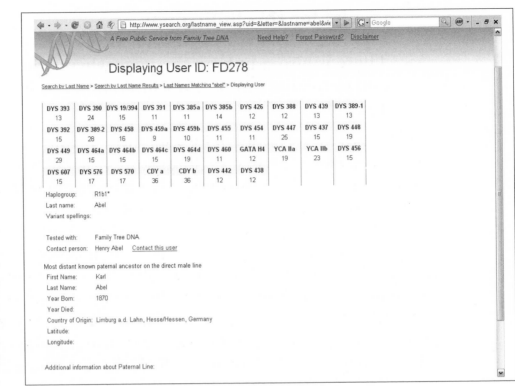

Figure 10-8: Results from Ysearch.org for the surname Abel.

Mitochondrial DNA testing

In the previous section, we looked at Y chromosome DNA testing that assists in the genetic identification of the direct male line of a family. In this section, we look at mitochondrial DNA testing that allows for the identification of the genetic information of the direct female line of a family.

Remember from the beginning of the chapter that the mitochondrion is the "power plant" of the cell. It's outside of the nucleus and has its own distinct genome, called mtDNA, which is inherited from the female parent by both male and female children. Because it also mutates at a very slow rate, the mtDNA is good for identifying genetic relationships over many, many years and generations.

372

Testing method

For testing purposes, mitochondrial DNA is divided into three regions — a coding region, a Hyper Variable Region One (HVR1), and a Hyper Variable Region Two (HVR2). Genealogical tests are usually conducted on a sequence of Hyper Variable Region One or a sequence of both Hyper Variable Regions One and Two. Some testing facilities fully sequence the entire mitochondrial DNA; however, it is a fairly expensive test. The results from these sequences are compared to a sample known as the Cambridge Reference Sequence (CRS). The CRS is the mitochrondrial sequence of the first individual to have their mitochrondrial DNA sequenced. The differences between the sample and the CRS are considered mutations for the purposes of assigning a haplogroup to the sample.

How is this done in practical terms? At the beginning of the chapter, we mentioned that DNA testing was used to identify the remains of the family of the last Czar of Russia. The results of the remains thought to be Czarina Alexandra were compared to Prince Philip and the results matched (Prince Philip and Czarina Alexandra were both descended from Queen Victoria). The results were listed as the following:

HVR1: 16111T, 16357C HVR2: 263G, 315.1C

Remembering back to when we talked about how DNA is coded (if you can't remember, just look at the "Getting down to bases" section earlier in this chapter), we mentioned that a DNA sequence was composed of four bases including adenine (A), guanine (G), cytosine (C), and thymine (T). These same bases are used in sequencing mitochondrial DNA.

The first result for Czarina Alexandra was 16111T. This

result is interpreted as the substitution of thymine in the location 16111 of the Hyper Variable One region. The second result translates as the substitution of cytosine at location 16357 of the same region. The next result, 263G, shows a substitution of guanine at location 263 in the Hyper Variable Two region. The fourth result is a bit different in that it has a ".1" in it. The ".1" indicates that an extra base was found at that location. This means the fourth result shows that an extra cytosine is found at the 315 location in the Hyper Variable Two region. Based upon the changes between Czarina Alexandra's sequence and the Cambridge Reference Sequence, her sample was classified in mitochondrial Haplogroup H.

Keep in mind that, although they are named in the same manner, Y chromosome haplogroups and mitochondrial haplogroups are two different entities.

Making sense of the results

Mitochondrial DNA changes (or mutates) at a slow rate. This makes its uses for genealogical purposes very different than the uses for Y chromosomes, which change at a faster rate and can link family members together at closer intervals. However, mtDNA is useful for determining long-term relationships, as in the case of the Romanov family.

When two individuals have the same mutations within the Hyper Variable One region, it is considered a *low resolution match*. If the individuals have a low resolution match and they are classified in the same haplogroup, there is about a 50 percent chance that they shared a common ancestor within the past 52 generations (or about 1,300 years). If they have a low resolution match and the haplogroups are not the same, it is considered a coincidence and the probability is that the two individuals did not share a common ancestor within a measurable time frame. Depending upon your result set, you might get a lot of low resolution matches. To see if there really is a connection, it is useful to test both the Hyper Variable One and Hyper Variable Two regions.

A *high resolution match* occurs when two individuals match exactly at both Hyper Variable One and Hyper Variable Two regions. Individuals having high resolution matches are more likely to be related within a genealogically provable time frame. With a high resolution match, there is about a 50 percent probability of sharing a common ancestor within the past 28 generations (about 700 years).

Testing companies

A lot of the same companies that provide Y chromosome tests also provide mitochondrial DNA tests. In fact, if you are male, you can have the tests done at the same time on the same sample. If you are interested, here are some places to consider:

- **African Ancestry:** africanancestry.com/mc.html

- **DNA Ancestry:** dna.ancestry.com/learnMoreMaternal.aspx

- **DNA Heritage:** www.dnaheritage.com/mtdna.asp

- **FamilyTreeDNA:** www.ftdna.com/maternal_test.html

- **Genebase:** www.genebase.com

- **Oxford Ancestors:** www.oxfordancestors.com/maternal-ancestry.html

- **Sorenson Molecular Genealogy Foundation:** www.smgf.org

- **Trace Genetics:**

www.tracegenetics.com/dnaancestry.html

Finding others with the same results

Similar to Y chromosome testing, you might want to post your mitochondrial DNA results to some public databases. One place to post results is mitosearch.org at www.mitosearch.org (see Figure 10-9). If you want to find results of mitochondrial tests performed by the Sorenson Molecular Genealogy Foundation, see the Mitochondrial Database at www.smgf.org/mtdna/search.jspx. To find more information on mitochondrial DNA scientific databases, check out MITOMAP at www.mitomap.org and MitEURO at www.miteuro.org.

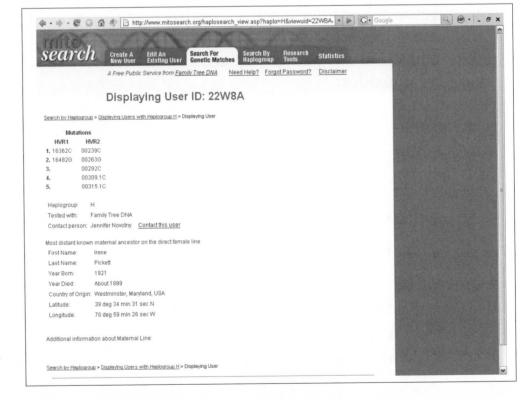

Figure 10-9: *An entry from MitoSearch.org.*

Autosomal DNA testing

Probably the most controversial of the DNA tests are autosomal tests (also known as admixture or bio-geographical tests). Earlier in the chapter, we mentioned that autosomal DNA consists of 22 pairs of non-sex chromosomes found in the cell nucleus. This DNA is found in both males and females and is the part of the DNA that is responsible for physical characteristics of an individual, like height and eye color. The DNA is inherited from both parents and all four grandparents.

Autosomal testing traditionally has been used for paternity testing and in forensic investigations. However, using autosomal DNA to predict percentages of ethnicity for genealogical purposes has begun to catch on.

When forensic scientists began looking into DNA, they recognized that certain genetic markers were common to particular ethnicities. Once enough markers were identified with ethnicities, they could begin to assess what percentage ethnicity a particular person might possess. Genealogists picked up on this and believed that the same types of tests might be able to shed some light on the ethnicities of their ancestors — especially, in the areas of identifying native American, Jewish, and African ancestry.

The controversial weakness with autosomal testing is that the DNA in each individual recombines differently. This means that two children born from the same two parents will measure with different ethnicities because their DNA does not recombine exactly the same. Also, the percentages quoted by testing companies can often have a significant error rate or change over time as new research comes to light.

If you take an autosomal DNA test, you can expect to receive a copy of the sequences examined and an interpretation of the results. The interpretation usually comes in the form of a percentage of a certain ethnicity. For example, you might receive results such as

European — 92%
Sub-Saharan African — 8%
East Asian — 0%
Native American — 0%

Some companies now offer more in-depth testing of European ethnicities. Results from these tests might look like the following:

Southeastern Europe — 73%
Iberian — 0%
Basque — 0%
Continental Europe — 6%
Northeastern Europe — 21%

If you are interested in taking an autosomal test, here are some companies to look at:

✔ **DNA Print Genomics:** www.dnaprint.com

✔ **DNA Tribes:** www.dnatribes.com

✔ **FamilyTreeDNA:** www.ftdna.com

Helpful DNA Sites

Within this chapter, we were able to cover only the tip of the iceberg in using DNA testing for genealogical purposes. There are some sites that can provide some additional information to help you decide if DNA testing is useful for your research or to keep abreast of the current developments in DNA research.

If you are looking for some basic information on using DNA testing in genealogy, see Chris Pomery's DNA Portal at freepages.genealogy.rootsweb.com/~allpoms/genetics .html or the DNA 101: Y-Chromosome Testing page part of the Blair DNA project at blairgenealogy.com/dna/

dna101.html.

As DNA testing methods and capabilities change on a frequent basis, it is a good idea to consult some sites that provide updates on the technology and issues related to using the technology. A couple of sites to consult include the Genealogy-DNA mailing list archives at lists5.rootsweb.com/index/other/DNA/GENEALOGY-DNA.html (you can also subscribe to the mailing list from this page) and the Genetic Genealogist blog at www.thegeneticgenealogist.com.

Part IV
Share and Share Alike

The 5th Wave — By Rich Tennant

"Tell the boss the 'Begets' aren't cutting it. The people are demanding online access."

In this part . . .

Discover how to maximize your online research by effectively using as many resources as possible. This part also addresses sharing information with others using reports, GEDCOM files, Web pages that you create yourself, and genealogical networking sites, as well as how to coordinate your research efforts with those of others. Along the way, you also find out a little history about GEDCOM and the best way to respect others' privacy and copyrights.

Chapter 11

Help Wanted!

Have you ever taken a long car trip by yourself? Was it difficult to pass the time without getting lost, bored, or tired? You can think of genealogical research as a long car trip. You may begin by yourself, but you quickly discover that the trip would go a lot faster if you have someone along for the ride. In your genealogical journey, these travel partners can take various forms — a single individual researching the same family, or a research group searching for several branches of a family in which you're interested, or a genealogical society that coordinates the efforts of many people researching different families.

You may be saying, "A research mate sounds great! But where can I find one of my own?" Lucky you — in the next few pages, we explore just that. We look at ways to find (and keep) research partners, as well as ways that research groups and genealogical societies can help you meet your research goals.

Getting Out of Your Comfort Zone

You might be thinking that it's better to do all of your own research. After all, that way you have a sense of control over how the research is done, whether it's documented correctly, and what piece of information you get next. For you, it may even be comfortable to be alone in your quest. It's time to step outside your comfort zone. Although researching alone some of the time is great, don't try to do all the research yourself. As you'll discover, an awful lot of people out there are digging for answers, and it would be a shame for you not to take advantage of the work they have done and vice versa.

We can't emphasize enough the benefits of sharing genealogical data. Sharing is the foundation on which the genealogical community is built. For example, when Matthew began researching his genealogy, he went to the National Archives, Library of Congress, and several regional libraries and archives. Along the way, he found a few books that made a passing mention of some of his ancestors, and he discovered some original records that helped him put some pieces together. It wasn't until he shared his information online that he began to realize just how many people were working on his surname. During the month following the creation of his Web site, he received messages from 40 other Helm researchers — one of whom lived in Slovenia! Although not all these researchers were working on Matthew's specific branch (only two of the 40 were directly related), he received valuable information on some of the areas that other researchers were working on. Matthew may never have known that some of these researchers existed had he not taken the first step to share his information.

By knowing the family lines and regions that other researchers are pursuing, you can coordinate your efforts with theirs — not only sharing information you've already collected, but also working together toward your common goal. Maybe you live closer to a courthouse that holds records relating to your ancestor than does a distant cousin with whom you're communicating online — but maybe the cousin lives near a family gravesite that you'd like to have a photo of. Rather than duplicating efforts to collect the court records and photographs, you can make arrangements for each of you to get the desired items that are closest to you and then exchange copies of them over the Internet or through traditional mail.

The Shotgun Approach

You're probably wondering how to find individuals with whom to share your information. Well, you could start by going through telephone books and calling everyone with the surname that you're researching.

However, given how some people feel about telemarketers, we don't recommend this as a strategy.

Sending mass e-mails to anyone you find with your surname through one of the online white-pages sites or through various non-genealogical Web sites is similar to the telemarketing strategy we've just warned you against. We refer to this mass e-mail strategy as the *shotgun approach* and many people refer to it as spamming. You shoot out a bunch of e-mail messages aimed in various directions, with hopes of successfully hitting one or two targets. Although you may find one or two people who answer you in a positive way, a lot of people may find such unsolicited e-mail irritating. And, quite honestly, gleaning e-mail addresses from online white-pages is not as easy as it was even just a few years ago. Most of the online directories that allow you to search for e-mail addresses no longer give the precise address to you. Rather, they enable you to send an e-mail from their site to the individual; it is up to that recipient to respond to you if he or she chooses to do so. (See Figure 11-1.) This is their way of protecting that person's online privacy, and the directories require you to jump through a few hoops in order to send the e-mail — for example, Info-Space.com requires confirmation from your e-mail address before it completes the process of sending your message to the intended recipient.

Instead of spending hours trying to find e-mail addresses through online directories and following a three- or four-step process to send an initial message to someone, go to a site that focuses on genealogy to find the names of and contact information for researchers who are interested in your surname — this is a much gentler, better way to go about finding others with the same interests as you.

Also, please note that we aren't saying that e-mail directories don't have a function in genealogy. E-mail directories can be a good means for getting in contact with a relative whose e-mail address you've lost or one you know is interested in your e-mail.

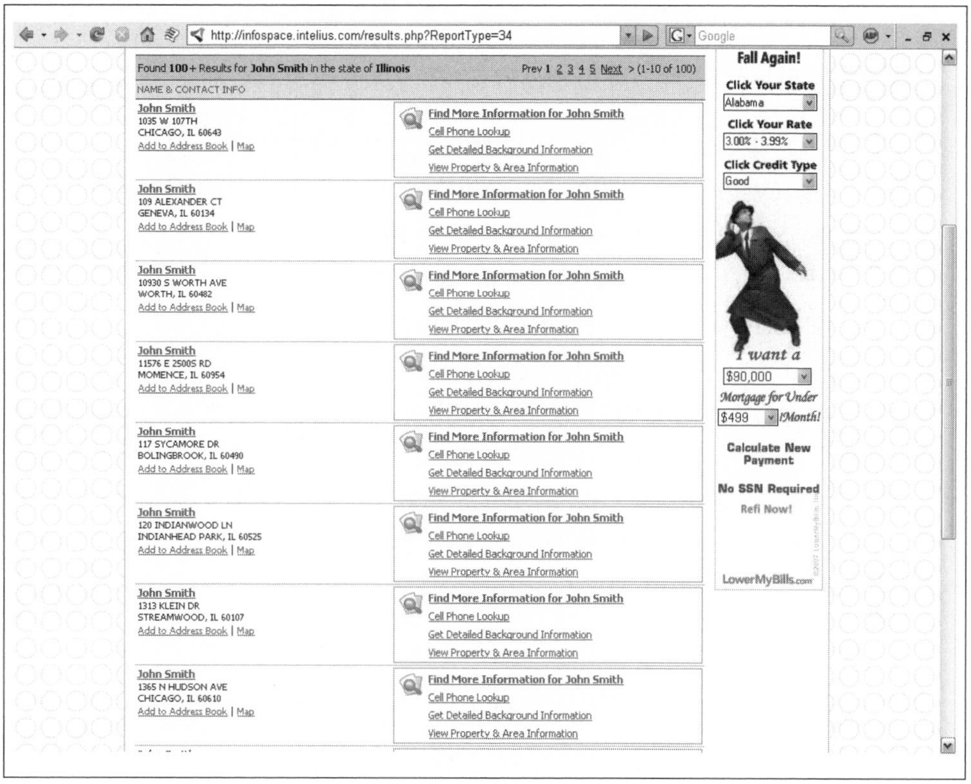

Figure 11-1: InfoSpace.com enables you to e-mail the person you've looked up directly from their results page.

Making Friends (and Keeping Them) Online

One place to begin your search for others who are doing similar research is the Roots Surname List. (See Figure 11-2.) The Roots Surname List (rsl.rootsweb.com) is one of the oldest genealogy resources on the Internet and consists of a list of individuals, the surnames they're researching, and where on the planet those surnames are found. (For more information on using the Roots Surname List, see Chapter 4.) Other places to find fellow researchers include query pages on the World Wide Web, newsgroups, and mailing lists. (If you need a refresher on using these or other surname resources, you can find more information in

Netiquette: Communicating politely on the Internet

Part of being a fine, upstanding member of the online genealogy community is learning to communicate effectively and politely on the Internet. Online communication is often hampered by the fact that you can't see the people with whom you're corresponding, and you can't hear the intonation of their voices to determine what emotions they're expressing. To avoid misunderstandings, follow some simple guidelines — called *netiquette* — when writing messages:

- Don't send a message that you wouldn't want posted on a bulletin board at work or the library, or that you wouldn't want printed in a newsletter. You should expect that every e-mail you send is potentially public.

- Make sure that you don't violate any copyright laws by sending large portions of written works through e-mail. (For more information on copyrights, see Chapter 13.)

- If you receive a *flame* (a heated message usually sent to provoke a response), try to ignore it. Usually, no good comes from responding to a flame.

- Be careful when you respond to messages. Instead of replying to an individual, you may be replying to an entire group of people. Checking the To: line before you hit the Send button is always a good idea.

- Use mixed case when you write e-mail messages. USING ALL UPPERCASE LETTERS INDICATES SHOUTING! The exception to this guideline is when you send a query and place your surnames in all-uppercase letters (for example, George HELM).

- If you participate in a mailing list or newsgroup, and you reply with a message that is most likely of interest to only one person, consider sending that person a message individually rather than e-mailing the list as a whole.

✔ When you're joking, use smileys or type **<grins>** or **<g>**, but use these symbols somewhat sparingly to increase their effectiveness. A *smiley* is an *emoticon* that looks like :-). (Turn the book on its right side if you can't see the face.) *Emoticons* are graphics created by combinations of keys on the keyboard to express an emotion within an e-mail. Here are a few emoticons that you may run into:

:-)	Happy, smiling
;-)	Wink, ironic
:->	Sarcastic
8-)	Wearing glasses
:-(	Sad, unhappy
:-<	Disappointed
:-o	Frightened, surprised
:-()	Mustache

Chapter 4.) After you identify some potential online friends, send them e-mail messages introducing yourself and briefly explaining your purpose for contacting them. Be sure to include a listing of the ancestors you're researching in your e-mail message.

Before we send you out to contact people, however, we must offer our most sage advice:

✔ **Before sending messages to a Web-site maintainer, look around the site to see whether that person is the appropriate one to approach:** More often than not, the person who maintains a Web site is indeed the one who is researching the surnames you find on that Web site. However, it's not unusual for site maintainers to host information on their sites for other people. If they do, they typically have separate contact addresses for those individuals and an explanation that they're not personally researching those surnames. Some even go so far as to post notices on their sites stating that they don't entertain research questions. So when you see a list of surnames on a site, don't automatically assume that the Web-site maintainer is the person to contact. Look around a little to ensure that you're addressing the most appropriate person.

✔ **Make your messages brief and to the point:** E-mail messages that run five or six pages long can overwhelm some people. If the person you send the message to is interested in your information and responds positively to you, you can send a more detailed message at a future date.

✔ **Ensure that your message has enough detail for the recipients to decide whether your information relates to their research and determine whether they can help you:** Include names, dates, and places as appropriate.

✔ **Use net etiquette, or *netiquette,* when you create your messages:** Remember, e-mail can be an impersonal medium. Although you may mean one thing, someone who doesn't know you may mistakenly misinterpret your message. (For more on netiquette, see the "Netiquette: Communicating politely on the Internet" sidebar in this chapter.)

✔ **Don't disclose personal information that could violate a person's privacy:** Information such as address, birth dates, and Social Security numbers for living persons is considered private and should not be freely shared with other researchers. Also, we don't recommend you send out much personal information about yourself until you know the recipient a lot better — when first introducing yourself, your name and e-mail address should suffice, along with the information about the deceased ancestors you're researching.

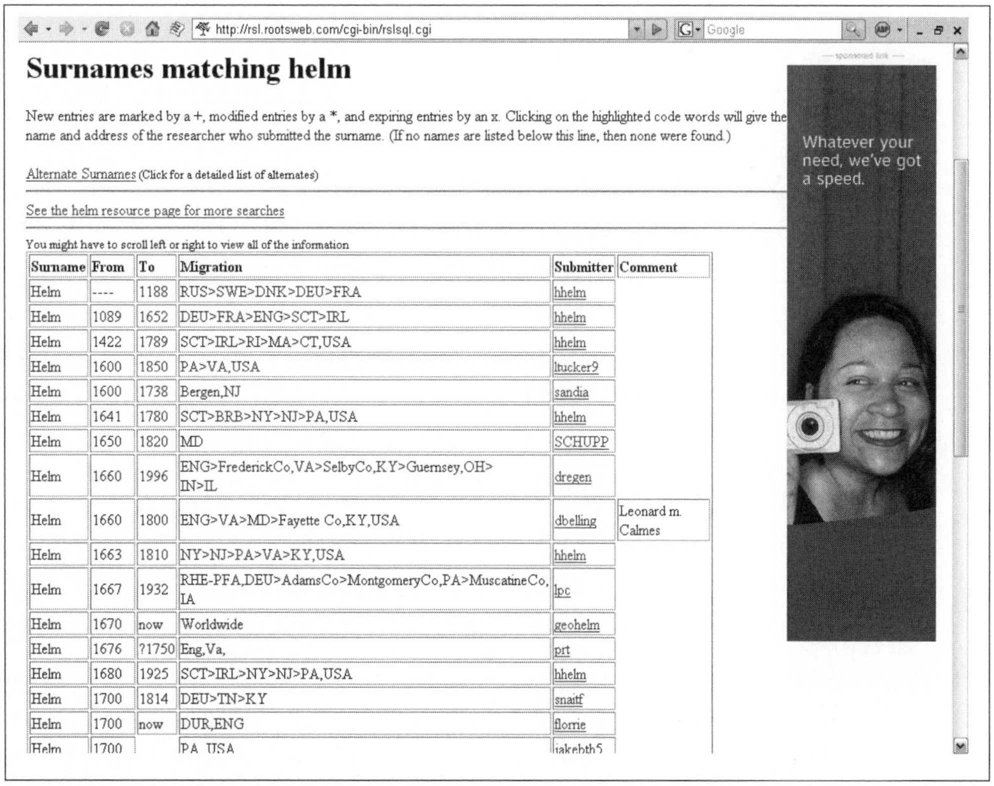

http://rsl.rootsweb.com/cgi-bin/rslsql.cgi

Surnames matching helm

New entries are marked by a +, modified entries by a *, and expiring entries by an x. Clicking on the highlighted code words will give the name and address of the researcher who submitted the surname. (If no names are listed below this line, then none were found.)

Alternate Surnames (Click for a detailed list of alternates)

See the helm resource page for more searches

You might have to scroll left or right to view all of the information

Surname	From	To	Migration	Submitter	Comment
Helm	----	1188	RUS>SWE>DNK>DEU>FRA	hhelm	
Helm	1089	1652	DEU>FRA>ENG>SCT>IRL	hhelm	
Helm	1422	1789	SCT>IRL>RI>MA>CT,USA	hhelm	
Helm	1600	1850	PA>VA,USA	ltucker9	
Helm	1600	1738	Bergen,NJ	sandia	
Helm	1641	1780	SCT>BRB>NY>NJ>PA,USA	hhelm	
Helm	1650	1820	MD	SCHUPP	
Helm	1660	1996	ENG>FrederickCo,VA>SelbyCo,KY>Guernsey,OH>IN>IL	dregen	
Helm	1660	1800	ENG>VA>MD>Fayette Co,KY,USA	dbelling	Leonard m. Calmes
Helm	1663	1810	NY>NJ>PA>VA>KY,USA	hhelm	
Helm	1667	1932	RHE-PFA,DEU>AdamsCo>MontgomeryCo,PA>MuscatineCo,IA	lpc	
Helm	1670	now	Worldwide	geohelm	
Helm	1676	?1750	Eng,Va,	prt	
Helm	1680	1925	SCT>IRL>NY>NJ>PA,USA	hhelm	
Helm	1700	1814	DEU>TN>KY	snaitf	
Helm	1700	now	DUR,ENG	florrie	
Helm	1700		PA USA	jakebth5	

Figure 11-2: *Example of the Roots Surname List for the Helm surname.*

- **Get permission before forwarding messages from other researchers:** Sometimes researchers may provide information that they do not want made available to the general public. Asking permission before forwarding a message to a third party eliminates any potential problems with violating the trust of your fellow researchers.

Joining a Herd: Research Groups

If your relatives are tired of hearing about your genealogy research trips or the information that you found on great-uncle Beauford, but you'd like to share your triumphs with someone, you may be ready to join a research group.

Research groups consist of any number of people who coordinate their research and share resources to achieve success. These groups may start conducting research because they share a surname, family branch, or geographic location. Individuals who live geographically close to each other may make up a research group, or the group may consist of people who have never personally met each other but are interested in descendants of one particular person. Research groups may have a variety of goals and may have a formal or an informal structure. They are quite flexible organizationally and depend entirely on the membership of the group.

A good example of a research group is one that Matthew discovered shortly after he posted his first Web page. An individual who was researching one of his surnames on the East Coast of the United States contacted him. After exchanging a couple of e-mails, Matthew learned that this individual was part of a small research group studying the origins of several different branches of the Helm surname. Each member of the group contributes the results of his or her personal research and provides any information that he or she finds, which may be of use to other members of the group. Additionally, the group as a whole has sponsored research by professional genealogists in other countries to discover more about their ancestors there and has spun off a more formal research group that focuses solely on molecular research (DNA-based) of the Helm bloodlines. The vast majority of the communication for these two research groups is through e-mail.

You can find an example of an online-based research group at the William Aaron Saunders Research Group site (www.wasrg.org/). The mission of this group is to collect and share genealogical data and stories relating to William Aaron Saunders (cir. 1735 VA to cir. 1785 NC). The site is constructed to help Saunders/Sanders researchers collaborate with each other. It has sections containing information about the research group members, family groups, stories, photos, and GEDCOM files. It also has links to other Web sites that have information about some of the same ancestors that are studied through the research group.

To find research groups, your best bet is to visit a comprehensive genealogical Web site or a site that specializes in surnames, such as the GeneaSearch Surname Registry at www.geneasearch.com/surnameregister.htm or SurnameWeb at www.surnameweb.org.

The following steps show you how to find groups pertaining to a surname on the site:

1. **Launch your Web browser and go to the SurnameWeb site at www.surnameweb.org.**
   After the page loads, you see a search field and the letters of the alphabet near the top center of the page.

2. **Choose the letter of the alphabet that's the first letter of the surname that you're researching.**
   For example, say the surname that you're researching begins with the letter *P*. Find the link to the letter *P* and click it. This action brings up a Web page with the *P* Index.

3. **Select the Po link near the top of the page.**
This brings up a list of surname links that begin with the letters *Po*.

4. **Scroll through the list and select a surname link.**
We want to find sites relating to the surname *Pollard,* so click the link for the Pollard surname, which takes us to a Results page titled Pollard Genealogy Center.

5. **Choose a site to visit.**
Scroll down past all of the links to search other commercial Web sites until you reach the links you're most interested in — in our case, those links that take us directly to personal and group Web pages that contain information about people named Pollard.

In addition to using comprehensive genealogy sites and specialized surname sites, you can use other strategies to identify possible research groups. One way to find research groups pertaining to surnames is to visit a one-name studies index. You can find a list of one-name studies sites at the Guild of One-Name Studies page (www.one-name.org). You can also look to existing larger groups that may have specific research components, such as genealogical societies. (The following section goes into more detail on genealogical societies.)

If you can't find an established online group that fits your interests, why not start one yourself? If you're interested in researching a particular topic, the chances are very good that others out there are interested as well. Maybe the time has come for you to coordinate efforts and begin working with others toward your common research goals. Starting an online research group can be relatively easy — just post a message stating your interest in starting a group at some key locations, such as message boards, newsgroups, or mailing lists.

Becoming a Solid Member of (Genealogical) Society

Genealogical societies can be great places to learn research methods and to coordinate your research. Several different types of societies exist. They range from the more traditional geographical or surname-based societies to *cyber-societies* (societies that exist only on the Internet) that are redefining the way that people think about genealogical societies.

Geographical societies

Chapter 7 introduces geography-based genealogical societies as groups that can help you discover resources in a particular area in which your ancestors lived, or as groups in your hometown that can help you discover how to research effectively. However, local genealogical societies can provide another service to their members. These societies often coordinate local research efforts of the members in the form of projects. To locate geographical societies, follow our advice in Chapter 7 or check out the site of a genealogical-society federation such as one of these:

- ✔ Federation of Genealogical Societies, Society Hall page, at www.familyhistory.com/societyhall/

- ✔ Federation of Family History Societies at www.ffhs.org.uk

These projects can take many forms. For example, the Illinois State Genealogical Society (www.rootsweb.com/

~ilsgs/) is working on several projects, including creating a database of county marriage records, updating a list of Illinois pioneers, compiling an index of Civil War certificates issued, and forming a list of all cemeteries in the state. (See Figure 11-3.)

Smaller groups of members sometimes work on projects in addition to the society's official projects. For example, you may belong to a county genealogical society and decide to join with a few members to write a history of the pioneers who settled a particular township within the county. If each member of the team shares the fruits of his or her research, you can cover three or four times more ground than you can by yourself.

Figure 11-3: Cemetery entries for Fayette County, Illinois, on the ISGS site.

Fayette County   Updated 1/16/2003

NAME	ALIAS	OL	C	R	V	ST	SEC	TOWNSHIP	LOCATION	QTR QTR	QTR SEC
Abel						DE	02	Sharon		NW	SW
Adcock	Causey or Depew or Devore or Donelson			Y	Y	IN	17	Bear Grove		SW	NW
Ambuehl				Y	Y	AC	13	Lone Grove		NE	NE
Amish				Y		IN	17	Sefton		SW	SE
Ammerman				Y	Y	DE	18	Loudon		NW	SW
Antioch			Y	Y	Y	AC	22	Bowling Green		NW	NE
Arm Prairie			Y	Y		AC	35	Otego		SW	SE
Augsburg	Immanuel Lutheran		Y	Y	Y	AC	18	Wilberton		SE	SE
Austin					Y	DE	30	Carson		SW	NW
Bails					Y	DE	?	Bowlling Green		?	?
Bear Creek				Y		AC	11	Pope		SE	SE
Beck				Y		IN	28	Ramsey		NE	NE
Beck Private	Snow			Y		IN	24	Bowling Green		SW	SW
Bethlehem	Brushy Point		Y	Y	Y	AC	07	Bear Grove		?	SE
Big Spring					Y	DE	?	Carson		?	?
Biggs	Pratt			Y	Y	AC	21	Pope		SE	SE
Blankenship				Y		AC	15	Carson		?	NW
Boaz				Y		AC	36	Vandalia		NW	NW
Bob Doane				Y	Y	AC	25	Carson		NE	SE
Bolt				Y		AC	25	Ramsey		?	NE
Bolyard				Y		IN	28	Ramsey		SE	NW
Bone				Y		IN	32	Bear Grove		?	SW
Brackenbush				Y		IN	06	Shafter		SW	NE
Britton				Y	Y	IN	02	Kaskaskia		NE	SW
Brown				Y		IN	04	Wilberton		SW	SW

Family and surname associations

In addition to geographically based associations, you can find groups tied to particular names or family groups. Typically, they are referred to as — you've probably already guessed — surname or family associations or research groups.

Family associations also frequently sponsor projects that coordinate the efforts of several researchers. These projects may focus on the family or surname in a specific geographic area or point in time, or they may attempt to collect information about every individual possessing the surname throughout time and then place the information in a shared database.

Chapter 4 covers family associations in a little more detail and provides some examples. You can find family and surname associations through comprehensive genealogy sites, general Internet search engines, or sites specializing in associations.

If a family or surname association isn't currently working on a project that interests you, by all means suggest a project that does interest you (as long as the project is relevant to the association as a whole).

Gathering Up Kinfolk: Using the Family Reunion for Research

You may have noticed that throughout this book, we strongly recommend that you interview relatives to gather information about your ancestors both to use as leads in finding records and to enhance your genealogy. Well, what better way to gather information from relatives than by attending a family reunion?

Family reunions can add a lot to your research because

you find many relatives all in one place and typically most are eager to visit. A reunion is an efficient way to collect stories, photographs, databases (if others in the family research and keep their records in their computers), and even copies of records. You might even find some people interested in researching the family along with you. And a family reunion can be great fun, too.

When you attend your next family reunion, be sure to take along your notebook, list of interview questions (see Chapter 2 if you haven't developed your list yet), and camera. You can take some printed charts from your genealogical database, too — we bet that lots of your relatives will be interested in seeing them.

Rent-a-Researcher

There may come a time when you've exhausted all of the research avenues directly available to you and you need help that family, friends, and society members can't give you. Maybe all the records you need to get past a research "brick wall" are in a distant place, or maybe you have too many other obligations and not enough time to research personally. You needn't fret. Professional researchers are happy to help you.

Professional researchers are people you pay a fee to dig around and find information for you. They will retrieve specific records that you identify or they will prepare an entire report on a family line using all of the resources available. And, as you might expect, the amount that you pay depends on the level of service that you require. Professional researchers are especially helpful when you need records from locations to which you cannot travel conveniently.

When looking for a professional researcher, you want to find someone who is reputable and experienced in the area in which you need help. Here's a list of questions you may want to ask when shopping around for a professional researcher:

✔ **Is the researcher certified or accredited and, if so, by what organization?** In the genealogy field, certifications function a little bit differently than in other fields. Rather than receiving a certification based upon coursework, genealogical certifications are based on demonstrated research skills. There are two main certifying bodies in the field — the Board for Certification of Genealogists (www.bcgcertification.org) and the International Commission for the Accreditation of Professional Genealogists (www.icapgen.org). The Board for Certification of Genealogists (BCG) awards two credentials — Certified Genealogist and Certified Genealogical Lecturer. You might also run into some old certifications such as Certified Lineage Specialist (CLS), Certified American Indian Lineage Specialist (CAILS), Certified Genealogical Records Specialist (CGRS), and Certified Genealogical Instructor (CGI) that are no longer used by the organization. The credentials are awarded based upon a peer review process — meaning that a group of individuals possessing the credentials evaluate a research project of an applicant. The International Commission for the Accreditation of Professional Genealogists (ICAPGen) awards the Accredited Genealogist (AG) credential. The accreditation program originally was established by the Family History Department of the Church of Jesus Christ of Latter-day Saints. In 2000, the program was launched as an independent organization called ICAPGen. To become accredited, an applicant must submit a research project and take an examination. Accredited Genealogists are certified in a particular geographical or subject-matter area. So, you want to make sure that the accreditation that the researcher possesses matches your research question. Of course, there are professional researchers that do not hold either of these credentials, who might hold a professional degree such as a Masters in Library and Information Science or advanced history degree from an accredited college or university. Depending on the research area, they could be just as proficient as a credentialed genealogist.

✔ **How many years experience does he have researching?** In general, we tend to think of a person as improving in knowledge and efficiency as he has more years of experience researching. But the answer to this question needs to be considered in context of some other questions. It might be that the researcher has only a little time under his belt actually researching genealogies for others, but might have an educational degree that required historical research experience.

✔ **What is his educational background?** The methods for researching and the type of reports that you will get from an individual can be directly influenced by his educational background. If the researcher has a degree in history, you may get more anecdotal material relating to the times and places in which your ancestor lived. If the researcher attended the school of hard knocks (and doesn't have a formal education per se but lots of experience researching), you may get very specific, bare-bones facts about your ancestor.

✔ **Does the researcher have any professional affiliations? In other words, does he belong to any**

professional genealogical organizations and, if so, which ones? Much like the question dealing with certification or accreditation, a researcher's willingness to belong to a professional organization shows a serious commitment to their calling. One particular organization to look for is membership in the Association of Professional Genealogists (www.apgen.org). The APG is an umbrella organization of all types of researchers and those providing professional services. It includes researchers credentialed under both BCG and ICAPGen, as well as other non-credentialed researchers. All members of the APG agree to be bound by a code of ethics and meet particular research standards.

✔ **What foreign languages does the researcher speak fluently?** This is a very important question if you need research conducted in another country. There are research firms that will send employees to other countries to gather information, but you need the reassurance that they have the qualifications necessary to obtain accurate information.

✔ **What records and resources does he have access to?** Again, you want the reassurance that the researcher can obtain accurate information and from reliable sources. You probably don't want to pay a researcher to simply read the same documents that you can access at your local library and put together a summary.

✔ **What is the professional researcher's experience in the area where you need help?** For example, if you need help interviewing distant relatives in a foreign country, has he conducted interviews in the past? Or if you need records pertaining to a particular ethnic or religious group, does he have experience researching those types of records?

✔ **How does the researcher charge for his services?** You need to know how you're going to be charged — by the record, by the hour, or by the project. And it's very helpful to know up front what methods of payment the researcher accepts so you're prepared when payment time comes. And although you hopefully never have a need to know this, you should ask what you can do if you're dissatisfied with his services.

✔ **How many other projects is the researcher working on presently and what kinds of projects?** It's perfectly reasonable to ask how much time the researcher will devote to your research project and when he will report his results. If he tells you that it's going to take him a year to get a copy of a single birth certificate from an agency in the town where he lives, you might want to rethink hiring him.

✔ **Does the researcher have references you can contact?** A researcher's willingness to provide references speaks to his ethics, in our opinion. And we recommend that you contact one or two of the references to find out what exactly they like about this researcher and if they see him as having any pitfalls of which you should be aware.

One way to find professional researchers is to look for them on comprehensive genealogy sites. Another is to consult an online directory of researchers, such as the Association of Professional Genealogists (www.apgen.org/directory/index.html) directory or genealogyPro (www.genealogypro.com).

Follow these steps to check the APG directory:

1. **Using your Web browser, go to the APG site at** www.apgen.org.

2. **Click the link from the list in the left column of the page under the Find a Specialist heading.** As an example, look for a researcher who specializes in adoption.

3. **Click the link for a researcher who — based on the description posted — sounds promising.** Figure 11-4 shows the researchers specializing in adoption.

When you find a professional researcher who looks promising, make your initial contact. Be sure to be as specific as possible about your needs. That helps the researcher pinpoint exactly what he or she needs to do, and makes it easier to calculate how much it will cost you.

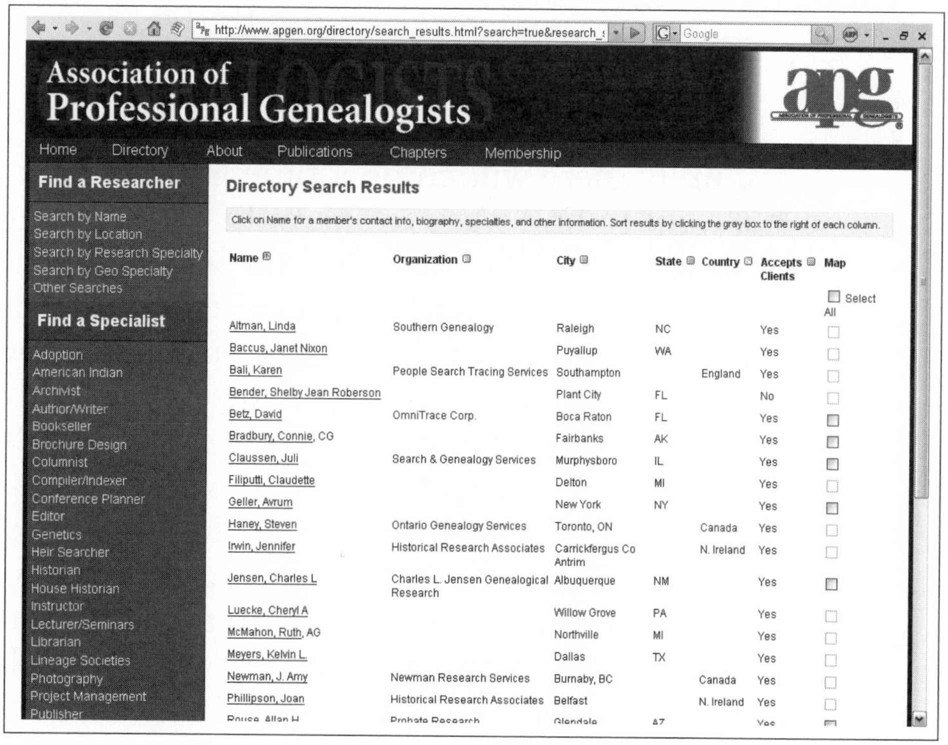

Figure 11-4: Researchers specializing in adoption at the Association of Professional Genealogists site.

Chapter 12

Giving Back to Your Online Community

Surely there will come a time in your research when you want to find ways to share the valuable information you discovered — after all, sharing information is one of the foundations of a solid genealogical community. When you share information, you often get a lot of information in return from other researchers. For example, shortly after we began the Helm/Helms Family Research Web page, several other Helm researchers throughout the world contacted us. We discovered that several Helm lines existed that we didn't even know about. Plus, we received valuable information on our own line from references that other researchers discovered during their research. Not to mention that we made contact with some really nice folks we probably wouldn't have met otherwise.

In this chapter, we focus on methods you can use to share information (except for placing your information on the World Wide Web, which we cover in Chapter 13) and ways to let other researchers know that you have information to share.

Why Would Anyone Want Your Stuff?

Why would anyone want my stuff? seems like a logical first question when you stop and think about making the many tidbits and treasures you collected available to others. Who would want a copy of that old, ratty-looking photograph you have of great-grandpa as a dirty-faced toddler in what appears to be a dress? Nobody else wanted it in the first place, and that's probably how you ended up with it, right? The picture has sentimental value only to you. Wrong! Some of great-grandpa's other descendants may be looking for information about him. They, too, would love to see a picture of him when he was a little boy — even better, they'd love to have their own electronic copy of that picture!

As you develop more and more online contact with other genealogists, you may find a lot of people who are interested in exchanging information. Some may be interested in your research findings because you share common ancestors, and others may be interested because they're researching in the same geographical area where your ancestors were from. Aren't these the same reasons that you're interested in seeing other researchers' stuff? Sharing your information is likely to encourage others to share theirs with you. Exchanging information with others may enable you to fill in some gaps in your own research efforts. Even if research findings received from others don't directly answer questions about your ancestors, they may give you clues about where to find more information to fill in the blanks.

Also, just because you haven't traced your genealogy back to the Middle Ages doesn't mean that your information isn't valuable. Although you need to be careful about sharing information on living persons, you should feel free to share any facts that you do know about deceased ancestors. Just as you may not know your genealogy any further than your great-grandfather, someone else may be in the same boat — and with the same person! Meeting up with that fellow researcher can lead to a mutual research relationship that can produce a lot more information in a shorter amount of time.

Share and Share Alike!

So you're at the point where you recognize the value in sharing your genealogical information online. How do you begin letting people know what you have? Well, the first thing to do is to come up with a marketing plan for your information — much like a business does when it decides to sell a product.

Masterminding a surname marketing plan

A *surname marketing plan* is simply a checklist of places and people to contact to effectively inform the right individuals about the information that you have to contribute to the genealogy community. As you devise your plan, ask yourself the following questions:

- ✔ **What surname sites are interested in my information?** To find surname sites, see Chapter 4.

- ✔ **What geographical sites are interested in my information?** For geographical sites, see Chapter 7.

- ✔ **What association sites (both family and geographical) are interested in my information?** See Chapters 4 and 7 for association sites.

- ✔ **What general sites (such as query sites and GEDCOM collections) are interested in my information?** See Chapters 4 and 7 for some examples of these sites.

You may want to use all available Internet resources to let people know about your information, including mailing lists, newsgroups, and Web sites.

For example, April has information on a McSwain family. She knows that they lived in Madison, Estill, Jessamine, and Nicholas counties in Kentucky. To identify sites where she may be able to post this information, she looked for one-name study pages on the surname *McSwain,* personal pages that have connections to the McSwain family, and any mailing lists dedicated to discussing the family. She also tried to find sites for each of the four counties in Kentucky that the McSwains resided in. Then she searched for family societies or county genealogical or historical societies in Kentucky that look for information on their past inhabitants. Finally, she looked for general-query sites and GEDCOM repositories (more about GEDCOM later in this chapter) that may accept her information.

Contacting your target audience

After you write down the names and addresses of sites that probably attract an audience that you want to target, you need to notify them. Create a brief but detailed e-mail message to make your announcement. When you submit your message, look at the format required by each resource that you're contacting. Some *query sites* (places where you can post genealogical questions to get help from other researchers) also have specific formats, so you may need to modify your message for each of these sites. (For more information about query sites and posting queries, see Chapter 4.)

Here's a sample message to give you some ideas:

> MCSWAIN, 1810-1910, KY, USA
> I have information on the family of William McSwain of Kentucky. William was born in 1802, married Elizabeth Hisle in March 1827, and had the following children:
> Thomas, Mary, Joseph, Sarah, Susan, Margaret, Elizabeth, Nancy, and James.

 Most people understand that you're willing to share information on the family if you post something to a site, so you probably don't need to say that within your message. Remember, people are more likely to read your message if it has a short-but-descriptive subject line, text that is brief and to the point, and contains enough information for the readers to determine whether your information can help them (or whether they have information that can assist you).

Exporting Your Information

Suppose you contact others who are interested in your research findings. What's the best way to share your information with them? Certainly, you can type everything up, print it, and send it to them. Or you can export a copy of your genealogy database file — which the recipients can then import into their databases and run as many reports as they want — and save a few trees in the process.

Generating GEDCOM files

Most genealogical databases subscribe to a common standard for exporting their information called *Genealogical Data Communication,* or GEDCOM. (Beware that some genealogical databases deviate from the standard a little — making things somewhat confusing.)

A *GEDCOM file* is a text file that contains your genealogical information with a set of tags that tells the genealogical database importing the information where to place it within its structure. For a little history and more information about GEDCOM, see Chapter 3. (Flip ahead to Figure 12-2 later in this chapter to see an example of a GEDCOM file.)

You may be asking, *Why is GEDCOM important?* It can save you time and energy in the process of sharing information. The next time someone asks you to send them your data, you can export your genealogy data into a GEDCOM file and send it to them instead of typing it up or saving a copy of your entire database.

Making a GEDCOM file using most software programs is quite easy. This is true for RootsMagic, too, if you're using the full version of the program. If you're using the full version of RootsMagic or you want to follow the steps in the trial version simply to familiarize yourself with exporting information, try this:

1. **Open RootsMagic.**
   Usually, you can open your software by double-clicking the icon for that program or by going to the Programs (or All Programs) menu from the Start button and selecting the particular program.

2. **Use the default database that appears, or choose File→Open to open another database.**

XML: GEDCOM's successor?

Although GEDCOM was originally designed to help researchers exchange information with each other using various genealogical software programs, it isn't necessarily the best way to present information on the World Wide Web. There have been efforts over the past several years to create a better way to display and identify genealogical information on the Web. Eventually, these efforts could produce the successor to GEDCOM.

One of the possible successors to GEDCOM is *eXtensible Markup Language,* more commonly recognized by the acronym, *XML.* XML is similar to HyperText Markup Language (HTML) in that it uses tags to describe information. However, the purpose of XML is different than HTML. HTML was designed to tell a Web browser, such as Netscape or Internet Explorer, how to arrange text and graphics on a page. XML is designed not only to display information, but also to describe the information.

An early version of XML for the genealogical community was *GedML* developed by Michael Kay. GedML uses XML tags to describe genealogical data on the Web, much like GEDCOM does for genealogical software. Here's an example of information provided in a GEDCOM file and its GedML equivalent:

GEDCOM:
```
  0 @I0904@ INDI
  1 NAME Samuel Clayton /ABELL/
  1 SEX M
  1 BIRT
  2 DATE 16 Mar 1844
  2 PLAC Nelson County, KY
  1 FAMS @F0397@
```

GedML:

```
<INDI ID="I0904">
<NAME> Samuel Clayton <S>ABELL</S></NAME>
<SEX>M</SEX>
<EVEN EV='BIRT'>
<DATE>16 Mar 1844</DATE>
<PLAC> Nelson County, KY</PLAC> </EVEN>
<FAMS REF="F397"/>
</INDI>
```

XML, whether it's GedML or some other XML structure, promises an enhancement of the searchability of genealogical documents on the Web. Right now, it's difficult for genealogically focused search engines to identify what's genealogical in nature and what's not (for more on genealogically focused search engines, see Chapter 4). Also, tags allow search engines to determine whether a particular data element is a name or a place.

XML also provides an efficient way to link genealogical data between Web sites, gives users more control over how particular text is displayed (such as notes), and allows genealogists to place information directly on the Web without using a program to convert databases or GEDCOM files to HTML.

For more information on GedML, see users.breathe .com/mhkay/gedml/.

3. **After you open the database for which you want to create a GEDCOM file, choose File→Export GEDCOM File.**
   The GEDCOM Export dialog box appears, as shown in Figure 12-1.

411

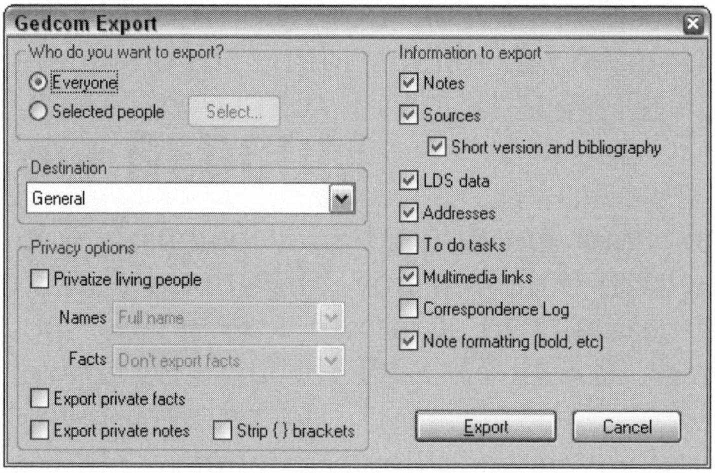

Figure 12-1:
The Export
dialog box
enables you to
choose who
and what to
include in your
GEDCOM file.

4. **Choose whether you want to include everyone in your database in your GEDCOM file or only selected people. You can also choose the output format and what types of information to include, and then click Export.**
   If you choose to include only selected people in your GEDCOM file, you need to complete another dialog box marking those people to include. Highlight the individual's name, and then select Mark People→Person to include him or her. After you select all the people you want to include, click OK.

   If you choose to include Everyone from the GEDCOM Export box or after you select certain people to include and click OK, the GEDCOM file to create dialog box opens, where you can enter a name for the file.

5. **Type the new name for your GEDCOM file in the File Name field and then click Save.**
   At this point, whether a file is actually created depends on whether you're using the full version of RootsMagic or the trial version.

After a GEDCOM file is created on your hard drive, you

can open it in a word processor (such as WordPad or NotePad) and review it to ensure that the information is formatted the way you want it. See Figure 12-2 for an example. Also, reviewing the file in a word processor is a good idea so you can ensure that you included no information on living persons. After you're satisfied with the file, you can cut and paste it into an e-mail message or send it as an attachment using your e-mail program.

Figure 12-2:
An example of a GEDCOM file opened in Windows WordPad.

```
1 NAME Samuel Clayton /Abell/
1 BIRT
2 DATE 1810
2 PLAC Cedar Creek,Nelson,Kentucky,USA
2 SOUR @S00001@
3 PAGE http://trees.ancestry.com/pt/person.aspx?pid=-2062150436&tid=516351
1 DEAT
2 DATE 1890
2 PLAC Lyons,Larue,Kentucky,USA
2 SOUR @S00001@
3 PAGE http://trees.ancestry.com/pt/person.aspx?pid=-2062150436&tid=516351
1 NOTE @N00001@
1 NOTE @N00024@
1 FAMC @F00007@
0 @I00002@ INDI
```

Reports

GEDCOM is a great option when two individuals have genealogical software that supports the standard. But what about all those people who are new to genealogy and haven't invested in software yet? How do you send them information that they can use? One option is to generate reports through your genealogical software, export them into your word processor, and then print copies to mail (or attach copies of the word-processing file to e-mail messages).

The process for generating a family tree or report should be similar for most genealogical software. RootsMagic is the software we use to demonstrate the process of creating reports. If you've not yet installed the version on the CD-ROM and entered or imported some information, you might want to check out Chapter 3. It gives step-by-step instructions for entering all your detailed family information

413

into RootsMagic.

Before you can generate a report, you have to find the person who will be the focus of that report. Here's a quick refresher on how to get to the appropriate person's record:

1. **Open RootsMagic.**
   Usually, you can open your software by double-clicking the icon for that program or by going to the Programs (or All Programs) menu from the Start button and selecting the particular program.

2. **Choose File→Open.**
   This action brings up the RootsMagic Database to Open dialog box, which lists the RootsMagic files on your computer.

3. **Select the family file for which you want to generate a chart/report by highlighting the file name and clicking Open.**

4. **Highlight the name of the person who will serve as the focus for your report.**
   On the Pedigree tab, highlight the name of the focal person of the family you select.

   For example, if Matthew wants to generate a report for his ancestor Samuel Clayton Abell, he highlights the Samuel Abell file.

5. **Click the Reports icon.**
   The Print Reports dialog box appears with a list of reports in the left column and options for the report in the right column.

6. **Choose the type of report on the left, set your options on the right, then click Create.**
   RootsMagic generates the report and displays it on your screen.

If You Post It, They Will Come

Instead of sending information to several different individuals, consider placing your information at a site where people can access it at their convenience. One option is to post your information on a Web site. (See Chapter 13 for more information.) But you have some other options if you're not ready to take the Web-designing plunge.

One option is to find others who are working on the same surnames or geographical areas and who already have Web pages, and ask them to post your information on their sites. Don't be offended if they decline — most Internet accounts have specific storage limits, and they may not have room for your information.

A second option is to submit your information to a general site that collects GEDCOM files. Examples of these sites include

- **Ancestry World Tree:**
  www.ancestry.com/share/awt/main.htm

- **GenServ:** www.genserv.com

- **WorldConnect:** worldconnect.rootsweb.com

Citing Your Sources

We can't stress enough the importance of citing your sources when sharing information — online or through traditional means. Be sure to include references that reflect where you obtained your information; that's just as important when you share your information as it is when you research it. Not only does referencing provide the other person with leads to possible additional information, but it also gives you a place to return and double-check your facts if someone challenges your facts. Sometimes, after exchanging information with another researcher, you both notice that you have conflicting data about a particular ancestor. Knowing where to turn to double-check the facts (and, with any luck, find out who has the correct information) can save you time and embarrassment.

Here are some examples of ways to cite online sources of information:

- ✔ **E-mail messages:** Matthew Helm, [<ezgeneal ogy@aol.com or 111 Main Street, Anyplace, Anystate 11111]. "Looking for George Helm," Message to April Helm, 12 October 2007. [Message cites vital records in Helm's possession.]

- ✔ **Newsgroups:** Matthew Helm, [<ezgenealogy@ aol.com > or 111 Main Street, Anyplace, Anystate 11111]. "Computing in Genealogy" in soc.genealogy.computing, 05 June 2006.

- ✔ **Web sites:** Matthew Helm, [<ezgenealogy@aol.com > or 111 Main Street, Anyplace, Anystate 11111]. "Helm's Genealogy Toolbox."<genealogy.tbox.com> January 2004. [This site contains numerous links to other genealogical resources on the Internet. On January 12, located and checked links on Abell family, found two that were promising.] (Of course, with a note like the preceding one in brackets, you expect that your next two citations are the two Web sites that looked promising. For each site, you should provide notes stating exactly what you did or did not find.)

 Although most genealogical software programs now enable you to store source information and citations along with your data, many still don't export the source information automatically. For that reason, double-check any reports or GEDCOMs you generate to see whether your source information is included before sharing them with other researchers. If the information isn't included, create a new GEDCOM file that includes sources.

Mandatory Lecture on Privacy

We couldn't sleep at night if we didn't give you the mandatory lecture on maintaining the privacy of living individuals when you share your genealogical information. Seriously, we cannot stress this information enough.

In the rush to get genealogical information posted on the Internet, people sometimes forget that portions of the information in their databases, and thus in their GEDCOM files, are considered private.

Why worry about privacy? Ah, allow us to enlighten you . . .

We've heard horror stories about Social Security numbers of living individuals ending up in GEDCOM files that are available on the Internet. We've also heard of people who didn't know that their biological parents weren't married (to each other, anyway) and found out through an online database. Private detectives and other people who search for information on living persons frequently use genealogical databases to track people. For these reasons, it is illegal in some states and countries to share information about living persons on the Internet without first getting each person's written permission to do so. To avoid an invasion of privacy and any legal problems that could arise from you sharing your information, you should always clean out (exclude) any information on living individuals from your GEDCOM file before you give it to anyone.

Chapter 13

Finding Your Online Home

So you've loaded your genealogical database with information about your relatives and ancestors, and you've started sharing data with others by e-mail. Now you're ready to find a home to which you can open the doors to guests, inviting others to come to you for information and advice.

In the not-so-distant past, our advice was to create from scratch and post your own home page (Web site). But these days, there are much easier options than mastering Hyper-Text Markup Language (HTML) and other coding programs. Online communities already exist where all you have to do is use a template to create a snazzy-looking site. After your site is up and running, you can invite all your family and friends over. You can even make your site available to the general public so that others you don't know who might be researching the same families can find you on the Internet.

In this chapter, we explore networking sites, blogs, and even basic home-grown HTML Web pages (for the die-hard do-it-yourselfers) where you can post your information on the Web. Also we review how to use genealogical utility programs to help put content in specific formats on your site.

Perfecting the Art of Networking

If you're an average person who likes to use the Internet to aid in your research but who doesn't have time to learn a whole computer programming language, the past few years have probably been like a dream to you. The growing number of Web sites intended to help people find other people with the same interests, talents, backgrounds, and locations is amazing!

It's hard to turn on the news without hearing some reference to one of these many networking sites — think Facebook and MySpace.com. Facebook (www.facebook.com) touts itself as a social utility meant to connect people with a common strand in their lives, whether that's working together, attending the same school, or living in the same or nearby communities. The catch-phrase for MySpace.com (www.myspace.com) — "A Place for Friends" — says it all. It's an online community where people with similar interests can interact. Although both of these popular networking sites have members with expressed interest in genealogy, we want to introduce you to networking sites with a more targeted focus on genealogy — after all, this is a genealogy-related book, right?

Like the number of networking sites in general, the number of genealogical-networking sites has grown at an incredible pace over the past couple of years. You might have heard of some of these:

- ✔ Geni (www.geni.com)
- ✔ Familyrelatives.com (www.familyrelatives.com)
- ✔ WeRelate.org (www.werelate.org)
- ✔ Famillion (www.famillion.com)
- ✔ OneGreatFamily (www.onegreatfamily.com)
- ✔ FamilyLink.com (www.familylink.com)

One curious but very appropriate thing that we've noticed about the genealogy-based networking sites is that instead of starting a new member's profile with personal information about that member, the profile at many of these sites typically begins with a pedigree chart (also called a family tree). Another neat feature of some of these sites is that they use mathematical algorithms to link your tree(s) with trees that other people have submitted. In essence, this means they are trying to help connect you to others with the same family lines.

If you're looking to set up a genealogy-networking site where others can discover your family lines and contribute information directly to you in a public forum, Geni is one place to start. Here's what to do to get started:

1. **Using your Web browser, go to www.geni.com.**
   The Geni Web site is easy to figure out, with its main purpose explicitly stated near the top: "Create your family tree and stay in touch."

2. **In the Start Here box, enter your first name in the Your First Name field.**

3. **Enter your last name in the Your Last Name field.**

4. **Type your preferred e-mail address in the Email field.**

5. **Click the radio button corresponding to your gender.**

6. **Click Start My Tree.**

And viola! You have officially started your genealogical networking profile. Of course, your profile doesn't have much information of substance yet. It simply has your name, e-mail address, and gender — not enough to let others know who and where you're researching. So, you want to go ahead and enter a little more information:

1. **Starting with the My Tree tab in the Geni profile, click on the parent whose information you are ready to add.**
   You can use the instruction dialog box that appears in the bottom center of the screen. Simply follow the instructions to add information about your parents.

   For this example, to enter information about your father, click the blue parental box above your box on the family tree. The Add a Person dialog box pops up.

2. **At the very top of the box, check the Divorced box if your parents are divorced.**

3. **Enter your father's first name in the First Name field.**

4. **If your father's last name is different from the one that auto-populates, fix it in the Last Name field.**

5. **Click on the appropriate radio button indicating whether your father is Living or Deceased.**

6. **If you like, type your father's e-mail address in the Email (Optional) field.**

7. **Click the <u>More</u> link if you want to add more birthdate information about your father, or click Add if you want to add only basic information.**

After you have added information about a person using one of the boxes in the family tree, the box becomes activated and little yellow arrows appear surrounding it (see Figure 13-1). You can click on these arrows to navigate to that person's parents, spouse(s), and children to add more individuals to your tree.

Figure 13-1:
After data about an ancestor has been entered, their box activates and enables the user to navigate to other ancestors to enter more information.

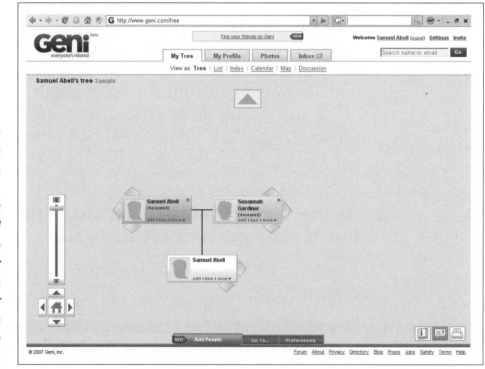

The Geni site is quite impressive in the ways it helps you share your family tree research with others. Here's a quick overview of the various parts of the site:

- **My Tree:** Under this tab, you can view information about the family members included in the tree as a family tree (pedigree chart) or a list. You can also search for people in the tree by their surname in the Index section. If you enter birthdates and anniversaries for your family members, the Calendar gives you a consolidated list that helps you remember special events. The Map shows you where your family members currently live and were born, if you include locations in the individualized data you record on the site. And the Discussion section allows you and visitors to your Geni tree to exchange written commentary on any topic you choose.

- **My Profile:** The Profile section is where you can store data specifically about you — everything from your birthdate and age, to educational information, to your work experience, to personal narratives about your life, aspirations, research interests, or whatever you'd like to say about yourself in a free-form text box. This is also where you can track who you've invited to view and participate in your Geni tree. You can view the Profile data in different ways — at the top, you choose the setting of You, Family, Tree, Friends, or Public. Depending on which setting you choose, various aspects of your profile may or may not be visible. This is a nice feature so you can see how much of your profile or personal information is accessible by the public, which enables you to fix your security settings to restrict information that you don't want available to everyone.

- ✔ **Photos:** Just as you would expect, the Photos section is where you can upload and sort photos into albums. There are various categories for your photos designated by content, such as whether you're included in the album, whether the photos are specifically of you, or which photos are your favorites.

- ✔ **Inbox:** The last tab in your Geni tree site is your online mail account. It's much like any other e-mail account. You have separate boxes for incoming mail, requests, saved messages, and sent mail.

It's worth noting that a couple of other sites that we would classify as social networking do not quite fit the family tree mold. They are interesting sites that we want to mention because they hold great potential in making your family history research a little more colorful and exciting. They are

- ✔ **Story of My Life (www.storyofmylife.com):** This is an online memoir site. You can record text narratives, videos, pictures, and even entire journals recounting anecdotal stories of your life. It's free to register and use the basic service, but if you want the Story of My Life Foundation to keep your stories forever, you have to pay a fee for Forever space.

- ✔ **Second Life (www.secondlife.com):** If you've been around for awhile and/or you've seen a previous edition of this book, you might be familiar with the old Geocities neighborhoods. They were online neighborhoods where you could create a Web page and link to others with similar interests in the neighborhood. (Geocities is now a Yahoo! domain and still offers Web hosting. Check out the "Building Your Own Home" section later in this chapter for more information about them.) Second Life is kind of like the old Geocities, only way more cool — like a third or fourth generation of neighborhoods built on new technology. Second Life is a three-dimensional (3D) online world of digital neighborhoods. It is created by the residents and has imagery reflecting their personalities. Although its intent is not solely for genealogy, it does have interesting potential and applicability for genealogists. Imagine creating an environment to resemble your great-grandfather's world in 1850 Virginia. Or presenting an ancestor's experience on an orphan train to the western United States. Or simply a depiction of your family tree in 3D. You lend your creativity to present your family history in new and exciting ways. The catch — there is cost involved for any services and functionality beyond the free basic membership.

Blogging for Attention

Blog is a common term around the Internet these days. But what exactly is a blog? *Blog* is an abbreviated name for a *Weblog,* and it's just what it sounds like: an online journal or log. Typically blogs include narratives on whatever topic the blogger (the person who maintains the blog) feels like writing about. Therefore genealogy blogs typically contain narratives on family history research. These narratives are much like the Web boards of years past where people could go and post information about their research findings or needs, and others would post replies. The main difference is that the blogger typically updates the blog on a regular and frequent basis, anywhere from daily to weekly to monthly, and the blogger is the one who initiates the topics of discussion that are welcome on a particular blog. Some blogs even contain photos, video or audio clips, and links to

Privacy

Sometimes, we genealogists get so caught up in dealing with the records of deceased persons that we forget one basic fact: Much of the information we've collected and put in our databases pertains to *living individuals.* In our haste to share our information with others online, we often create our GEDCOM files and reports, and then ship them off to recipients without thinking twice about whether we may offend someone or invade his or her privacy by including personal information. The same thing goes for posting information directly to Web sites and in our blogs — we write the data into the family tree or include anecdotal information in our blog narratives without thinking about the consequences to living individuals. We need to be more careful.

Well, okay, why *shouldn't* you include everything you know about your relatives?

✔ **You may invade someone's right to privacy:** Your relatives may not want you to share personal information about them with others, and they may not have given you permission to do so. The same thing goes for photos and video clips. Just because you're gung ho to show the world the group photo from your family reunion does not mean that every one of your parents, siblings, aunts, uncles, and cousins feels the same way. So don't share the information or the image without the permission of everyone involved.

✔ **Genealogists aren't the only people who visit genealogical Internet sites:** For example, private detectives are known to lurk about, watching for information that may help their cases. Estranged spouses may visit sites looking for a way to track down their former partners. Also, people with less-than-honorable intentions may visit a genealogical Web site looking for potential scam or abuse victims. And some information, such as your mother's

426

maiden name, may help the unscrupulous carry out fraud.

When sharing genealogical information, your safest bet is to include only the data that pertains to people who have long been deceased — unless you've obtained written consent from living persons to share information about them. By *long been deceased,* we mean deceased for more than ten years — although the time frame could be longer depending on the sensitivity of the information. You may also want to keep in mind that the U.S. Government standard dictates that no record covered under the Privacy Act is released until it's at least 72 years old.

other sites — all depending on the blogger's interests and abilities to include these things.

There are blogs available about all aspects of genealogy including how-to, news, ethnic-based research, surnames, conferences, technology, and document preservation.

Hunting blogs

Looking for genealogy blogs to aid in your family history research? There are a lot available these days and the number is growing rapidly. Of course you can find them by using a general Internet search engine, like Google.com. Or you can use a couple of other simple options for finding blogs. The first is to visit the Genealogy Blog Finder search engine at blogfinder.genealogue.com/. Here's how to use it:

1. **Open your Web browser and go to blogfinder.genealogue.com/, as shown in Figure 13-2.**

2. **In the Quick Finder field, enter the name of the family or location you are researching.**

3. Click Quick Finder.

This brings up a list of results with links to each. Click on any that interest you.

If you're not sure of a spelling or you just want to browse to see what's available, you can also use the menu system to navigate the Genealogy Blog Finder. All of the topics under which the blogs are organized are accessible from the main Web page.

There is a second, relatively simple way to find blogs. Go to one of the blog-hosting sites that we mention in the next section of this chapter and use the search functionality on the site to see if there are any blogs available through that service that fit your needs. For example, if you're looking for anything available on the Helm family in Fayette County, Illinois, you can search using the terms "Abel" and "Illinois" or "Abel" and "Fayette." Although this method of searching is not difficult, it can become more time-consuming than the blog-specific search engine route.

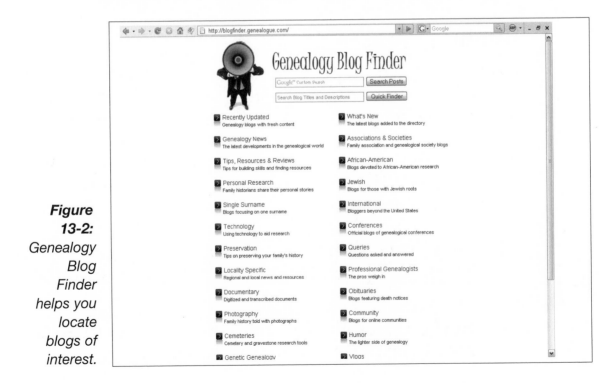

Figure 13-2: *Genealogy Blog Finder helps you locate blogs of interest.*

Getting a blog of your own

If you're ready to start your own blog where you can share information about your research pursuits and genealogical interests, there are several sites ready and willing to help you. Three that come to mind are

- Blogger.com (www.blogger.com)

- Blog.com (www.blog.com)

- Blogthing (www.blogthing.com)

- BlogoMonster (www.blogomonster.com)

- WordPress.com (www.wordpress.com)

Each of these three sites offers easy-to-use instructions for creating your blog. You can choose from templates for the overall design at each site, and privacy controls so you can determine who has access to your blog and what levels of permission they have (whether they can just read your narratives or post replies, as well as whether they can contribute original narratives initiating online discussions). All three also offer the ability to post photos and files.

Here's a walk-through on how to set up your own blog at Blogger.com:

1. **Open your Web browser and go to www.blogger.com.**
   This opens the Blogger.com site. The site has several areas, including an online tour, a sign-in area for returning bloggers, and step-by-step instructions for creating a blog.

2. **Click Create Your Blog Now(the button looks like an arrow).**
   This brings you to Step 1 in the Blogger process,

which is to create a Google account. If you already have a Google account, it offers you the opportunity to log in using your existing account instead of creating a new one.

3. **In the Email Address field, type in your current or preferred e-mail address.**

4. **In the Retype Email Address field, type the same e-mail address again.**

5. **Complete the Enter a Password field, typing in a password that is at least eight characters long.**
   Remember that when setting up a password, you want to choose a combination of letters, numbers, or characters that won't be easy for others to decipher. We recommend you do not use your pet's name or your mother's maiden name. Instead, it's better if you choose something that is not common knowledge about you — the name of your favorite book character with your favorite number on the end or a special text character like $, #, or %. Click on the Password Strength link if you want Blogger.com–specific information about selecting a password. Blogger.com provides some excellent hints on making your password as safe as possible.

6. **Provide the same password again in the Retype Password field.**

7. **Choose the name you want to show to others on the blog in the Display Name field.**
   This is where you select an alias if you don't want your real name posted on the blog. You might choose to use just your first name, or just your last name, or a nickname, or to select some totally new and

random name that is catchy and fun.

8. **In the Word Verification box, you need to retype the word that you see above the field. The word is usually presented in a wavy, distorted way.**

9. **Click on the Terms of Service and read through them. If you agree to Blogger.com's terms for using their service, click the I Accept the Terms of Service check box.**

10. **Click Continue.**
    This takes you to Step 2: Name Your Blog.

11. **In the Blog Title field, enter a name for your blog.**

12. **Type part of a Web address for your blog in the Blog Address (URL) field.**
    When choosing what to use for the section of the Web address that you get to designate, think about using something that fits with the title of your blog. For example, if your blog will be called Anna's Ancestral Avenues, you might try using AncestralAve or AAncestralAve or even AnnasAncestralAvenue in the URL.

    There's a Check Availability link under the field where you can see whether your preferred URL is already taken. If you click the Check Availability link and find that your choice is already taken, Blogger.com proposes some similar alternatives that are still available. You can choose to use one of the alternatives or to try starting from scratch in selecting the URL.

13. **Click Continue.**
    The next part of Step 2 pops up, where you select

the template to use in designing the look of your blog.

14. **Scroll through the list of templates and select the one that you like best.**
    If you want to see the template a little bigger and better, click the Preview Template link under the template. This enables you to see whether you really like that template.

15. **Click Continue.**
    Congratulations! You have just created your blog. You get a message confirming that you have completed the blog creation process and you are now ready to begin posting to your blog.

16. **Click Start Posting to continue on and begin adding content to your blog.**
    The next screen that pops open has three tabs (Posting, Settings, and Template) and a link to View Blog. You need to navigate through this part of the site, providing the specific information that you wish to include on your blog. Each of the tabs has several sub-tabs where you can control various aspects of your blog. The site is easy to use and intuitive by simply clicking through the tabs and sub-tabs. Here's a high-level description of what you can do in each tab:

    • In the Posting section, you can compose narratives including research findings, your personal thoughts on how to research in certain areas, your opinions about new methods for researching or recent findings on celebrity ancestries — pretty much whatever you think others would be interested in reading about you and your genealogy. Just keep in mind that if you make your blog available to anyone and everyone, you may get good and bad responses to your thoughts and opinions.

- In the Settings section, you provide a description of your blog's intent, determine whether your blog is listed for public consumption, and choose some other editing settings, as well as set your preferences for archiving and e-mail, and assign permissions to others for using your blog. This is also where you can go if you decide to delete your blog — removing it forever and ever.
- In the Template section, you can edit the look of your blog, including the layout, colors, and fonts, or custom-write HTML or change templates.

After you have your first blog set up, you're ready to start posting information about your genealogical insights and discoveries.

Building Your Own Home

Are you the type of person who prefers to create things personally? If so, you might want to learn HTML and build your own home page. But before you can build anything, you need to find a home (that is, a *host*) for it. Although you can design a basic home page on your own computer using no more than a word processor, others won't be able to see it until you put the page on a Web server on the Internet. A *Web server* is a computer that's connected directly to the Internet that serves up Web pages when you request them using your computer's Web browser.

Commercial Internet service providers

If you subscribe to a commercial *Internet service provider*

(ISP) like America Online, AT&T, or MSN, or if you subscribe to a local provider, you may already have a home for your Web pages. Most commercial ISPs include a specific space allocation for user home pages in their memberships, as well as some tools to help you build your site. Check your membership agreement to see whether you have space. Then you can follow the ISP's instructions for creating your Web site (using the service's page builder or editor) or for getting your independently created Web pages from your computer to the ISP's server. (If you didn't keep a copy of your membership agreement, don't fret! Most ISPs have an informational Web page that you can get to from your ISP's main page; the informational page reviews membership benefits.) You may as well take advantage of this service if you're already paying for it.

If your particular membership level doesn't include Web space, but the ISP has other membership levels that do, hold off on bumping up your membership level. You can take advantage of some free Web-hosting services that may save you money. Keep reading . . .

Free Web-hosting services

There are some Web sites that give you free space for your home page provided that you agree to their rules and restrictions. We can safely bet that you won't have any problems using one of these freebies, because the terms (such as no pornography, nudity, or explicit language allowed) are genealogist-friendly.

If you decide to take advantage of Web space, remember that the companies providing the space must pay their bills. Often they can make space available free to individuals by charging advertisers for banners and other advertisements. In such cases, the Web host reserves the right to require that you leave these advertisements on your home page. If you

434

don't like the idea of an advertisement on your home page, or if you have strong objections to one of the companies that advertises with the site that gives you free space, you should find a fee-based Web space for your home page.

Here are a few free Web hosting services that have been around for awhile:

- Yahoo! Geocities (geocities.yahoo.com)

- Tripod (www.tripod.lycos.com)

- Rootsweb.com (accounts.rootsweb.com/index.cgi?op=show&page=freagree.htm)

Allow us to show you how to register for free space on Tripod:

1. **Browse on over to** www.tripod.lycos.com **and click the Start Now link.**
   This takes you to the Tripod Plan Options page, where you can do a quick comparison of all that Tripod has to offer.

2. **Click Sign Up in the Tripod Free section.**
   The Choose a Membership Plan page pops up.

3. **Complete the online membership application.**
   The online form asks you to provide a username and password, as well as your first name, last name, mailing address with ZIP code, country of residence, birth date, e-mail address, and gender. It also asks about educational level and occupation, although you are not required to complete these fields in order to sign up. You can also indicate your marketing preferences — whether you want to receive additional items or information from Lycos

and partner companies. Lastly, you must complete a registration verification section where you have to type a code that is provided in a wavy, hard-to-read format.

5. **Upon completing the form and reading the consent statement, click I Agree.**
   After you submit the registration form, Tripod takes you to a page with information on how to get started building your Web site.

Do You Speak HTML?

HyperText Markup Language (or HTML) is the language of the World Wide Web. HTML is a code in which text documents are written so Web browsers can read and interpret those documents, converting them into graphical images and text that you can see through the browser. HTML is a relatively easy language to learn, and many genealogists who post Web pages are self-taught. If you prefer not to read about it and teach yourself by experimenting instead, there are sure to be classes as well as other resources in your area that could teach you the basics of HTML. Check with a local community college for structured classes, local genealogical societies for any workshops focusing on designing and posting Web pages, or the World Wide Web itself for online courses.

Here are a couple of things to remember about HTML:

✔ You write HTML as a text document using a text editor, an HTML editor, or a word processor, and you save it as a text document (with the file name extension of htm or html).

✔ You use a Web browser to interpret HTML documents as graphical and text pages on the Internet.

What does HTML look like?

To get an idea of what HTML looks like — both as the text document and as the converted graphical image — take a look at some extremely simple HTML tags that April created for a Web page called My Favorite Abe. Figure 13-3 shows the Web page that's created by the tags.

Here's what the HTML codes (also called tags) look like:

```
<HTML>
<HEAD>
<TITLE>My Favorite Abe</TITLE>
</HEAD>
<BODY BGCOLOR = "White" ALINK = "Blue" VLINK = "Gray">
<H1><FONT COLOR = "Green"><CENTER>My Favorite
Abe</CENTER></FONT></H1>
```

```
While there are several famous Abes (Abe Vigoda, Abe Kobo, and
Abe Fortas, to name a few), by far the most famous and my favorite
is Abe Lincoln.<P>
Abraham Lincoln was born February 12, 1809, in Kentucky and died
April 14, 1865, in Washington, D.C. He married Mary Todd with
whom he had four sons. Here are the dates of some of Abe's
accomplishments:
<UL>
<LI>1858: Ran for Senator
<LI>1860 and 1864: Elected President
<LI>1863: Issued Emancipation Proclamation
</UL><P>
If you'd like to read more about Abe, check out his official entry on
<A HREF = "http://www.whitehouse.gov/history/presidents/
al16.html"> The White House</A> Web site.
</BODY>
</HTML>
```

The tags are placed within angle brackets, like this: <BODY>. These tags tell the browser how to interpret the text that follows and whether to actually show that text on the Web page. Just as you have to tell the browser when to begin interpreting text in a certain manner, you also have to tell it when to stop. This ending command consists of an open bracket, a front slash, the tag word, and a close bracket, like this: </BODY>.

For example:

<TITLE>My Favorite Abe</TITLE>

In this line, the <TITLE> tag tells the browser where to begin treating text as a title and </TITLE> also tells it where to end that treatment. Think of HTML tags as on and off commands where < > indicates *on* and </ > indicates *off.*

Some basic tags for writing your own HTML

If you've been reading along systematically in this chapter, you know that just preceding this section is an example of what HTML codes or tags look like. But what are the tags themselves? HTML involves too many tags to do justice here when the main point is to create and post a basic genealogical Web page. We really only have space here to cover just a few of the many tags.

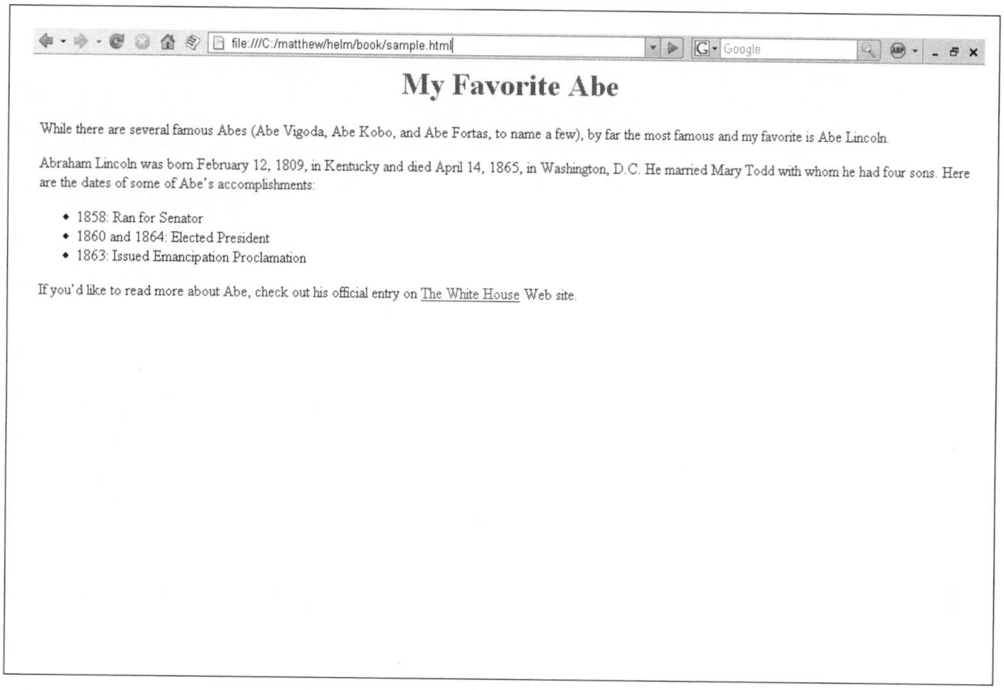

The following is a screenshot of a Web browser window with the URL file:///C:/matthew/helm/book/sample.html

My Favorite Abe

While there are several famous Abes (Abe Vigoda, Abe Kobo, and Abe Fortas, to name a few), by far the most famous and my favorite is Abe Lincoln.

Abraham Lincoln was born February 12, 1809, in Kentucky and died April 14, 1865, in Washington, D.C. He married Mary Todd with whom he had four sons. Here are the dates of some of Abe's accomplishments:

- 1858: Ran for Senator
- 1860 and 1864: Elected President
- 1863: Issued Emancipation Proclamation

If you'd like to read more about Abe, check out his official entry on The White House Web site.

Figure 13-3:
The My Favorite Abe Web page as displayed in a Web browser.

If you're interested in more advanced HTML programming, we recommend that you check out these other *For Dummies* books (all published by Wiley Publishing, Inc.): *Creating Web Pages For Dummies,* 8th Edition, by Bud E. Smith and Arthur Bebak; *The Internet For Dummies,* 11th Edition, by John R. Levine, Carol Baroudi, and Margaret Levine Young; and *HTML 4 For Dummies,* 5th Edition, by Ed Tittel and Mary Burmeister.

Take a look at Table 13-1 for some basic tags and their functions. For each tag identified, the *off* (or ending) command would be the same word in brackets preceded by a / (slash symbol). (We explore a few exceptions to the off-command rule in Table 13-2.) You must turn off tags in the reverse order that you turned them on. For example, if you use the tags <HTML><HEAD>, you close them with </HEAD></HTML>.

Table 13-1 explains what some common HTML tags tell Web browsers to do.

439

Table 13-1		Tag, You're It!
Tag	**What It Means**	**What It Tells the Browser**
<HTML>	HTML	This text document is written in HTML and should be interpreted as such.
<HEAD>	Head element	The following text is the header of the document. (This is where you put the title and any descriptive information.)
<TITLE>	Title	The following text is the title of the Web page. (It appears in the title bar at the top of your browser.)
<BODY>	Body	The body or main part of the document. (Here you put all pertinent information that you want to appear on your Web page.)
<H1>	Heading	Denotes a heading for the page or section of text and the size that it should be. (Headings come in six levels: <H1>, <H2>, <H3>, <H4>, <H5>, and <H6>. <H1> is the largest print, and <H6> is the smallest.)
<CENTER>	Center	Center the following text on the page or within a table cell or column.
<B>	Bold	Bold the following text.

<I>	Italicize	Italicize the following text.
<U>	Underline	Underline the following text.
<A HREF= "URL">	A hypertext link	The following text is a link to another reference page/site and should take people there when they click it. (The URL for the other site goes in the quotation marks; the off command for this code is simply </A>.)
<FONT COLOR=" (color)">	Font color	The following text should be a particular color. (The color, written in either code or plain English, goes in the quotation marks; the off command is </FONT>.)
<FONT SIZE=" (number)">	Font size	The following text should be a particular size. (The size goes in the quotation marks; the off command is </FONT>.)
<FONT FACE=" (font name)">	Font face	The following text should be printed in a particular font or typeface. (The font or typeface name goes in the quotation marks; the off command is </FONT>.)
<OL>	Ordered list	The following is a numbered list. (Use this code with <LI>, identified in Table 13-2. The off command is </OL>.)
<UL>	Unordered list	The following is going to be a

bulleted list. (Use this code
with <LI>, identified in Table
13-2. The off command is
</UL>.)

You don't necessarily have to close all HTML tags. Table
13-2 shows codes that are exceptions to the off-command
rule. For these codes, you don't have to use a </> code to
tell the browser when to stop interpreting something.

Table 13-2   Closing-Tag Exceptions

Tag	What It Means	What It Tells the Browser
<P>	Paragraph break	Skip a line and begin a new paragraph.
 	Line break	End a line here, then go to the next line to begin the next command or line of text.
<LI>	List item	This is a new item to identify on its own line in a list.
<IMG SRC "image URL">	Image source	Picks up a graphical image from a URL to insert here. (The URL or address of the graphical file goes between the quotation marks.)
<HR>	Horizontal rule	Puts a horizontal line across the page here to divide up the page.
<BODYBG COLOR= "(color) ">	Body background	The background color of the document should be a particular color. (The color, written in either code or plain English, goes in the quotation

442

		marks.)
<ALINK COLOR=" (color) ">	Active link color	Colors each link on the page a certain color until it's visited by people who load the page into their browsers. (The color, written in either code or plain English, goes in the quotation marks.)
<VLINK COLOR=" (color) ">	Visited link color	The color that each link on the page becomes after the person clicked through to the link and then returns to the page. (The color, written in either code or plain English, goes in the quotation marks.)

 You probably noticed that we use all uppercase letters in our coding, but that's just our own preference. You can use lowercase, uppercase, or a combination of both when programming in HTML. We prefer all uppercase so we can more easily identify where the codes are when we need to edit an HTML document. We also like to skip lines between commands so we can more easily look through the HTML document to see how we coded it.

Using an HTML editor

An *HTML editor* is a program that walks you through HTML programming so you don't have to learn all the codes and remember to turn them on and off. Some editors use text that you've already written in your word processor, whereas others have you type text directly into the editor. To tell the editor how particular text should appear on a Web page (such as the format it should take — title, body of text, a list, and so on), you click an icon or drop-down menu option, and the editor applies the necessary codes.

Including Your GEDCOM

After you've designed your basic home page or acquired space on a networking site, you may find that you want to upload your GEDCOM file to it. In Chapter 12, we discussed how to generate GEDCOM files to share through e-mail. Now, we're going to examine how to format the GEDCOM file without manually converting it to HTML.

First and foremost, make sure that your GEDCOM file is ready to share with others. By this, we mean that it's free from any information that could land you in the doghouse with any of your relatives — close or distant! (For more about ensuring that your GEDCOM file has no information about living individuals, head to Chapter 12. You can also take a look at this chapter's sidebars, "Privacy" and "Copyrights.")

Some genealogical software programs enable you to indicate whether you want information on each relative included in reports and GEDCOM files. Other programs don't allow you to do this. This may mean that you need to manually scrub your GEDCOM file to remove information about all living persons.

After you have a GEDCOM file that is free of information about all living persons, you're ready to prepare it for the Web. You can choose from several programs to help you convert your GEDCOM file to HTML. GED2HTML may be the most commonly known GEDCOM-to-HTML converter available, and it's available for downloading at www.starkeffect.com/ged2html/. Here's how to use it with your cleaned GEDCOM file:

1. **Open the GED2HTML program that you**

downloaded from www.starkeffect.com/ ged2html/.

A dialog box asks you to enter the location of your GEDCOM file. (You can browse if you can't remember the path name for the GEDCOM file.)

2. **Type the path for your GEDCOM File and then click Go.**

   A typical path looks like this: c:\my documents\ helm.ged

   GED2HTML runs a program using your GEDCOM file. You can watch it going through the file in a black window that appears.

3. **After the program is done, press Enter to close the program window.**

   GED2HTML saves the output HTML files in a folder (appropriately called HTML) in the same directory where the GED2HTML program is saved.

4. **Use your Web browser to open any of the HTML output files.**

   After seeing what your output looks like and reviewing it to make sure it doesn't contain any information that shouldn't be posted, you're ready to add it to your Web site (or link to it as its own Web page).

5. **Follow any instructions from your Web host, and upload your GED2HTML files to your Web server. Put any links to those files on your home page so you can share your GEDCOM information online.**

   For example, suppose GED2HTML saved an HTML-coded index of all of the people in your GEDCOM to a file called persons.html. After uploading or copying this file to your Web host's

Copyrights

Copyright is the controlling right that a person or corporation owns over the duplication and distribution of a work that the person or corporation created. Although facts themselves can't be copyrighted, *works in which facts are contained* can be. Although the fact that your grandma was born on January 1, 1900 can't be copyrighted by anyone, a report that contains this information and was created by Aunt Lola may be. If you intend to include a significant portion of Aunt Lola's report in your own document, you need to secure permission from her to use the information.

With regard to copyright and the Internet, remember that just because you found some information on a Web site (or other Internet resource) does not mean that it's not copyrighted. If the Web site contains original material along with facts, it is copyrighted to the person who created it — regardless of whether the site has a copyright notice on it!

To protect yourself from infringing on someone's copyright and possibly ending up in a legal battle, you should do the following:

- ✔ Never copy another person's Web page, e-mail, blog, or other Internet creation (such as graphics) without his or her written consent.

- ✔ Never print out an article, story, report, or other material to share with your family, friends, genealogical or historical society, class, or anyone else without the creator's written consent.

- ✔ Always assume that a resource is copyrighted.

- ✔ Always cite sources of the information in your genealogy and on your Web pages.

- ✔ Always *link* to other Web pages rather than copying their content on your own Web site.

446

server, you can use a link command such as <A HREF = "[directory path]/persons.html"> from your main home page to this index of persons to share it on the Web.

Deciding Which Treasures to Include

Although the content of genealogical Web pages with lots of textual information about ancestors or geographic areas may be very helpful, all-text pages won't attract the attention of your visitors. Even we get tired of sorting through and reading endless narratives on Web sites; we like to see things that personalize a Web site and are fun to look at. Graphics, icons, and photographs are ideal for this purpose. A couple of nice-looking, strategically placed photos of ancestors make a site feel more like a home.

If you have some photographs that have been scanned and saved as .jpg or .gif images or some media clips (such as video or audio files) that are in a format that meet the compatibility requirements for your Web hosting service, you can post them on your Web site. If you're uploading photos or media clips to a networking site or blog, be sure to follow the Web host's instructions. And if you're uploading to a Web page that you coded personally, make sure that a copy of the .jpg or .gif file is uploaded to your Web host's server in a directory that you can point to with HTML codes on your home page. By using the <IMG SRC = " "> code, you can tell browsers where to go to pick up that image or photograph. (Be sure to type the filename for that image exactly as it appears on your hard drive or other resource.)

Just as you should be careful about posting factual information about living relatives, be careful about posting photos or recordings of them. If you want to use an image that has living relatives in it, get their permission before doing so. Some people are very sensitive about having their pictures posted on the Web. Also, use common sense and taste in selecting pictures for your page. Although a photo of little Susie at age 3 wearing a lampshade and dancing around in a tutu may be cute, a photo of Uncle Ed at age 63 doing the same thing may not be so endearing!

Part V
The Part of Tens

The 5th Wave   By Rich Tennant

"That's strange — according to your birth certificate I got from Tommy's genealogy project, you're not the Queen of the Universe and Master of All Men."

In this part . . .

Ah, The Part of Tens — a staple of the *For Dummies* books. Use these chapters as quick references when you're looking for the following:

- ✔ Items to think about when you travel for research

- ✔ Some things to ponder when designing your own genealogical Web pages

- ✔ Places to visit when you need a bit of help with your research

- ✔ Tips for making the most of your research

Chapter 14

Ten Tools for Your Genealogical Travels

Researching your family history online may jumpstart your genealogical pursuits, but there will come a time when you'd like to make a pilgrimage to your ancestor's birthplace or travel to another location to get original records or pictures. In this chapter, we discuss ways you can make your trip easier by planning your travels and taking along a few aids.

Hit the Road, Jack!: Planning Your Genealogy Travels Using the Web

A wealth of information is available to help you plan your travels — and it's all at your fingertips! You can surf the Web to check out hotels/motels, car-rental places, airlines, local attractions, and a host of other things related to research trips and vacations. Two sites that provide links to all sorts of travel-related information are MapQuest (www.mapquest.com) and the Yahoo! Travel section (dir.yahoo.com/recreation/travel). Each has sections for transportation, lodging, dining, and a variety of other things you need while traveling. You can even use MapQuest to plan your route if you're driving in North America.

Follow these steps to get driving directions from MapQuest:

1. **Using your World Wide Web browser, open the MapQuest site** (www.mapquest.com).

2. **Click the Directions icon or scroll down to the Directions block.**
   The Directions page appears, offering two columns of boxes to complete.

3. **In the first column, complete the fields indicating your Starting Location or where this part of your journey will begin.**
   You can type an actual street address in the Address or Intersection field.
     Type the city from which your journey will begin in the City field.
     Type the state or province from which you'll begin your trip in the State/Prov field. You can type the ZIP Code too, if you'd like, but it is not required.

4. **In the second column, complete the fields indicating your destination or Ending Location.**
   The destination fields are titled just like the starting fields and accept the same sort of information.

5. **Click Get Directions.**

MapQuest determines the directions from your starting point to your destination. If MapQuest can't determine a route for you, it provides an explanation and recommends revising your Directions information.

Narrowing Your Target

Before you jump in the car and start heading west, you should do a little research on the places you plan to visit. Fire up your computer at home and determine the days and hours that repositories you plan to visit are open to the public. Review their holdings to determine exactly what types of records you are looking for at particular locations. And review their rules and policies — you do not want to haul in all of your gadgets if they only allow you to bring in paper and a writing utensil.

If you are traveling during cold months, you might want to see if your destination offers lockers or a coat closet to store your jacket, umbrella, or backpack. If you plan to spend an entire day in one location, you might want to see whether they have a cafeteria or food court where you can purchase lunch, or if they have a place designated where you can eat a sack lunch you bring with you. You can iron out all sorts of details before you embark on your journey.

If you are traveling within the United States, the USGen-Web Project (www. usgenweb.com) provides links for every state and details on many of the resources that are available.

Remembering Your Laptop or Notebook

It would be frustrating if you reached your destination and found that you didn't have any of your past findings and leads for research on this trip with you, and you couldn't remember much about the ancestors you set out to research. It's easy to get caught up in packing and meeting departure times, and to forget some of the most important things you need to have with you. We don't expect you to have all of your research memorized, so be sure that you set your laptop computer or your notebook full of family charts, pictures, and notes in an obvious place so you don't forget to take them along. While you're at it, keep a printed copy of the directions you just received from MapQuest (in the preceding section) with your laptop or notebook so you don't forget them either.

Flashing Your Treasures

Our title for this section caught your attention, didn't it? Well, it's really not risqué — we're talking about flash drives (also sometimes called JumpDrives). Flash drives are tiny devices that store files, presentations, music, and/or photos. They are relatively inexpensive and store lots of information — typically up to 2 GB. They plug into the USB port on any computer (provided the computer has a USB port, that is) and can help you transfer files from one location to another quickly. Most flash drives fit on your keychain or a necklace so you can carry them almost anywhere with you.

This is a nice gadget to have if you're going to share your genealogical treasures with others at a family reunion or society meeting, or if you plan to give a presentation at a genealogical meeting or conference.

Capturing a Picture-Perfect Moment

If your mother is like April's mother, she drilled it into your head when you were young that you should always carry a camera with you when you travel. It doesn't have to be a digital camera, although we highly recommend them. The point-and-click digital cameras have come down a lot in price over the past few years and they are handy to have around for many reasons — photos at family reunions, pictures of headstones in cemeteries, or snapshots of the family homestead or some landmark near it. If you're visiting a library or archive that allows you to bring it inside with you, it might even be used to photograph documents.

Be sure to take plenty of film for your traditional camera or an extra memory card or stick for your digital camera, and extra batteries.

Of course, you may be one of those people who have a camera with you at all times in the form of your cellular phone. We have to admit that we were a bit skeptical about cellular phones with cameras built in when they were first introduced. However, we have grown to understand the practical applications that such a gadget offers. The ability to take photos on a whim is a luxury that truly can benefit a genealogist.

Using Your Cell Phone As a Cell Phone

In the preceding section, we talk about using your cell phone as a camera — provided your cell phone has that functionality. But you should take your cell phone with you on your research jaunts and ensure that it is charged at all times so that you have it to use as a phone, too. We probably don't have to explain that you will want it if you have an emergency while traveling. It's also useful when you need to call a relative or research buddy if you have questions about a particular ancestor that you're researching in a location away from home.

For example, recently we were visiting a cemetery we'd never been to before and we found ourselves having trouble locating Matthew's ancestor because of conflicting information in the family file. It was a wonderful convenience to be able to call his aunt and ask her immediately for some clarification rather than having to travel home to phone her, or waiting to see her and then making a return trip to the cemetery at a later date.

Positioning Yourself for Success

If you have had the opportunity to work much with land records, you know the difficulty in translating the land descriptions into an actual place on the ground. One way to help you find a specific location is to use latitudes and longitudes to tell you a precise location.

Latitude is the distance of a point either north or south of the Equator and longitude is the distance of a point either east or west of the Prime Meridian. If you want a primer on latitude and longitude, we recommend the WorldAtlas.com site at worldatlas.com/aatlas/imageg.htm.

In genealogy, you might encounter latitude and longitude associated with descriptions of historical landmarks, land measurements, and burial locations, among other things.

Global positioning systems (GPSs) are devices that pick up satellite signals that determine your precise location in terms of latitude and longitude. They are also designed to guide you to specific locations based on latitude and longitude. This is useful if you're looking for a plat of land where your great-great-grandfather lived but all of the natural markings have changed over time.

There are varieties of GPS devices — from hand-held systems, to navigation systems built into cars, to cellular phones that can give you position readings. While the cost of the first two options (hand-held GPS devices and automobile navigation systems) can be expensive, cellular phones with built-in GPS are quite common and a good alternative. So check your cell phone to see if it has positioning capabilities before rushing out to buy a GPS on our recommendation.

Diversifying Your Currency

If you travel for pleasure or business much, you know it's a good idea to have various forms of currency with you. Traveling for genealogical pursuits is no different. You will want to carry some cash, not only in the form of paper money but also in coins: Change is often needed for toll roads, parking meters, and copy machines in libraries and archives. These days, credit cards are more readily accepted at institutions such as courthouses, libraries, and archives, so you may not need to carry oodles of cash — in fact, we do not recommend carrying a lot of cash for safety reasons. And it doesn't hurt to carry the checkbook or at least one or two checks in your wallet or pocketbook. There are still some courthouses that will accept checks, and many genealogical and historical societies are happy to take them.

Have Scanner, Will Travel

At first, it may sound a bit strange to say you should take your flatbed scanner with you on your travels. However, many document repositories now allow you to bring a small scanner in with you and your laptop. Scanning the documents that you discover on location saves you the cost of having them reproduced on a copier and saves you time that you would typically lose waiting for a staff member to copy the document (if it is a large document that requires staff copying). Be sure to check the policies of the repository online to make sure that they allow scanners on-site before trying to bring it into the repository.

If you need a refresher on what scanners are and how they benefit you as a genealogist, flip back to Chapter 3.

Packing Necessities

We are going to sound a little condescending here, so we apologize, in advance, if we offend you. Please remember to pack your necessities. Clothing is not optional at most public places you will be visiting on your research trip — it is required. And while you wouldn't dream of forgetting prescription medications, it is easy to overlook convenient over-the-counter products that you already have on hand that can make your trip go a little more smoothly. We're talking about things like pain relievers and bug repellent (for those mid-summer cemetery excursions). Depending on your destination and how you spend your days while traveling, these items could save you lots of misery and enable you to make the most of your research time.

Chapter 15

Ten Handy Databases

Throughout the book, we talk about different online databases that are available. Here's a list of some databases that we think you may find useful in your research. Each database entry in this chapter has a brief description of what the database contains and how you may use it to further your research goals.

Social Security Death Index

www.genealogybank.com/gbnk/ssdi.html

A good place to get your feet wet in using databases containing genealogical data is the Social Security Death Index — commonly known as the SSDI. The Social Security

Death Index is a listing of individuals whose deaths were reported to the Social Security Administration since 1962. Currently, this database contains more than 80 million records. The information that is available here includes name, birth date, death date, last residence, last benefit, Social Security Number, and the state of issue of the deceased's Social Security card. With this information, you can request a copy of the Social Security card application that provides more information on the individual. This database is a good resource when you try to fill in the gaps of missing information on individuals after the 1930 Census. There are a few different online sources for the SSDI — the most up-to-date copy is located at Genealogy-Bank.com, so that's the Web address we provide above. At GenealogyBank, you can conduct a search for free, but you will have to subscribe to see the entire record. Several other versions of SSDI are also available on the Web. Here are a few that are free (although they are not updated as frequently as the subscription versions):

- RootsWeb at ssdi.genealogy.rootsweb.com

- Family Finder Search at www.genealogy.com/ifftop.html

- FamilySearch at www.familysearch.org/Eng/Search/frameset_search.asp?PAGE=ssdi/search_ssdi.asp&clear_form=true

- World Vital Records at www.worldvitalrecords.com/indexinfo.aspx?ix=ssdiall

- New England Historic Genealogical Society at www.newenglandancestors.org/research/Database/ss/default.asp

American Family Immigration History Center

www.ellisisland.org/search/passSearch.asp

If you know that you have a relatively recent ancestor who was an immigrant and may have come through Ellis Island, the Ellis Island Foundation database is the place to go. The American Family Immigration History Center (AFIHC) holds a collection of immigrant arrival records for those who entered the United States through Ellis Island and the Port of New York between 1892 and 1924. The online site contains a passenger-list database of information such as the name of the passenger, residence, arrival date, age upon arrival, gender, marital status, ship name, and port of departure. You can also view a digitized version of the complete ship manifest — and, in some cases, view a photograph of the ship. To use all of the resources the site has to offer, you will need a free registration. If you would like copies of the manifests or ship photographs, you can order them directly from the site.

FamilySearch: Family History Library Catalog

www.familysearch.org/eng/Library/FHLC/frameset_fhlc.asp

In Chapter 4, we highlight several features of the Family-Search site. One that we don't talk about is the Family History Library Catalog. This catalog lists over 3 million microfilms/microfiches and 300,000 books in the Family History

Library collection. This is a good resource for finding family histories that are already completed on branches of your family. You can search the catalog by author, microfilm/fiche, place, surname, keyword, title, subject, and call number.

National Archives and Records Administration Archival Research Catalog

www.archives.gov/research/arc/

To do research in the United States, it's a good idea to know what federal records can help your search. The National Archives and Records Administration Archival Research Catalog (ARC) database houses descriptions of 56 percent of the Archives holdings. It also contains a number of digitized documents including 325 maps, over 58,000 pictures, and 15,000 textual documents. You can query the system through a basic-search or advanced-search interface. Other helpful resources available on the Archives site include

- ✔ Microfilm publications search at eservices.archives .gov/orderonline/start.swe?SWECmd=Start& SWEHo=eservices.archives.gov

- ✔ Access to Archival Databases (AAD) at aad.archives.gov/aad/

Bureau of Land Management, General Land Office Records

www.glorecords.blm.gov

Wondering how your ancestor ended up settling in a particular state? This site might shed some light. The BLM site contains the images of over 3 million land records issued in Eastern Public Land States between 1820 and 1908. Also, you can find serial patents issued after 1908 until the mid-1960s, as well as images of survey plats and field notes going back to 1810. Keep in mind that this site has information on only the first transfer of land title from the federal government to an individual. If that individual sold that land to someone else, it's not shown in this database. You can view the land patent images here in a variety of ways, including GIF images, TIFF images, and Adobe Acrobat (PDF) files — and order a certified copy suitable for framing.

Google Book Search

books.google.com

Sometimes there are nuggets of information on your ancestor or the place where they lived locked away in local histories. Although it's not strictly focused on local histories, Google Book Search does index the full text of several local histories. These local histories were digitized from large, collegiate library collections in the United States, as well as some large foreign universities.

WorldCat

www.worldcat.org

If you don't find what you are looking for in Google Book Search, that doesn't mean that a book on your subject doesn't exist. A great place to search for genealogies and local histories held by libraries throughout the world is WorldCat. WorldCat contains information on more than 1 billion items held in more than 10,000 libraries. When you enter your search term, the database tells you what library holds the work — along with information on how far away the library is from you (you can tell WorldCat where you are located).

Alexandria Digital Library Gazetteer Server

testbed.alexandria.ucsb.edu/gazclient/index.jsp

Looking for a particular place in the world? Trying to figure out just where Metropolis, Illinois is so you can scan for the names of neighboring towns to look for ancestors? The Alexandria Digital Library Gazetteer contains over 4 million features throughout the world. You can search by place name and define what feature type that you're looking for (buildings, cities, drainage basins, landmarks, parks, and rivers, for example). You can also limit the area searched by clicking a map to define the search area.

HyperHistory Online

www.hyperhistory.com/online_n2/History_n2/a.html

Although it's not a genealogical database per se, Hyper-History Online contains some interesting resources for genealogists who want to see what historical events occurred during their ancestors' lives. The site contains over 2,000 maps, charts, and articles recounting 3,000 years of world history. It's divided into four topical areas, including People, History, Events, and Maps. The People area contains lifelines of individuals from 1000 B.C. to 1996 A.D. Historical timelines are available from before 1000 B.C. to 1998 A.D. The Event index covers significant occurrences in science, culture, and politics between 1791 A.D. and 1999 A.D. The Map section contains several maps covering ancient times to the twentieth century.

Topozone

www.topozone.com

Location, and the terrain surrounding it, often played an important role in the lives of our ancestors. Although we may not be able to see maps of the terrain as it existed a hundred years ago, we can see modern-day topographic maps produced by the United States Geological Survey for the entire United States. To find a map, just type a place name in the search field (or you can search by latitude or longitude), select a state (if known), and you're off to the races. The Results page of the search lists the place name, county, state, type of feature, elevation, USGS quad (the title of the USGS map where the place is located), latitude, and longitude. Clicking the place name brings up the appropriate topographical map. You can view maps at different scales (if available) and in different image sizes (small, medium, and large).

Chapter 16

Ten Things to Remember When Designing Your Web Site or Blog

Y ou've probably seen them: Web sites that look like the maintainers simply copied someone else's site and then plugged their surnames in specified spots and maybe changed the background color of the page. Typically, such pages don't contain much information of value to anyone — they're simply lists of surnames with no context and maybe lists of links to some of the better-known genealogical Web sites. Some might say that these sites are clones. We agree. You don't want your genealogical Web site to contain almost exactly the same information as sites created by others. You want yours to be unique and useful to other genealogists so a lot of people will visit your site and recommend it to others. At the same time, you don't necessarily want your site to be overwhelming complicated or ugly. The same thing goes for your blog — you don't want your blog

466

to sound just like another's. So what can you do to avoid the genealogical Web-site ruts that some genealogists find themselves in? Here we offer a few ideas and places to get help.

Be Unique: Don't Copy Other Web Sites

Please, please, please tell us that you want to set your home page apart from all other genealogical Web sites! You don't really have to be told not to copy the content from other sites, right? But when you design your site, the pressure is on, and coming up with ideas for textual and graphical content can be pretty hard sometimes. We understand that this pressure can make it awfully tempting for you to take ideas from other Web sites that you like. Although you can certainly look to other sites for ideas on formatting and types of content, don't copy them verbatim! Web sites are copyrighted by the person(s) who created them — even if they don't display a copyright notice — and you can get in trouble for copying them. (See Chapter 13 for more information about copyrights.)

The other reason you shouldn't copy other Web sites is that you want your page to attract as many visitors as possible — and in order to do this, you need to offer something unique that makes it worth people's time to stop by. After all, if your site has the same old information as another site, people have no particular need to visit your page. For example, because several comprehensive genealogical sites already exist, posting a Web site that merely has links to other genealogical pages doesn't make much sense. Likewise, if you're thinking about making a one-name study site on a surname for which four or five one-name study sites already exist, you may want to focus your home page on another surname you're researching.

Be creative. Look around and see what existing genealogical Web sites offer, and then seek to fill the void — pick a unique topic, name, or location that doesn't have much coverage (or better yet, one that doesn't have any coverage at all). If you really want to post a surname site, think about making a site for your surname in a particular state or country. Or think about posting some transcribed records that would benefit genealogists who are researching ancestors from a particular county.

 If you find it challenging to come up with enough unique and original content for your site, consider involving others in your efforts. You can turn to relatives or other researchers who are interested in the same family lines as you — perhaps someone who doesn't have Internet access with whom you correspond, or others who have access but don't have the time or motivation to create their own sites.

Include the Surnames That You're Researching and Provide Your Contact Information

If the purpose of your Web site or blog is not only to share your collection of genealogical information but to get information from others as well, be sure to include a list of the names you're researching. And don't be stingy with information. We encourage you to share at least a little information about your ancestors with those surnames. Just a list of surnames alone isn't going to be very helpful to visitors to your site, particularly if any of the surnames on your list are common — Smith, Johnson, Jones, Martin, and so forth. An online version of the information contained in your GEDCOM file (a text file that contains the contents of your genealogical database, created using GED2HTML or another similar program — see Chapter 13 for more information) will do because it includes an index of surnames that people can look through, and also has information about your ancestors with those surnames. Also be sure to include your name and e-mail address so that people know how to get in touch with you to share data.

 If you're comfortable doing so, you can include your mailing address on your Web site so those who don't have e-mail access can contact you. Or, if you're not comfortable providing such personal information but you want other researchers to be able to contact you, you may want to consider getting a post-office box that you can post on your Web site and use for receiving genealogy-related mail.

Make It Attractive Without Being Too Flashy

Choose your colors and graphics wisely! Although using some color and graphics (including photographs) helps your Web site stand out and makes it more personal, be careful about using too much color or too many graphics. By *too much color,* we mean backgrounds that are so bright that they almost blind your visitors (or make the rest of the site hard to look at), or backgrounds that drown out the colors of your links. You want your site to be appealing to others as well as to you; before using neon pink or lime green, stop and think about how others may react. The especially good news here is that if you use a networking site, like Geni, you can choose from standard templates using subdued, easy-to-look-at colors and fonts. The variety of templates gives you an opportunity to distinguish your site from others without being fully responsible for determining all of your own layout and formatting, including things like colors.

The more graphics you use and the larger they are, the longer a computer takes to load them. (And animated graphics are even worse! Not only do they take a long time to load, but they can make your visitors dizzy and disoriented if you have several graphics moving in different directions at the same time.) Graphics files aren't the only factor that affects how quickly computers load files: the amount of bandwidth of your Internet connection and the amount of space available on your hard drive also affect download time. Waiting for a page to load that has more graphics than useful text content is frustrating. You can pretty much bet that people won't wait around, so concentrate on making your page as user-friendly as possible from the beginning. Use graphics tastefully and sparingly.

If you have a large amount of family photos that you really want to share, put each on its own page and then provide links to the photo pages from your home page. This way, visitors who aren't interested in seeing any of the photos don't have to wait for the images to load on their computers just to view the other contents of your site, and visitors who are only interested in a particular image don't have to wait for all the other photos to load.

The "Where to Go for Help" section later in this chapter identifies some online resources that lead you to sites with Web-safe colors and graphics that you can download and use on your Web site.

To shrink the size of the graphics on your Web site, try using a graphics optimizer (a tool that formats your graphics to make them load faster in someone's Web browser) such as NetMechanic GIFBot available at www.net mechanic.com/accelerate.htm.

Be Careful What You Post

Be careful and thoughtful when designing your Web site

and posting information contributed by others. Don't post any information that could hurt or offend someone. Respect the privacy of others and post information only on people who have been deceased for many years. (Twenty-five years is a good conservative figure to use when in doubt.) Even then, be cautious about telling old family stories that may affect people who are still alive. (For more information about privacy, see Chapter 13.)

Always Cite Your Sources

We can't stress this enough! Always cite your sources when you put genealogical narrative on your Web site, or when you post information from records that you've collected or people you've interviewed. That way, people who visit your page and get data from it know exactly where you got the information and can follow up on it if they need or want to. (Also, by citing your sources, you keep yourself out of trouble because others may have provided the information to you, and they deserve the credit for the research.)

Not All Web Browsers Are Created Equal

World Wide Web browsers interpret HTML documents differently depending on who created the software. Also, some Web browsers have HTML tags that are specific to the browser. So, although you may create a Web site that looks great using Microsoft Internet Explorer, it may look off-center or somewhat different when using Netscape Navigator or Opera. Because of this problem, try not to use tags that are specific to any one browser when you create your Web site. For that matter, whenever possible, test your page in several browsers before posting it for public access. Better yet, use a testing service that allows the "experts" to look at your page and give you feedback. The Yahoo!

HTML Validation and Checkers page at

```
dir.yahoo.com/Computers_and_Internet/Data_Formats/HTML/
Validation_and_Checkers/
```

provides a decent list of programs that check your Web site and notify you about broken links.

Another consideration when designing your Web page is to make your Web pages "readable" by screen-reading browsers. Screen-reading browsers allow visually impaired researchers the ability to access information on the World Wide Web. To see if your content is accessible, you can find scanning utilities at WebsiteTips.com at

```
websitetips.com/accessibility/tools/
```

Check and Recheck Your Links

If you include on your home page links to other Web sites that you've designed or sites maintained by someone else, double-check the links when you post your pages. Make sure that the links work properly so that visitors to your site don't have problems navigating around sites that you recommend or that support your home page. A lot of genealogical Web sites tend to be transient — the maintainers move them for one reason or another, or take them down entirely — so you should also check back periodically (once a month or so) to make sure that the links still work.

If you have a lot of links on your Web site and you don't have the time to check every single one yourself (which is a common scenario), look to the Yahoo! HTML Validation and Checkers page at

dir.yahoo.com/Computers_and_Internet/Data_Formats/

HTML/Validation_and_Checkers/

It links to a list of programs that check your Web site and notify you about broken links.

Market Your Genealogical Web Site or Blog

After you put together your Web site and post it on your provider's server, or create your blog, you need to let people know that it exists so they can stop by and visit, as well as contribute. How do you do this? We recommend that you follow some of the same tips in Chapter 4 for marketing the research that you've done on your surnames (using mailing lists if the site deals with particular surnames or geographic areas). In particular, one of the best ways to promote your Web site is to register it with several comprehensive genealogical Web sites that receive a lot of traffic from people looking for genealogy-related pages.

Also, most of the major search engines have links to registration or submission pages within their sites that enable you to submit your URL. Of course, in the interest of saving time, you can visit Add Me Site Submission at

www.addme.com/submission.htm

which forwards your Web site information to up to 14 search engines for free.

Helping Others Is Its Own Reward

Don't go overboard patting your own back — you know, promoting your home page or blog for the sake of receiving awards from other sites, magazines, societies, or other sources. Post your genealogical site or blog with the intent of helping other genealogists and encouraging a sharing genealogical community. If you use the majority of your page to advertise your awards and beg people to vote for your site in popularity contests, you lose a lot of valuable space where you can post information that's useful to genealogists. And you may lose credibility with your visitors, causing them to turn away — which defeats the purpose of self-promotion in the first place.

Now, we're not saying that you shouldn't acknowledge awards that your site or blog receives if it has good and sound genealogical content. We recognize that it's good business to give a little traffic back to the sites, magazines, societies, or other sources that send visitors your way by awarding your page some honor. We're simply saying that you can acknowledge the honors you receive in a tasteful and humble manner. You don't have to plaster all the graphics for every single award across the top of your page. Rather, you can set up a separate Web page for awards and provide a link from your home page so that those who are interested in seeing your honors can go to that page.

Where to Go for Help

Chapter 13 tells you how to create a simple Web site and discusses some HTML editors that are available from Web hosts. But these resources may not even begin to cover all the wonderful things that you intend to do with your home-grown Web site. Maybe you want to learn more about how to do fancier things with your Web site. If this is the case, you should check out community colleges in your area or workshops offered by local libraries or genealogical societies. Community colleges and workshops often offer classes or sessions on how to make a Web site, walking you through the basics of HTML — what the tags are, how to use them, and how to post a Web site.

If the thought of attending a structured class gives you hives or just makes you roll your eyes, you can learn more about HTML and Web design in other ways. You can teach yourself; many books and online sites are out there to help you. In fact, Wiley Publishing, Inc. offers several *For Dummies* books you may want to consider: *Creating Web Pages For Dummies,* 8th Edition, by Bud E. Smith and Arthur Bebak; *The Internet For Dummies,* 11th Edition, by John R. Levine, Carol Baroudi, and Margaret Levine Young; and *HTML 4 For Dummies,* 5th Edition, by Ed Tittel and Mary Burmeister.

The following online sites are additional resources for designing and programming Web pages:

✔ **About.com's Personal Web Pages section:** personalweb.about.com

✔ **Web Building Tutorial:** www.w3schools.com/site/default.asp

Chapter 17

Ten Sites That Offer Help

In This Chapter

▶ Finding how-to sites
▶ Subscribing to mailing lists

Do census records make you feel senseless? Panicked at the idea of using the Soundex? Just plain confused about where to start? These ten sites may relieve some of the anxiety you feel toward researching your genealogy.

Ancestors

byubroadcasting.org/ancestors/

Ancestors — a unique multi-part television series about genealogy — has a companion Web site that contains several resources for beginners. The first *Ancestors* series premiered in 1997, and the second series was released in 2000. The companion Web site has information on various types of records and sources that you collect as a genealogist, tips from other researchers, and a resource guide with locations of genealogy resources in each state. There's also information about the television series, a teacher's guide, and PDF charts you can download if you want to use paper copies when researching.

Ancestry.com Learning Center

www.ancestry.com/library/archive.asp

Although Ancestry.com is well known for its collection of databases and digitized images, perhaps equally of value is its little known collection of articles, columns, and other online resources to assist genealogists. The Learning Center contains thousands of articles (taken from multiple sources, including *Ancestry* magazine, *Genealogical Computing,* and online columnists) divided into categories that include

How-to	Preserving Family History
Record Sources	Home sources
Family Origins	Religion
Technology	Genealogy Products
Organizations	Current Events
Geography	Historical Context

Roots Television

www.rootstelevision.com

Roots Television contains free videos on a variety of genealogical topics. To see the video lineup, click on the Program Guide link on the main page of their Web site. You can find excerpts from the Ancestors television series, lectures from genealogical conferences, and instructional videos.

Genealogy Today: Getting Started

www.genealogytoday.com/genealogy/newbie.html

Genealogy Today's Getting Started resources include tips for beginning your research, hints for organizing your findings and planning research, articles on specific types of documents you're looking for, a searchable "knowledgebase" (online database), and a recommendation for a tutorial CD that demonstrates how to research. (Please be aware that you must purchase the CD.) Also there are links to other parts of the Genealogy Today site, which has a plethora of general genealogical resources such as podcasts, news, and book and record transcriptions.

GeneaSearch

geneasearch.com

GeneaSearch offers help in the form of look-ups (a service in which others will look up information for you in geographic locations that you can not easily access) and online resources. Some of the online resources include a surname registry, military rosters, transcribed records, directories, obituaries, family newsletters, information about researching female ancestors, and a beginner's guide.

GEN-NEWBIE-L

www.rootsweb.com/~newbie

This is the home page for the GEN-NEWBIE-L mailing list. This mailing list is a forum for individuals who are new to computers and genealogy and are looking for a place to discuss a variety of topics in a comfortable environment.

To subscribe to the GEN-NEWBIE-L mailing list, follow these steps:

1. **Open your favorite e-mail program and start a new e-mail message.**

2. **Type** Gen-Newbie-L-request@rootsweb.com **in the Address line.**

3. **Leave the Subject line blank and type only the word** subscribe **in the body of your message. Also make sure that you turn off any signature lines present in your email.**

4. **Send your e-mail message.**

Soon you receive a confirmation message with additional details on unsubscribing from the mailing list (if you want to do so down the road) and other administrative items. If you have questions about the mailing list, consult the home page for help.

National Genealogical Society

www.ngsgenealogy.org

The National Genealogical Society is an organization for

individuals whose research interests include the United States. At its Web site, you can find information on the society's home-study genealogy course, starting your genealogy research, research services, the society's library catalog, and conferences. The site also has information about membership — no surprise there — and does a good job of keeping visitors abreast of genealogical news and events. There's even a "bookstore," which actually carries a lot more than just books on its virtual shelves.

ROOTS-L

www.rootsweb.com/roots-l

This is the home page for the ROOTS-L mailing list. If you're looking for an all-purpose mailing list on genealogy, ROOTS-L may be for you. ROOTS-L is the oldest and largest genealogical mailing list. List members discuss all types of genealogical issues. On the mailing list's companion Web page, you can find subscription information, help files, a searchable archive of past ROOTS-L messages, and a brief history of the list.

If you decide to join after reviewing the ROOTS-L mailing list Web site, you may want to consider subscribing to the digest mode of the ROOTS-L mailing list. Because it's one of the largest lists, your e-mail inbox may quickly fill up if you receive every message that's posted to the list separately. *Digest mode* enables you to receive a single message with the text of several messages embedded within it periodically throughout the day. So instead of receiving some 50 to 200 messages per day, you may receive only five. For more information on subscribing to digest mode, see the ROOTS-L home page.

Getting Started in Genealogy and Family History

www.genuki.org.uk/gs/

The GENUKI (U.K. and Ireland Genealogy) Web site provides a list of helpful hints for starting out in genealogical research. The extensive list covers these elements: deciding the aim of your research, using Family History Centers, joining a genealogical society, tracing immigrants, and organizing your information. You also find a list of reference materials — should you want to read more about the topics GENUKI discusses.

About.com Genealogy: One-Stop Beginner's Genealogy

genealogy.about.com/library/onestop/bl_beginner.htm

If you are looking for information on a wide range of genealogical topics, hop on over to the About.com Genealogy site. The One-Stop Beginner's Genealogy section of the site has a large collection of articles that are categorized by subject: Articles and Tips, Learning Corner, and Tools and How-To. There are many subcategories under each of these topics as well. Some of the resources within these categories include information on surname origins, mistakes you can avoid, a genealogy chat room, and publishing your family history.

Chapter 18

Ten Tips for Genealogical Smooth Sailing

You want to make optimal use of your time when researching your genealogy — online and offline. Being time-efficient means planning well and keeping organized notes so that bad leads don't distract you. Making the most of your time also means staying motivated when and if a bad lead does distract you. Your genealogy research is worth continuing. This chapter offers some tips to help you plan, organize, and execute your research.

Start with What You Know

Sure, this concept seems basic, but it's worth repeating: When you begin researching your genealogy, start with what you know — information about yourself and your immediate family. Then work your way back in time, using information from relatives and copies of records that you obtain. Solving the mystery of your heritage is easier if you have some clues to start with. If you begin directly with your great-great-grandpa and all you know about him is his name, you may get frustrated very early in the process — especially if great-great-grandpa has a relatively common name like John Sanders or William Martin! Can you imagine trying to track down records on *all* the John Sanderses or William Martins who turn up in one year's census? (We believe in thoroughly covering the basics, so if you want to hear this again, go to Chapter 2.)

Get Organized

The better organized you are, the more success you're likely to have with your research efforts. If you know ahead of time where you stand in researching your family lines, you can identify rather quickly which records or other materials you need to find about a particular surname, location, or time frame. Knowing your gaps in information enables you to get right down to the nitty-gritty of researching instead of spending the first hour or two of your research rehashing where you left off last time.

To help yourself get organized, keep a *research log* — a record of when and where you searched for information. For example, if you ran a Google (www.google.com) search on the name Emaline Crump on January 1, 2007, and found 13 pages that you wanted to visit, record that in your research log. Also record when you visited those pages and whether they provided any useful information to you. That way, next time you're online researching your Crump ancestors, you know that you already ran a Google search and visited the particular resulting pages, so you don't have to do it again. (Of course, you may want to check back in the future and run the search again to see whether any *new*

Crump-related sites turn up. Again, your research log can come in handy because it can remind you of whether you've already visited some of the resulting sites.)

You can print a copy of a research log at the Church of Jesus Christ of Latter-day Saints site at

www.lds.org/images/howdoibeg/Research_Log.html

Although this particular log is intended for offline research, you can modify it for your online pursuits — substituting the URL of a site you visit for the Location/Call Numbers section of the form. Or you can find a *research table* (which is basically a research log by another name) at the Genealogy.com site:

www.genealogy.com/00000002.html?Welcome=10 16426690

A couple of other options are to create your own research log with a plain old notebook or a spreadsheet on your handy-dandy computer, or to use an already-prepared form that comes with your genealogical database (if available).

Always Get Proof

Unfortunately, not all researchers take the same amount of care when gathering sources and presenting the fruits of their research. So it's not a good idea to trust that everything that other researchers print or post is an undisputable fact.

Always be a little skeptical about secondhand information and seek to get your own proof of an event. We're not saying that if Aunt Dorothy gives you a copy of great-grandma's birth certificate that you still need to get your own copy from the original source. However, if Aunt Dorothy merely tells you that great-grandma was born in Hardin County, Kentucky, and that she knows this because great-grandma said so, you do need to get a copy of great-grandma's birth certificate or some other primary record that verifies this fact.

Even when using primary sources, evaluate the information that you find on each record. If the information does not add up, it is possible that the record could be wrong. If you suspect this is the case, it's a good idea to find another record that can help clear up the inconsistency.

If you assume that everything you hear or read is true, you're likely to get distracted frequently by bad leads. You could end up tracing an entire branch of a family that you're not even related to. And just think of all the lost time you could have spent working on your family line!

Always Cite Your Sources

We can't say this enough! Always — and we mean *always* — cite your sources. In other chapters (Chapter 12, for example), we explore why citing your sources is a smart thing to do when sharing your genealogical information with others. We also touch on the importance of citing sources for your own research — so important, in fact, that we reiterate the point here. Make sure you know where, when, and how you obtained a particular piece of information about your ancestors just in case you ever need to verify the information or get another copy of the record. Doing so saves you a lot of grief. It also brings you greater respect from others for your efforts.

Focus, Focus, Focus

If you're trying to remember all your ancestors in all your family lines and research them all at the same time, you're bound to get confused and burnt out! Focus on one or two branches at a time. Even better — focus on one or two people within a branch at a time. By maintaining a tight focus, you can still find information on other relatives in that branch of the family and collect records and data that pertain to them — but you're able to do so without driving yourself crazy.

Share Your Information

One of the best ways to facilitate getting genealogical information from others is to share some information first. Although most genealogists are rather generous people to begin with, some still believe in protecting their discoveries like closely guarded treasures — it's "every man for himself" in their minds. However, after they realize that you want to *give* information as well as receive it, some of them lighten up and are much more willing to share with you. By sharing information, you can save each other time and energy, as well as begin to coordinate your research in a manner that benefits both of you.

Sharing information is one area where the Internet has proven to be an invaluable resource for genealogists. It provides easy access for unconditional and conditional sharing of information among genealogists. Those of you who are willing to share your knowledge can go online and post information to your heart's content. And in return, simply ask the researchers who benefit from your site to share their findings with you. And for those of you who are a little more apprehensive about sharing your knowledge, you can post messages describing what you're looking for and state that you're willing to share what you have with anyone who can help you.

You have several different ways to share your information online. We cover many of these methods in various chapters of this book. You can share in one-on-one e-mail messages, mailing lists, newsgroups, and Web pages — just to name a few.

Join a Society or Research Group

You've probably heard the phrase "Two heads are better than one," right? Well, this theory holds true for genealogy. Joining a society or a research group enables you to combine research efforts with others who are interested in a particular surname or geographic location, so that together you save time and energy obtaining documents that benefit everyone. A society or research group also provides you with a support group to which you can turn when you begin to get discouraged or whenever you want to share a triumph.

You can find genealogical societies and research groups in several ways. Check out your favorite comprehensive genealogical site and look under both the category that lists societies and the place category for the location where you live. Or, if you're interested in finding a society in the United States, take a look at the Federation of Genealogical Societies home page at www.fgs.org (which identifies member societies by location) or the USGenWeb Project at www.usgenweb.org (which links to state pages that identify resources for the state and its counties).

If you're interested in finding a society in a country other than the United States, check out the WorldGenWeb site at www.worldgenweb.org to link to any resource pages for the region that you're researching. These resource pages should include at least general information about societies in the area.

Attend a Conference or Workshop

Conferences and workshops that are hosted by genealogical societies can be a great resource for you. They can help you get organized and find out how to research a particular place or look for specific records, and motivate you to keep plugging along with your research even if you have days when you feel like you haven't accomplished a thing. Conferences and workshops also enable you to meet other researchers with whom you have something in common, whether it's researching a specific surname or geographic location, or just research in general. Being in the company of someone with whom you can share your genealogical successes and failures is always nice.

Typically, conferences and workshops offer sessions that instruct you on various traditional researching topics like the following:

- ✔ Using local libraries and archives

- ✔ Finding and using land records

- ✔ Obtaining vital records

- ✔ Converting Soundex codes and using the census

- ✔ Publishing a genealogical report or book

And most workshops offer some computer-based components like the following:

- ✔ Using genealogical software

- ✔ Designing and posting your own genealogical Web page

- ✔ Joining online societies and mailing lists

- ✔ Presenting overviews of the Internet's genealogical offerings

- ✔ Using a computer in general

You can use your trusty computer and Internet connection to find genealogical and historical conferences and workshops in your area. The Federation of Genealogical Societies (www.fgs.org/fgs-calendar.asp) provides information about conferences coming up within the next couple of months. For events in the United Kingdom, look at the GENEVA: the GENUKI calendar of Genealogical Events and Activities (geneva.weald.org.uk/). You can also use these sites to get the word out about a conference or workshop that you're helping to plan!

Attend a Family Reunion

Family reunions enable you to see and share information with relatives you haven't seen in a long time and to meet new relatives you never would have known. While we cover family reunions in more detail in Chapter 11, we want to reiterate here that reunions are a wonderful opportunity to build your genealogical base by just chatting with relatives about old family stories, ancestors, and the like. Although a reunion doesn't feel like a formal interview, it can give you much of the same information that you would receive if you sat down and formally interviewed each of the people in attendance. Taking along a tape recorder or video camera is a good idea because you don't have to worry about writing down everything your relatives say right at that moment — you can just sit back and enjoy talking with your family. Plus, your genealogy records are greatly enhanced by audio or video. (Just make sure that, when you're going to tape a conversation, you have the permission of the relatives you plan to record and that you set aside *lots* of time later on to transcribe the tapes if you don't attach them directly to your genealogical database as media files.)

Family reunions also offer you the opportunity to share what you know about the family and exchange genealogical records and reports. If you know ahead of time that several of your relatives are also into genealogical research, you can better plan with them what records, pictures, reports, and other resources to bring. If you're not sure that any of your relatives are into genealogical research, we recommend that you take a notebook with some printed reports and maybe a narrative family history or genealogy (if you've already put one together) that you can share. Remember, your work doesn't have to be complete (in fact, it probably won't be) or perfect in grammar for others to enjoy seeing what you've collected.

To find out about family reunions, watch the family association and one-name study Web sites of the surnames that you're researching. Typically, this type of Web site has sections set up for reunion announcements. Also, see the Reunions Magazine site at

www.reunionsmag.com

Planning a reunion can often be a challenging experience. Fortunately, software is available to help you with all the details. Family Reunion Organizer by Formalsoft is just such a program. You can find a demo copy of the software at the software's Web site:

family-reunion.com/organizer/

Don't Give Up

You're going to have days where you spend hours at the library or archives — or on the Internet — with no research success whatsoever (or so you may think). Don't let those days get you down, and certainly don't give up! Instead of thinking about what you didn't learn about your ancestors on such days, think in terms of what you *did* learn — that your ancestors were not in that record for that particular place at that particular time. By checking that record, you eliminated one more item on your to-do list. So the next time you get ready to research, you know exactly where *not* to look for more information.

Glossary

abstract: A brief overview or summary of what a document or Web site contains.

Adjutant General's report: Published account of the actions of military units from a particular state during a war.

adoption: To legally be declared part of a family into which you were not born.

Ahnentafel: A well-known genealogical numbering system. Ahnentafel is a method of numbering that has a mathematical relationship between parents and children. The word itself means *ancestor* and *table* in German; also referred to as the *Sosa-Stradonitz System* of numbering.

albumen print: A type of photograph that was produced on a thin piece of paper coated with albumen and silver nitrate and usually mounted on cardboard; typically taken between 1858 and 1910.

allele: The form a gene takes which drives human characteristics such as eye color.

ambrotype: A type of photograph that was printed on thin glass and usually had a black backing; typically taken between 1858 and 1866.

America Online: A popular commercial Internet service provider.

Americanized: The process of changing one's surname (last name) to make it easier to pronounce or as the result of a misspelling on a record when an immigrant entered the United States.

ancestor: A person from whom you are descended.

ancestor chart: A chart that runs horizontally across a page and identifies a primary person (including that person's name, date and place of birth, date and place of marriage, and date and place of death), his/her parents, and then each of their parents, and so on until the chart runs off the page. Usually called a *pedigree chart.*

ancestral file: A database created and maintained by the Church of Jesus Christ of Latter-day Saints, with millions of names available in Family Group Sheets and Pedigree charts; part of the FamilySearch collection of CD-ROMs, which are accessible at Family History Centers. See also *Family History Center* and *Family History Library.*

archive: A physical location where historical documents and records are stored.

autosomal DNA: DNA that consists of 22 chromosomes that are non-sex specific chromosomes found in the cell nucleus.

banns: See *marriage banns.*

baptismal certificate: A certificate issued by a church at the time of baptism; sometimes used to approximate a birth date in the absence of a birth certificate.

bases: Also called nucleotides. Rungs of the DNA ladder that hold the molecule together. There are four types (adenine, guanine, cytosine, and thymine).

bibliography: A list of books or other materials that were used in research; also a list of books or other materials that are available on a particular topic.

biographical sketch: A brief written account of a person's life.

biography: A detailed written account of a person's life.

birth certificate: A legal record stating when and where a person was born.

blog: An abbreviated name for a Web log, which is an online journal or log of the author's interests and activities.

blogging: The act of recording your thoughts, opinions, news, or research findings in a Web log.

bounty land: Federal land given to a person in exchange for military service or some other civic service.

Brick Wall Syndrome: A situation when you think you have exhausted every possible way of finding an ancestor.

browser: See *World Wide Web browser.*

Bureau of Refugees, Freedmen, and Abandoned Lands: Established in 1865, the bureau had programs to assist ex-slaves after the American Civil War. Also called *Freedman's Bureau.*

cabinet card: A larger version of the carte-de-visite photograph; typically taken between 1865 and 1906.

Canon Code: A code that explains the bloodline relationship in legal terms by identifying how many degrees of separation (or steps) exist between two people related by blood. Canon law counts only the number of steps from the nearest common ancestor of both relatives.

carte-de-visite: A type of photograph that was a small paper print mounted on a card; collections were usually bound together in photo albums. Typically taken between 1858 and 1891.

CD-ROM: Acronym for Compact Disc-Read Only Memory; used in your computer's compact disc drive. A CD-ROM stores large amounts of information (including multimedia) that can be retrieved by your computer.

cells: Basic building blocks of the human body.

census: The counting of a population undertaken by a government.

census index: A listing of people who are included in particular census records, along with references indicating where you can find the actual census records.

census return: The record/form on which census information is collected. Also called a *census schedule.*

census schedule: Another term for a *census return* form.

charter: A formal or informal document that defines the scope of a newsgroup.

chromosome: The container that holds the strands of

deoxyribonucleic acid (DNA); each chromosome has a different set of instructions and serves a different purpose.

cite: To name the source of some information and provide reference to the original source.

Civil Code: A code that explains the bloodline relationship in legal terms by identifying how many *degrees of separation* (or kinship steps) exist between two people related by blood; civil law counts each step between two relatives as a degree.

civil records: Government documents that contain information on the civic duties of your ancestors, proceedings of municipal governments, or any other records of your ancestors' interaction with the government; often found in local and state archives or courthouses.

civil registration: Primary record of a vital event in life: birth, death, or marriage; for the most part, originals are kept by local governments. Also called *vital records* in the United States and Canada.

compiled genealogy: An online or print publication of one's genealogical findings. It can be a traditional narrative or a lineage-linked database.

comprehensive genealogical index: A Web site that identifies a large number of other genealogical sites containing information on a number of families, locations, or a variety of other genealogy-related subjects.

conscription: Also called draft; this is the act of enrolling men for compulsory service in the military.

cookies: Pieces of information that are sent to your computer by other computers when you visit certain Web pages. Generally, cookies are used for navigation purposes or by commercial sites that want to rotate banner advertisements for you so you don't get tired of the same old advertisement.

copyright: Copyright is the exclusive right of a creator to reproduce, prepare derivative works, distribute, perform, display, sell, lend, or rent his/her creations.

county clerk: The clerk of the county court that records or maintains records of transactions and events in that county. Sometimes called the *county recorder.*

cyber society: A genealogical or historical society that exists only on the Internet.

cyberspace: A slang term for the Internet.

daguerreotype: A type of photograph that required a long exposure time and was taken on silver-plated copper; typically taken between 1839 and 1860.

database: A collection of information that is entered, organized, stored, and used on a computer.

death certificate: A legal record stating when and where a person died.

declaration of intent: A sworn statement by a person who intends to become a naturalized citizen of the United States.

deed: A document that records the transfer of ownership of a piece of property or land.

deoxyribonucleic acid (DNA): Part of your molecular structure that determines your characteristics.

descendant: A person who descended from a particular ancestor.

descendant chart: A chart that contains information about an ancestor and spouse (or particular spouses if there was more than one), their children and their spouses, grandchildren and spouses, and so on down the family line; usually formatted vertically on a page like a list.

diary: A book containing one's innermost thoughts and findings in life.

digest mode: An option for receiving postings to some mailing lists in which several messages are batched together and sent to you instead of each message being sent separately.

digital camera: A camera that captures images to computer memory instead of to film, and then downloads the images to your computer.

digitized record: A copy or image of a record that has been made using electronic means.

directory: A collection of information about individuals who live in a particular place.

divorce decree: Decision and document that legally ends a marriage.

download: Getting a file (information or a program) to your computer from another computer.

draft: Also called conscription; this is the act of enrolling men for compulsory service in the military.

electronic mail: Messages sent from one person to another electronically over the Internet. Also called *e-mail.*

e-mail: Short for *electronic mail.*

emigrant: A person who leaves or moves away from one country to settle in another country.

emoticons: Graphics created by combinations of keys on the keyboard to express an emotion within a message.

enumeration district: The area assigned to a particular enumerator of the census.

enumerator: A person who collected details on individuals during a census.

estate: The assets and liabilities of a person who dies.

family association: An organized group of individuals who are researching the same family.

family association site: A Web site that's designed and posted by an organization devoted to researching a particular family.

Family Group Sheet: A summary of a particular family, including biographical information about a husband, wife, and their children.

family history: The written account of a family's existence over time.

Family History Center: Local branches of the *Family History Library.*

Family History Library: The Church of Jesus Christ of Latter-day Saints' main library in Salt Lake City, Utah. The Family History Library has the world's largest collection of genealogical holdings, including print sources and microfilmed records, as well as records and other information shared by genealogical researchers worldwide.

Family History Library Catalog: A listing of records (books, films, microfiche, CDs, cassette tapes, videos, and microfilms) available at the Family History Library in Salt Lake City, Utah; part of the FamilySearch collection of CD-ROMs, which are accessible at Family History Centers.

Family Outline report: A list of the descendants of a particular ancestor.

Family Tree Maker: A popular genealogical database.

family reunion: A gathering of people who share ancestors.

FAQ: Acronym for Frequently Asked Questions.

FHC: Acronym for Family History Center.

FHL: Acronym for Family History Library.

flame: A verbal (written) attack online.

forum: A subject-specific area where members post messages and files.

fraternal order: A service club or organization of persons.

Freedman's Bureau: Abbreviated name for the Bureau of Refugees, Freedmen, and Abandoned Lands.

Freedman's Savings and Trust Company: Established in 1865, this was a bank for ex-slaves.

freeware: Software that you usually obtain and use for free by downloading it off the Internet.

Frequently Asked Questions: A Web page or message posted to a mailing list or newsgroup that explains answers to the most-asked questions to the particular Web site, mailing list, or newsgroup. Usually serves as a starting point for people new to a site or resource.

gazetteer: Geographical dictionary that provides information about places.

GEDCOM: Acronym for GEnealogical Data COMmunication.

gene: A section of a chromosome that contains specific sequences of information that determine a particular inheritable characteristic of a human.

genealogical database: Software in which you enter, store, and use information about ancestors, descendants, and others relevant to your genealogy.

Genealogical Data Communication: The standard file format for exporting and importing information between genealogical databases; intended to make data translatable between different genealogical software programs so you can share your family information easily. Also called GEDCOM.

genealogically focused search engine: A program that indexes the full text of Web sites that are of interest and value to genealogists, and allows you to search the index for particular keywords.

GENDEX: An index of online genealogical databases that comply with the GEDCOM converted to HTML indexing format.

genealogical society: An organized group that attempts to preserve documents and history for the area in which the society is located; often a genealogical society has a second purpose, which is to help its members research their ancestors.

genealogy: The study of *ancestors, descendants,* and family origins.

genome: Complete set of instructions for how a cell will operate.

geographic-specific Web site: A Web site that has information pertaining to a particular locality (town, county, state, country, or other area).

geographical information systems (GIS): Software that allows you to create maps based upon layers of information.

glass-plate negative: A type of photograph made from light-sensitive silver bromide immersed in gelatin; typically taken between 1848 and 1930.

global positioning service (GPS): A satellite system that receives and sends signals to a receiver enabling the person controlling the receiver to determine his/her exact geographical coordinates.

haplogroup: A grouping of several similar haplotypes.

haplotype: Set of results of markers for a particular individual.

Helm Online Family Tree Research Cycle: A five-phase research model that explains the ongoing process of genealogical research.

Henry System: A widely used and accepted genealogical numbering system, it assigns a particular sequence of numbers to the children of a family's progenitor and to subsequent generations.

hierarchy: In terms of a newsgroup, a hierarchy is the major grouping to which a newsgroup belongs; for example, soc.genealogy.computing belongs to the soc hierarchy.

historical society: An organized group that attempts to preserve documents and history for the area in which the society is located.

home page: The entry point for a World Wide Web site.

HTML: Acronym for HyperText Markup Language.

HyperText Markup Language: The programming language of the World Wide Web. HTML is a code that's translated into graphical pages by software called a World Wide Web browser.

IGI: Acronym for International Genealogical Index.

immigrant: A person who moves into or settles in a country.

immigration record: A record of the entry of a person into a specific country where he or she was not native-born or naturalized.

index: A list of some sort. An index can be a list of Web sites, types of records, and so on.

interface: An online form or page.

interlibrary loan: A system in which one library loans a book or other material to another library for a person to borrow or use.

International Genealogical Index: A list of births and marriages of deceased individuals reflected in records collected by the Church of Jesus Christ of Latter-day Saints. The International Genealogical Index (also called IGI) is part of the FamilySearch collection of CD-ROMs, accessible at Family History Centers.

Internet: A system of computer networks joined together by high-speed data lines called *backbones.*

Internet service provider: A company or other organization that provides people with access to the Internet through a direct connection or dial-up connection. Also called *ISP.*

intestate: The estate status of a person who died without leaving a valid will.

ISP: Acronym for Internet service provider.

junk DNA: A non-coding region of a DNA strand.

kinship report: A list of family members and how they relate directly to one particular individual in your database; usually kinship reports include the Civil Code and Canon Code for the relationship to the individual.

land grant: Permission to purchase land or a gift of land in exchange for military service or other civic service.

land patent: A document that conveyed the title of a piece of land to a new owner after that person met required conditions to own the land.

land record: A document recording the sale or exchange of land; most land records are maintained at a local level where the property is located.

lineage-linked database: A database that is organized by the relationships between people about whom information is stored in the tables.

listowner: A person who oversees a mailing list.

listserv: A software program for managing electronic mailing lists.

locus: The specific location of a marker on a chromosome. Plural is *loci*.

lurking: Reading messages that others post to a mailing list or newsgroup without posting any messages of your own.

maiden name: The surname with which a woman is born; sometimes reflected as *née* on records and documents.

mail mode: The method for mailing lists in which each message is sent to you separately as it's posted.

mailing list: An e-mail exchange forum that consists of a group of people who share common interests; e-mail messages posted to the list come directly to your e-mail in full-format (mail mode) or digest mode; the list consists of the names of everyone who joins the group. When you want to send a message to the group, you post it to a single e-mail address that subsequently delivers the message to everyone on the list.

manumission papers: Documents granting slaves their freedom.

marker: A sequence of DNA at a specific location on a chromosome.

marriage banns: A proclamation made in front of a church congregation expressing one's intent to marry.

marriage bond: A financial contract guaranteeing that a marriage was going to take place; usually posted by the groom and another person (often the father or brother of the bride).

marriage certificate: A legal document certifying the union of two individuals.

marriage license: A document granting permission to marry from a civil or ecclesiastical authority.

maternal: Relating to the mother's side of the family.

microfiche: A clear sheet that contains tiny images of documents, records, books, and so on; you must read it with a microfiche reader or other magnifying equipment.

microfilm: A roll of clear film that contains tiny images of documents, records, books, and so forth; you must read it with a microfilm reader.

military index: A list of those killed in the Korean and Vietnam Wars; part of the FamilySearch collection of CD-ROMs, which are accessible at Family History Centers.

mitochondrian: The power plant of a cell; sits outside the nucleus and contains its own genome.

modem: A piece of equipment that allows your computer to talk to other computers through a telephone or cable line; modems can be internal (inside your computer) or external (plugged into one of your computer's serial ports or card).

moderator: A person who determines whether a post to a newsgroup or mailing list is appropriate, and if so, posts it.

mortgage: Legal agreement to repay money borrowed with real property as collateral.

muster record: A type of military pay record reflecting who was present with a military unit at a particular time and place.

mutation: A difference in the number of repeats within a marker.

naturalization: The official process of becoming a citizen or subject of a particular country in a manner other than birth in that country.

naturalization record: The legal document proving one is a naturalized citizen.

netiquette: Simple guidelines for communicating effectively and politely on the Internet.

networking site: A Web site intended to help people find other people with the same interests, talents, backgrounds, and locations.

newbie: A person who is new to the Internet.

newsgroup: A place to post messages of a particular focus so groups of people at large can read them online; messages are posted to a news server which, in turn, copies the messages to other news servers.

nucleotides: Also called bases. Rungs of the DNA ladder that hold the molecule together. There are four types (adenine, guanine, cytosine, and thymine).

nucleus: The center of a cell which contains the *deoxyribonucleic acid* (DNA).

obituary: An account of one's death that usually appears in a newspaper or other type of media.

one-name study: A page on the World Wide Web that focuses on research involving one particular surname regardless of the geographic location in which it appears.

online: Gaining access to and using the Internet or something that is available through the Internet.

online database: A collection of tables containing data that is accessible through the Internet.

orphan: An infant or child whose parents are both deceased. In some earlier times and places, a child was considered an orphan if his/her father had died but the mother was still living.

passenger list: Listing of the names of passengers who traveled from one country to another on a particular ship.

paternal: Relating to the father's side of the family.

pedigree chart: A chart that runs horizontally across a page, identifying a primary person (including that person's name, date and place of birth, date and place of marriage, and date and place of death), his/her parents, and then each of their parents, and so on until the chart runs off the page. Sometimes called an *ancestor chart.*

pension record: A type of military record reflecting the amount of a pension that the government paid to an individual who served in the military; pension records also showed the amount of pension paid to the widow or orphan(s) of such an individual.

personal genealogical site: Another name for a personal Web page that contains information relating to a person's or family's ancestry.

personal Web page: A page on the World Wide Web that was designed and posted by an individual or family. It may also be called a *personal genealogical site.*

petition for land: An application that your ancestor may have filed for a land grant.

plat map: A map of lots within a tract of land, usually showing the owners' names. Also spelled "platte map."

platinum print: A type of photograph with a matte surface that appeared to be embedded in the paper. Images were often highlighted with artistic chalk, giving the photo a hand-drawn quality; typically taken between 1880 and 1930.

primary source: A document, oral account, photograph, or any other item that was created at the time a certain event occurred; information for the record was supplied by a witness to the event.

probate: Settlement of one's estate after death.

probate records: Types of court records that deal with the settling of an estate upon one's death. Probate records include contested wills and will readings; often the file contains testimonies and the ruling.

professional researcher: A person who will research your genealogy — particular family lines — or obtain copies of documents for you for a fee.

progenitor: The farthest-back ancestor you know about in a particular family line.

query: A research question that you post to a particular Web site, mailing list, or newsgroup so that other researchers can help you solve your genealogical research problems/challenges.

research groups: A group of people who coordinate their research and share resources to achieve success.

robot: A program that travels throughout the Internet and collects information about sites and resources that it comes across. Also called a *spider*.

RootsMagic: A popular genealogical database.

Roots Surname List: A list of surnames, their associated dates, and locations accompanied by the contact information for persons researching those surnames that is maintained by RootsWeb.com. Also called *RSL*.

RSL: Acronym for Roots Surname List.

scanner: A device that captures digital images of photographs and documents into your computer.

search engine: A program that searches either a large index of information generated by robots or a particular Web site.

secondary source: A document, oral account, or any other record that was created after an event took place or for which information was supplied by someone who was not an eyewitness to the event.

server: A computer that makes information available for access by other computers.

service record: A type of military record that chronicles the military career of an individual.

shareware: Software that you can try before you pay to license and use it permanently; usually you download shareware off the Internet.

short tandem repeat polymorphisms (STR): Segments of repeating bases in DNA.

shotgun approach: A bad idea; the process of sending mass e-mails to anyone you find with your surname through one of the online white pages sites.

single nucleotide polymorphism (SNP): Differences on a chromosome.

site: One or more World Wide Web pages; also called a *Web site*.

snail mail: Mail delivered by hand — such as U.S. Mail.

Social Security Death Index: An index of those persons for whom Social Security death claims were filed with the United States government. Although there are a few records in the index that pre-date 1962, most date from 1962 to the present.

Sosa-Stradonitz System: See *ahnentafel.*

sound card: An internal computer device that enables you to hear the audio features of software or audio files that you download off the Internet.

Soundex: A system of indexing the U.S. federal census that groups names that sound alike but are spelled differently; the Soundex code for a name includes a letter followed by three numbers.

source: Any person or material (book, document, record, periodical, and so on) that provides information for your research.

spam: Unsolicited junk e-mail that tries to sell you something or offers a service.

spider: A program that travels throughout the Internet and collects information about sites and resources it comes across. Also called a *robot.*

spreadsheet: A worksheet that allows you to arrange data and track in a particular format.

stereographic card: A type of photograph that was paired and rendered a three-dimensional effect when used with a viewer; developed in the 1850s.

subclade: Subgroup of a haplogroup.

subscription database: An online database that is accessible if you subscribe to it.

surname: A last name or family name.

surname marketing plan: Checklist of places and people to contact to effectively inform the right individuals about information that you have to contribute to the genealogy community.

survey: Detailed drawing and legal description of the boundaries of a land parcel.

tax record: A record of any tax paid, including property, inheritance, and church taxes; most taxes were collected at the local level, but some of the records have now been turned over to government archives.

tertiary source: A source of information that is not considered *primary* nor *secondary*.

thread: A group of messages with a common subject on a newsgroup.

tintype: A type of photograph that was made on a metal sheet; the image was often coated with a varnish. Typically taken between 1858 and 1910.

tiny tafel: A compact way to show the relationships within a family database. Tiny tafel provides a Soundex code for a *surname* and the dates and locations where that surname may be found according to the database.

toggling: The process of flipping back and forth between open programs on your computer by using the Alt and Tab keys in Windows or the Application Switcher in Macintosh.

tract book: A book describing the lots within a township or other geographic area.

transcribed record: A copy of the content of a record that has been duplicated word for word.

Uniform Resource Locator: A standard online address provided for resources on the World Wide Web; also called *URL.*

URL: Acronym for Uniform Resource Locator.

USGenWeb Project: Online project that provides a central resource for genealogical information (records and reference materials) pertaining to counties within states in the United States.

U.S. Colored Troops database: An online database of information on more than 230,000 soldiers of African descent who served in the U.S. Colored Troops; part of the Civil War Soldiers and Sailors System sponsored by the National Park Service.

video-capture board: A device that enables your computer to grab images from your video camera or VCR.

vital record: Primary record of a vital event in life — birth, death, or marriage; for the most part, local governments keep the originals. Often called *civil registrations* outside the United States.

warrant: A certificate to receive land when your ancestor's petition for a land grant was approved.

Webmaster: A person responsible for creating and maintaining a particular Web site.

Web log: An online journal or log of one's interests and activities.

Web server: A computer that is connected to the Internet that serves up Web pages when you request them using your computer's Web browser.

Web site: One or more World Wide Web pages created by an individual or organization; also called a *site.*

will: A legal document that explains how a person wishes his/her estate to be settled or distributed upon death.

witness: One who attests that he/she saw an event.

word processor: Software that allows you to write and edit text.

World Wide Web: A system for viewing and using multimedia documents on the Internet; Web documents are created in HyperText Markup Language (HTML) and are read by World Wide Web browser programs.

World Wide Web browser: Software that enables you to view HTML documents on the Internet.

World Wide Web page: A multimedia document that is created in HTML and is viewable on the Internet with the use of a World Wide Web browser.

XML: A specialized computer code, similar to HTML, that uses tags to describe information. The broader purpose of XML is not only to display information, but also to describe the information.

Index

Virtual Reference Library, 84
vital records, 66, 69–72, 108–9, 186–96, 506
Vivisimo, 153

W
Wales, 242, 261
Walsh, Bruce (author), 361
War of 1812 records, 217–18
warrant, 88, 507
Washington, 206
Washington, Reginald (author), 296
Washington Post records, 346
Web browsers, 410, 471–72, 493
Web Building Tutorial, 475
Web-hosting services, 434–36
Web log, 507
Web queries, 160–66
Web server, 433, 507
Web sites, 507. *See also* personal genealogical sites; *specific sites*
weblog, 425
Webmaster, 507
WebsiteTips.com, 472
WeRelate.org, 420
Wesleyan Methodist Baptismal Register, 330
West Virginia, 196
will, 507
William Aaron Saunders Research Group, 393
William Madison Randall Library, 60
wills, 303–4
Wingfield Family Society, 135–36
Wisconsin, 90, 192, 210
Witcher, Curt B. (author), 307
witness, 507
word processor, 507
WordPress.com, 429